AUTHORITIES

Authorities

Conflicts, Cooperation, and Transnational Legal Theory

NICOLE ROUGHAN

Great Clarendon Street, Oxford, OX2 6DP,
United Kingdom

Oxford University Press is a department of the University of Oxford.
It furthers the University's objective of excellence in research, scholarship,
and education by publishing worldwide. Oxford is a registered trade mark of
Oxford University Press in the UK and in certain other countries

© N Roughan 2013

The moral rights of the author have been asserted

First Edition published in 2013

Impression: 1

All rights reserved. No part of this publication may be reproduced, stored in
a retrieval system, or transmitted, in any form or by any means, without the
prior permission in writing of Oxford University Press, or as expressly permitted
by law, by licence or under terms agreed with the appropriate reprographics
rights organization. Enquiries concerning reproduction outside the scope of the
above should be sent to the Rights Department, Oxford University Press, at the
address above

You must not circulate this work in any other form
and you must impose this same condition on any acquirer

Crown copyright material is reproduced under Class Licence
Number C01P0000148 with the permission of OPSI
and the Queen's Printer for Scotland

Published in the United States of America by Oxford University Press
198 Madison Avenue, New York, NY 10016, United States of America

British Library Cataloguing in Publication Data
Data available

Library of Congress Control Number: 2013943935

ISBN 978–0–19–967141–0

Printed and bound in Great Britain by
CPI Group (UK) Ltd, Croydon, CR0 4YY

Links to third party websites are provided by Oxford in good faith and
for information only. Oxford disclaims any responsibility for the materials
contained in any third party website referenced in this work.

For Alex, Elle, Mum, and Dad

Acknowledgements

This book has been four years, four countries, and seven cities in the making. At each stage and through each move I have been fortunate to have the direct and indirect support of a number of people, without whom the book could not have been written.

First, I wish to thank the supervisors whose advice was critical to the completion of the thesis on which this book is based. It was truly a 'dream team' of complementary approaches, styles, and ideas. To Jules Coleman, for his generosity in encouraging, critiquing, and interpreting my ideas, and giving me the space to pursue them even when they led to dead-ends and backpedalling. To Daniel Markovits for his precise, detailed, and insightful feedback on my early thesis drafts; and to Bruce Ackerman, for always encouraging me to think big, and giving me the confidence to do so. I am grateful too for the ongoing advice of both Jules and Bruce as I worked to turn that thesis into this book.

Moving back to New Zealand and to Victoria University of Wellington, I was fortunate to be able to draw upon the insights and advice of my colleagues at the Faculty of Law, in particular Claudia Geiringer, and to have the institutional support provided by the Faculty as I combined teaching with work on my Doctorate. A move to Brussels then led to a spell at Kent University's Brussels School of International Studies, which provided critical access to resources and the welcome support of colleagues.

From Brussels the shorter move to Cambridge for a two-year University Lectureship gave me a phenomenal opportunity to discuss my work with colleagues within and outside the Law Faculty. In particular I wish to thank Nigel Simmonds for his insights into my project and more general discussions of the state of jurisprudence, Paul McHugh for his sharing of strategic and sage advice, and the Law Fellows at Trinity College for their support.

I have been fortunate to receive feedback on working papers presented to a number of audiences. The input of participants in the Cambridge Political Philosophy Workshop and the Oxford Jurisprudence Discussion Group helped me to revise and consolidate the early version of the relative authority account. Later in the project, I appreciated the critical comments of Roger Cotterrell and Maksymilian Del Mar, in particular, and other participants in Queen Mary University of London's Legal Theory and Legal History Seminar. Law Faculty presentations at the National University of Singapore and the University of Auckland generated very helpful discussion, as did a presentation for members of the New Zealand Society for Legal and Social Philosophy.

I am grateful to the other scholars, friends, colleagues, and teachers who were willing to discuss my work more informally. In addition to those already mentioned, I wish to acknowledge the insights offered at different stages of the project, in conversations with Samantha Besson, Claire Charters, Jim Evans, Dean Knight, Janet McLean, Matthew Palmer, Judith Resnik, Scott Shapiro, Andrew Sharp, Jeremy Waldron, and Bas Van der Vossen, as well as the critical input of two anonymous manuscript reviewers and those who sent informal feedback in response to working papers available online.

The institutional support of the New Zealand Centre for Public Law at Victoria University of Wellington, appointing me a Research Fellow, and the University of Auckland, hosting me as a Visiting Academic, has been critical for the final stages of editing. I am also grateful to Palgrave Macmillan for granting permission to reproduce extracts from an earlier publication in Chapter 9 of this work, to James Blackie for facilitating permission to use the cover image, and to Ngatai Taepa, whose beautiful work 'Tiki 2' is represented on the front cover.

Finally, and most importantly, my family has helped me more than I can say. I wish to thank my parents, for travelling multiple times to the other side of the world to help, for supporting every personal and professional goal I have set, and for being wonderful role models. Elle arrived halfway through and has brought so much laughter and love into our lives, while teaching me that work-life balance means writing during nap times so I could be there to help practise animal noises or go sliding at the playground. Thanks to Ryan and Chandra for giving us all a home away from home in London, to Nick and Mary for their help with childcare and shared holiday breaks, and to my extended family. Lastly, I wish to thank Alex, for being an inspiration and a true partner, living this project with me from the very beginning and sharing each exciting step, each tentative breakthrough, and each international move. His support made the whole project possible.

Contents

Table of Cases	xiii
1. Introduction	1
1. The Target of this Book	3
2. Outline of the Core Argument	7
3. Structure of the Book	8
Part I: Plurality and Authority	8
Part II: The Puzzles of Plurality	9
Part III: A Pluralist Conception of Authority	10
Part IV: Relative Authority in International, Transnational	
(and) Constitutional Law	10
4. Preliminary Objections and Clarifications	12
a. Authority or sovereignty?	12
b. Legitimate or de facto authority?	15
c. Methodological objections	15

PART I: AUTHORITY AND PLURALITY

2. Understanding Authority	19
1. What is Authority?	19
a. Authority as power	20
b. Authority's normativity	20
c. Authority's subjects and domains	26
2. 'Public' Authority—General or Special Justification?	27
3. Legitimate Authority	29
a. Justification to subjects	31
b. Justification simpliciter	36
3. Plural Authorities and Inter-Authority Relationships	43
1. Introducing Plurality and Inter-Authority Relationships	44
a. 'Same-domain' and 'interactive-domain' plurality	45
b. Integrated and disjunctive authorities	47
2. Types of Inter-Authority Relationships	48
a. Compatible authorities: deference and toleration	48
b. Complementary authorities: cooperation and coordination	51
c. Conflict: actual and 'false' conflict	56

4. Plurality of Authority in Legal/Constitutional Theory	60
1. Constitutionalism, Pluralism, and Constitutional Pluralism	61
2. Conceptions of Sovereignty	65
3. Law and Legality	67
a. 'Transnational' law	72
4. Authority	74
5. Outstanding Puzzles	81

PART II: THE PUZZLES OF PLURAL AUTHORITY

5. Compatible and Complementary Relationships	87
1. Procedural Justifications and Plurality	87
2. The Waldron-Raz Exchange	89
3. Initial Clarifications	93
4. Compatible/Complementary Authorities and the Normal Justification Thesis	95
5. Compatible/Complementary Authorities and Procedural Justifications	101
6. Actual and Apparent Conflict	105
1. The Possibility of Conflicting Authorities	105
2. Conflict and the Service Conception	107
a. The de facto condition	107
b. The moral condition	109
3. The Identification Problem, the Rankings Problem, and Reasonable Enquiry	114
a. The rankings problem	114
b. The identification problem	115
4. The Limitations of the Service Conception	119

PART III: A PLURALIST CONCEPTION OF AUTHORITY

7. A Conjunctive Justification	125
1. Standing and Standards of Authority	126
a. Standing	126
b. Standards	128
2. Reasons in a Conjunctive Justification	130
a. Plural reasons for decision	130
b. Plural reasons for action	133

3. Is a Conjunctive Justification Satisfactory to Explain
   Plurality of Authority?   134
8. 'Relative Authority'   136
   1. Relative Authority and the Relativity Condition   137
   2. A Pluralist Theory of Legitimate Authority
      (Why it is Preferable to a Monist Account)   143
   3. The Case for Pluralism   145
9. The Relative Authority of Law: 'Pluralist Jurisprudence'   149
   1. Why Care about Authority?   150
   2. Relative Legal Authority   154
      a. Law's claim to supremacy   154
      b. Law's claim to authority   158
      c. The interaction of legal systems   161
   3. The Value of Relative Legal Authority   163
   4. The Place of Relative Authority amid
      'Pluralist Jurisprudence'   168

PART IV: RELATIVE AUTHORITY IN INTERNATIONAL, TRANSNATIONAL, (AND) CONSTITUTIONAL LAW

10. Relative Authority in Public International Law and
    Transnational Law   173
    1. Relative Authority in Public International Law   173
    2. Conceptualizing International Law   175
       a. States as subjects and authorities   175
       b. Sovereignty   178
       c. International law's fragmentation/constitutionalization   179
       d. Legitimacy   179
    3. The Relative Authority of International Law   180
       a. The significance of consent   180
       b. Inter-authority relationships   185
    4. Monism and Dualism about the Relationship between
       International Law and Domestic Law   189
    5. The Relative Authority of Transnational Law   190
11. Understanding Europe: From Constitutional Pluralism
    to Relative Authority   193
    1. Characterizing Authority: Plurality or Constitutionality?   194
    2. Relative Authority in Europe: A Fourth Way   197

3. Relative Authority's Empirical and Normative Credibility	201
a. Relative authority in practice	201
b. Relative authority as a normative theory	205
12. Relative Authority Inside the State	208
1. Inter-Branch Relationships	208
a. Separation of powers	209
b. Judicial review and oversight	210
2. The Relative Authority of Governments within the State	212
a. Federal-local relationships	212
b. Federal/state relationships with indigenous authorities	215
13. A Case Study in Relative Authority: Crown–Māori Relationships in New Zealand	216
1. Background to Crown–Māori Relationships in New Zealand	217
a. Identifying the authorities	219
2. Are These Parties Candidates for Legitimate Relative Authority?	222
a. Justifying Māori authorities	225
b. The overlap or interaction of Crown–Māori authority	231
3. 'Relational' Self-Determination and Relative Authorities	233
4. The Crown and Māori as Relative Authorities	236
a. Justified relationships and specific problems	237
b. Constitutional issues	241
Bibliography	247
Index	261

Table of Cases

European Courts
Amministrazione delle Finanze dello Stat v Simmenthal (Case 106/77) [1978] ECR 629... 195, 201
Bosphorus Hava Yollari Turizm v Ireland (2006) 42 EHRR 1........................... 202
Costa v Enel (Case 6/64) [1964] ECR 585 .... 195, 201
Kadi v Council and Commission (Case T-315/01) [2005] ECR II-3649, 21 Sept. 2005....... 202
Yassin Abdullah Kadi v Council of the European Union and Commission of the European Communities, Case C-402/05 P, *3 Sept. 2008* 202–5

German Federal Constitutional Court
BVerfGE 37, 271 (1974) (*'Solange I'*).. 195, 202
BVerfGE 73, 339 (1986) (*'Solange II'*) 195, 202
BVerfGR 89, 155 (1993) (*'Maastricht'*) 195, 201
BVerfGE 123, 267 (2009) (*'Lisbon'*)... 195, 201

New Zealand Cases
Attorney-General v. Ngati Apa, [2003] 3 N.Z.L.R. 643........................... 219, 245
Manukau Urban Maori Authority v Treaty of Waitangi Fisheries Commission
    (Privy Council, Appeals 67-68/2000, 2 July 2001)............................. 222
New Zealand Māori Council v Attorney-General [1987] 1 NZLR 641 218
New Zealand Māori Council v Attorney-General [1994] 1 NZLR 513 218
New Zealand Māori Council v Attorney-General [2013] NZSC 6............. 218, 238–40, 244
Taiaroa v Minister of Justice [1995] 1 NZLR 513 218
Te Runanga o Te Ika Whenua Inc Society v Attorney-General [1994] 2 NZLR 20 218
Wi Parata v. Bishop of Wellington (1877), 3 N.Z. Jur. (N.S.) 72 (S.C.) 218–9

United Kingdom
Airbus Industries GIE v Patel 1 AC 199 (1999)..................................... 50

United States
Roper v. Simmons 125 S.Ct. 1183 (U.S., MO., 2005)........................... 167, 214

World Trade Organisation
GATT Dispute Settlement Panel Report: *United States- Restriction on Imports on Tuna*,
    GATT Doc. DS21/R, August 16, 1991 (not adopted), GATT BISD (39th Supp.)
    155 (1993).. 187
GATT Dispute Settlement Panel Report: *United States- Restrictions on Imports of Tuna*,
    GATT Doc. DS 29/R, June 16, 1994, reprinted in 33 I.L.M. 839 (1994) 187
WTO Report of the Appellate Body: United States-Import Prohibition of Certain
    Shrimp and Shrimp Products, WT/DS58/AB/R (Oct. 12, 1998), reprinted in 38
    I.L.M. 118 (1999) 187

1
Introduction

Law is not tidy. It is not contained by the boundaries of modern states nor generated solely by the work of public officials, within or even above those states. Nor is law lonely. It is frequently found overlapping or interacting with other instances of law. Yet somehow, despite this messiness and multiplicity, law still can, or at least claims to be able to, create obligations for its subjects. Despite its plurality, law still has or at least claims some kind of authority.

Scholars working in jurisprudence are beginning to analyse the expanding practice of plurality of law that is familiar from studies of supra-state, inter-state, sub-state, or non-state legal systems. That attention stands in contrast to the core of the jurisprudential canon, and indeed much conventional jurisprudential wisdom, which has either isolated or even ignored law beyond the central case of state law. Any reputation for being staid or static, which jurisprudence may once have deserved, is being sternly tested by this recent flurry of activity challenging the core focus of the subject, and re-forging a connection with doctrinal legal analysis.

That flurry can be described as an emerging 'pluralist jurisprudence',[1] which seeks to analyse purported instances of law beyond, between, within, and/or outside state borders; and any resulting interactions or overlaps between different legal systems.[2] In different ways, pluralist jurisprudents argue that a

---

[1] Nicole Roughan, 'The Relative Authority of Law: A Contribution to "Pluralist Jurisprudence"', in Maksymilian Del Mar (ed), *New Waves in Philosophy of Law* (Palgrave MacMillan, 2011).

[2] The most extensive recent examples of these in English include WL Twining, *General Jurisprudence* (Cambridge University Press, 2009); Keith Charles Culver and Michael Giudice, *Legality's Borders: An Essay in General Jurisprudence* (Oxford University Press, 2010); D Von Daniels, *The Concept of Law from a Transnational Perspective* (Ashgate Pub Co, 2010); Nico Krisch, *Beyond Constitutionalism: The Pluralist Structure of Postnational Law* (1st edn, Oxford University Press, 2010); Peter Calliess and Peer Zumbansen, *Rough Consensus and Running Code: A Theory Of Transnational Private Law* (Hart Publishing, 2010); Mireille Delmas-Marty, *Ordering Pluralism: A Conceptual Framework for Understanding the Transnational Legal World* (Hart Publishing, 2009). Much of this work builds upon the groundwork of MacCormick: see Neil MacCormick, *Institutions of Law* (Oxford University Press, 2007); Neil MacCormick, *Questioning Sovereignty: Law, State, and Nation in the European Commonwealth* (Oxford University Press, 1999).

concentration upon the law-state within modern jurisprudence has led to a blinkered approach to the subject, and limited answers to both its analytical and normative questions. Instead, jurisprudence must ask its key analytical questions about legality and normative questions about legitimacy, but seek answers that can account for international, supra-national, sub-national, and transnational legal orders, as well as the more familiar state/municipal legal systems.

Within this movement are a series of quite distinct interests. One seeks to revise an account of legality so that it can accommodate law and legal systems that are different from the Hartian model. A second challenges the idea of law's systematic character by emphasizing overlap, interaction, or simply blurred boundaries between different instances of law. For all their differences, these interests are both reactionary in a positive sense, as they seek to understand actual instances of 'transnational law' that are becoming more and more influential in legal practice and legal theory. Their bottom line is that general jurisprudence must not ignore such developments, nor isolate them to specialized (or indeed methodologically separate) studies of plurality of law[3] and 'legal pluralism'.[4] Their fundamental question is to ask how all these developments might be explained by existing understandings of law.

A recurring theme in all this work is the idea of overlap or interaction between legal systems, institutions, officials, orders, and norms. Such overlap means that, sometimes, a single legal question might admit different answers at different levels of law, or trigger complex jurisdictional possibilities for inter-level forum-shopping or avenues of appeal. Plurality of law can also generate constraints upon law-makers in one system, imposed by another system or set of rules, as occurs in the orthodox interaction of international and municipal law. The practical implications of all this plurality of law need not be troubling, but they will be if they generate uncertainty for law subjects over which law they are bound by, or for law-makers over the limits of their

---

[3] Plurality is used here as a synonym for multiplicity, as opposed to a normative concept of 'pluralism'.
[4] Substantial recent contributions to legal pluralist theory include Paul Schiff Berman, 'Global Legal Pluralism' (2007) 80 *Southern California Law Review* 1155; PS Berman, *Global Legal Pluralism: A Jurisprudence of Law Beyond Borders* (Cambridge University Press, 2012); Calliess and Zumbansen, *Rough Consensus and Running Code*; Brian Z Tamanaha, A *General Jurisprudence of Law and Society* (Oxford University Press, 2001). The canonical literature on legal pluralism includes Marc Galanter, 'Justice in Many Rooms: Courts, Private Ordering, and Indigenous Law' (1981) 19 *Journal of Legal Pluralism* 1; John Griffiths, 'What Is Legal Pluralism' (1986) 24 *Journal of Legal Pluralism and Unofficial Law* 1; Sally Engle Merry, 'Legal Pluralism' (1988) 22 *Law and Society Review* 869; Gunther Teubner, 'Global Bukowina: Legal Pluralism in the World-Society', in Gunther Teubner (ed), *Global Law without a State* (1996); Franz von Benda-Beckmann, 'Who's Afraid of Legal Pluralism' (2002) 47 *Journal of Legal Pluralism and Unofficial Law* 37.

authority. In both cases, the practical problem is not plurality of law in itself, but confusion over law's authority.

1. The Target of this Book

This book takes such confusion about authority to generate the key theoretical puzzle generated by circumstances of plurality. Unlike work focusing upon conditions of legality, systemic closure/openness, or options for managing jurisdictional overlap/interaction, this work seeks to revise an understanding of the authority that law claims, and that law can have. It aims to show that plurality of law puts pressure on the authority of law at a number of junctures. Plurality unsettles the finality of law's authority, its location, its identifiability, and, most significantly, its independence. I will argue that understanding authority in such pluralist circumstances requires a new conception of 'relative authority', and a new theory of its legitimacy.

This work thus has dual interests. The first is to treat plurality and relationships between legal orders/institutions/officials/norms as matters concerning legitimate authority, and thus as being part of any question about the existence and/or legitimacy of authority over subjects. The second is to consider what all this plurality, and the variation of the circumstances of justification from a monist assumption to a pluralist one, means for theories of authority themselves. I will argue that there are insights to gain in both directions. Although theories of authority help us understand and evaluate relationships between authorities, the practice of plural authority also has implications for understanding what authority is and when it is justified.

In adopting this approach, my work sets aside two other important projects within the legal pluralism/transnational law fields. First, it does not set out to prove or defend the impact of plurality of law upon contemporary legal scholarship and practice. It is not filled with case studies detailing the array of interactions and overlaps between various legal regimes and their institutional managers.[5] I take it to be settled, now, that such plurality not only exists, but is also significant for a theory of law.[6] Second, this project does not advocate a set of procedural or institutional changes to better manage the overlap

---

[5] For studies rich in such examples, see Berman, 'Global Legal Pluralism'; essays in Jeffrey L Dunoff and Joel P Trachtman, *Ruling the World?: Constitutionalism, International Law, and Global Governance* (Cambridge University Press, 2009); Günther Handl and Joachim Zekoll, *Beyond Territoriality: Transnational Legal Authority in an Age of Globalization* (Martinus Nijhoff Publishers, 2012).

[6] Among many others offering a similar observation, Peer Zumbansen's account is particularly vibrant, arguing that transnational law 'works itself like a drill through the few remaining blankets

and interaction of legal authorities. It neither advocates creating further room for pluralism nor defends moves towards universalism, constitutionalism, or harmonization. It does not contain a programme for eliminating or resolving inter-authority conflicts, nor for deepening the integration of interacting regimes.[7]

This book rather seeks to provide the theoretical tools needed to bring the disciplines examining legal/constitutional pluralism, broadly conceived, into more direct engagement with theories of authority, by examining the one practice in which they are all interested: the practice of public authority. It makes no sense for 'mainstream' jurisprudence and legal pluralism to exist in convenient isolation, when the impact of plurality and resulting interactions generate puzzles that should interest both fields. For instance, both fields should seek answers to questions such as:

- How can theory make sense of the multilevel, dispersed, and fragmented practice of public authority?
- How should subjects understand their relation to all these different authorities, and their standing in relation to each other?
- If there are multiple public institutions with the authority to create legal obligations for the same subjects, what happens if those obligations conflict?
- What happens when there are conflicting norms applying to subjects of different legal authorities who are proximate or interactive with one another?
- How should relationships between legal authorities be evaluated?
- Does plurality of legal authority generate possibilities for either enhancing or impinging upon authorities' legitimacy?
- Does such plurality affect the justification of authority?

One way to answer these questions would be to insist upon a technical account of legal authority, in which authority is constituted and limited by institutional norms. That approach would treat the existence of authority as a matter of rules, and would be interested in plurality only as a generator of overlap or conflict between those rules. It would equate legal authority with

---

covers hastily thrown over an impoverished and internally decaying conceptual body': Peer Zumbansen, 'Transnational Law', in JM Smits (ed), *Elgar Encyclopedia of Comparative Law* (2006). See also A Halpin, 'Conceptual Collisions' (2011) 2 *Jurisprudence* 507; and Roger Cotterrell, 'Transnational Communities and the Concept of Law' (2008) 21 *Ratio Juris* 1, at 8, arguing that a theory of law must 'adopt criteria of the legal that are sufficiently flexible to recognise many different forms of law in currently indeterminate but potentially developing relations with each other'.

[7] Others have set about that task with considerable complexity: see, eg Delmas-Marty, *Ordering Pluralism*.

jurisdiction and/or treat an institution's constitutional rules as constitutive and determinative of its authority. For many scholars in both the jurisprudential and legal pluralist fields, that is the proper way to conceive of legal authority, and doing so opens up an array of important questions surrounding both hierarchy and heterarchy between institutional authorities at various levels of governance.[8]

My own work, however, begins from the position that such a jurisdictional account of authority is insufficient for capturing the full impact of plurality because plurality can unsettle the very rules that are supposed to delimit the authority and cause confusion over their relative status, force, or enforcement prospects. Even if a jurisdictional approach to legal authority is convincing in the context of a monist, statist account, it is analytically unhelpful when the very rules that are supposed to be determinative of authority cannot be clearly deciphered or demarcated from one another. Instead, if authority is conceived as a moral power, which law has or claims to have, authority can be separated from jurisdiction so as to generate a tool for evaluating the very rules that institutionalize authority into a jurisdictional form. When these rules are overlapping and conflicting, an analysis of their (morally) legitimate authority offers a way to evaluate them or rank them without simply resorting to a description or explanation of the brute force or respective power behind various rules or regimes.[9]

My work thus condenses the puzzles of plurality into one complex topic: whether, and if so how, plurality of authority and relationships between authorities affect or even effect the existence and legitimacy of authority. The target of the study becomes a variation upon the familiar question of when authority can be legitimate. It asks: when can authority be legitimate in circumstances of its plurality? My answer here makes two core arguments:

(a) First, that understanding how authority structures obligations and reasons applying to subjects, requires consideration of both the implications of plurality and inter-authority relationships, and the overall legitimacy of a practice of plural authority. Such consideration reveals

---

[8] The equation of legal authority with jurisdiction impacts upon theoretical understandings of both concepts. Jurisdiction implies more than simply the 'authorization of law' or the demarcation of law's authority, and these other facets of jurisdiction are not integrated into what I am calling a jurisdictional understanding of legal authority as something technical and formal. For a critical engagement with these and other aspects of jurisdiction, see Shaun McVeigh and Shaunnagh Dorsett, 'Questions of Jurisdiction', in Shaun McVeigh (ed), *Jurisprudence of Jurisdiction* (Routledge-Cavendish, 2006).

[9] Throughout this work, the authority I am interested in is legitimate, rather than de facto authority. See section 4.b of this chapter, and Chapter 2.3. I accept Raz's argument for the explanatory priority of legitimate authority. In Raz's view, de facto authority includes a claim to legitimate authority (and is thus distinguished from other de facto powers); thus, an understanding of de facto authority

that plurality of authority, and the relationships that exist between holders of authority, must be built into any justification of authority.

(b) Second, that the best explanatory and normative account includes a pluralist conception of authority in which authority can be a *relative* power shared between different authorities in the same domain, or mutually dependent between authorities in interactive domains. Relationships between these 'relative authorities' then amount to a 'relativity condition' upon their legitimacy. Together, these arguments make up my account of relative authority.

The goal is to find a persuasive account of authority and its legitimacy, while simultaneously suggesting how that account might help illuminate the plurality that exists within, between, and outside of states. In other words, by offering a theory of authority that can stand up to the problems posed by overlap, coordination, and conflict between authorities, we can explore the options for legitimate inter-authority relationships within each of the fields where those relationships are significant. Though not a prescription for institutional development or modification, the relative authority account offered here is a model for thinking about how and when institutional authorities ought to work with, alongside, or against one another, and a tool for evaluating how well actual institutions are engaging in relative authority relationships.

That model is neither monist nor dualist; and neither constitutionalist nor pluralist. It can be applied, however, to all the examples that are characteristically subjected to those other distinctive approaches. It would be easy to become repetitive when discussing relative authority across each of these different locations, as similar insights apply in the case of, for instance, federal, devolved, or multi-sovereign state examples, as they do for transnational, international, and regional authorities. Indeed, the examples all begin to look similar precisely because relative authority integrates the justification of overlapping and interacting authorities wherever they are located—inside, between, above, or at state borders. To an extent it does not matter which set of inter-authority relationships are plugged in to the relative authority equation.

In order to present a persuasive account of relative authority, however, it remains important to illustrate those examples that have attracted the most interest among scholars of constitutional and international theory. The difficulty in doing so is that each particular example requires a rich social-scientific

---

is parasitic upon an understanding of legitimate authority: Joseph Raz, *The Morality of Freedom* (Clarendon Press, 1986), 25–26. For an argument favouring the alternative interest in de facto authority, see Arie Rosen, 'The Normative Fallacy Regarding Law's Authority', in WJ Waluchow and S Stefan (eds), *Philosophical Foundations of the Nature of Law* (Oxford University Press, 2013).

analysis upon which descriptive conclusions can be drawn before the normative analysis is layered over the top.[10] My aim here is to isolate key aspects of the inter-authority relationship examples in order to show what the relative authority tool can add to their analysis, but will offer only one full analysis of a specific set of relationships—between state and indigenous authorities in New Zealand.

Some of my observations about the constitutional pluralist or international or transnational fields will, I hope, seem obvious to those who work in these fields or have theorized about the specific inter-authority relationships that inhabit them. They may be less obvious, however, to those working to understand authority or who study inter-authority relationships without assessing their impact upon authority, as well as those whose focus upon one location of inter-authority relationships has obscured similar or parallel insights to be gained from relationships in other locations. Those reading this book with either jurisprudential or pluralist expertise, therefore, will find some material familiar and some foreign. My hope is that the ideas and arguments are clear enough that, for both audiences, the foreign material might come to shed new light on the familiar.

2. Outline of the Core Argument

In brief, my argument proceeds as follows.

Familiar puzzles from international, constitutional, and transnational law reveal that legal practice is rife with overlap, interaction, and sometimes conflict between legal/constitutional orders, regimes, or norms. These interactions may be governed by rules; often they are not. In either case, rules or doctrinal approaches designed to manage or deflect conflicts and overlaps do not determine the authority of the different legal orders, nor, crucially, their interaction. Plurality of law should be understood to involve conflicting claims to legitimate authority, so that to explain how those claims interact or might be integrated we need the help of a concept of authority and a theory of its legitimacy.

However, existing work on authority and its legitimacy are not adequate to assist in explaining or assessing plurality. Existing work explains authority as an independently held power, and offers justifications that depend upon being able clearly to identify who or what has authority. Leading accounts, including Raz's substantive service conception and its contending procedural theories, are rendered unstable by plurality, suggesting that authority collapses in the face of pluralist conflict, or at least that it cannot be independently legitimate. Nor

---

[10] Berman, 'Global Legal Pluralism', 10–11, for instance, observes legal pluralism's susceptibility to 'excruciatingly difficult case-by-case questions.'

is there much assistance from work on legal or constitutional pluralism itself, which often eludes to a complex notion of overlapping authority but does not analyse just what that means or what would make it legitimate.

These defects necessitate both a revision to the concept of authority and to a theory of its justification, in order to better explain and assess practices of plurality of authority. I argue that an initial revision must combine procedural and substantive elements into a complex conjunctive justification, but that intractable problems remain surrounding the ranking and identification of multiple legitimate authorities. Further revision, which I suggest is necessary, must treat authority as a relative power that can be held interdependently, rather than independently. Just as two parents can be conceived as having authority that is relative to each other, so too can public authority be regarded as relative—shared by authorities whose subjects are overlapping or interactive. When authority is relative, relationships between relative authorities become a condition of their legitimacy. In other words, authorities might, depending on context, need to cooperate, coordinate, or tolerate one another if they are to have legitimacy. In some contexts, conflicts themselves are justified. In others they are not. The legitimacy of conflicts, cooperation, and other relationships, however, depends upon the balance of reasons assessed in relation to both or all relative authorities, rather than each one independently.

This conception of relative authority, and theory of its legitimacy, require a revised account of the (claimed) authority of law. Where there is plurality, overlapping legal systems should be understood to claim, and perhaps have, relative rather than independent legitimate authority. This opens the door for an analysis of what law must be like if it is to claim relative authority, as well as the potential to integrate the idea of relative authority into jurisprudential wisdom more generally.

The idea of relative legal authority can then be deployed to explore its implications for international and transnational law, and for constitutional pluralism and intra-state relationships. For each different field, there are some similar and some specific insights to be gained by shifting away from an independent conception of authority, to one that is interdependent, shared, and relative.

3. Structure of the Book

This work proceeds in four parts.

Part I: Plurality and Authority

Chapter 2 follows this introduction with an outline of contending conceptions of public authority and theories of its legitimacy. The chapter examines the key distinctions that divide theories both of what authority is, and when it is justified. The distinctions drawn do not aim to provide a comprehensive analysis of conceptions of authority, rather to isolate the familiar points of theoretical dispute that will prove most significant for the work on plurality of authority to follow.

Chapter 3 then examines the practice of plural authority and inter-authority relationships. It briefly describes the phenomenon of plurality of authority, paying special attention to inter-authority conflict and cooperation, and drawing distinctions between different types of inter-authority relationships.

In Chapter 4 I examine the literature in legal and constitutional theory, from which many examples of plurality are drawn, to examine how the practice of plurality of authority is currently conceived and explained. I argue that these accounts, for all their richness, do not adequately address the puzzles raised by plurality *of authority*, which requires more sustained attention. In particular, it is not clear if plurality of legitimate authority is conceptually possible, and/or how different types of coordinated, cooperative, or conflicting relationships can be explained.

Part II: The Puzzles of Plurality

Part II takes up these puzzles and argues that existing accounts cannot address them. Special attention is given here to Raz's service conception of authority, which presents both the most promise, and the biggest challenge, for explaining plurality of authority. Raz's theory of authority is not only the most widely discussed and most well-developed of contending theories; it is also the only full account of authority that addresses, albeit minimally, the possibility of plurality and the phenomenon of inter-authority relationships. Yet while Raz has turned some attention to the possibility of plurality, he has also argued that plurality is not problematic for his approach as a whole. Chapters 5 and 6 reject the ease with which Raz thinks plurality can be explained. In Chapter 5, I examine the possibility and explanation of compatible and cooperative relationships between authorities, in response to an exchange between Raz and Jeremy Waldron on the subject of inter-authority 'deference'. I argue that neither theorist adequately addresses the impact of plurality upon the practice of public authority, especially when such plurality occurs among disjunctive authorities.

Chapter 6 then turns Razian theory upon an analysis of conflicts of authority—when there is more than one legitimate authority, establishing conflicting obligations. This is a more difficult task, and I argue that conflicts generate two problems for Raz's theory—problems of ranking and identification. The latter, in particular, shows that Raz's normal justification for authority cannot sustain authority in the face of actual or even apparent conflicts of authorities. The effect of both chapters in Part II is to argue that the Razian account is not complete or conclusive for explaining plurality of authority.

Part III: A Pluralist Conception of Authority

Chapter 7 begins the task of offering a pluralist theory of authority by setting out a 'conjunctive justification', which combines procedural and substantive justifications in order to address the puzzles raised by plurality. I argue that the procedural and substantive justifications do different normative work, and that both are necessary for explaining legitimate authority in circumstances of plurality. However, the conjunctive justification does not solve the identification or rankings problems completely; rather, it reveals their intractability.

Chapter 8 responds to that intractability by developing a conception of relative authority, in which authority is mutually shared or interdependent between two authorities, generating what I call a 'relativity condition' upon their legitimacy. The condition entails that where there is relative authority (either in a single or in interacting domains), the authorities concerned must engage in appropriate relationships with one another if they are to enjoy legitimate authority. To establish whether a relationship is appropriate, standards can be derived from the procedural and substantive reasons applicable to each participant, in light of their relationship. This derivation of standards by which relationships can be evaluated is not always straightforward, nor will those standards require uniform types of engagements between authorities. Sometimes relationships of cooperation will be required; other times, the conditions for legitimate authority will require that one authority exclude another.

In Chapter 9, I return to the problem that animated the investigation into plurality of authority—namely the need to explain the authority of interacting or overlapping legal regimes. To do this, I argue that law's claim to authority can be reconceived as a claim to relative authority, and that, in order for that claim to be justified, law must not simply be open to other systems of law, but also responsive to them. I suggest here that the account of relative authority may serve as a building block for what I call 'pluralist jurisprudence', by offering a theory of law's authority that replaces supremacy and exclusivity with relativity and relationships.

Part IV: Relative Authority in International, Transnational (and) Constitutional Law

The remaining chapters outline the implications of a conception of relative authority, and a theory of its legitimacy, for the key areas in which it arises.

To examine relative authority in detail, concrete examples must be employed. Each of these is, by necessity, more truncated than is desirable. The examples examined here are intended to be food for further thought, rather than definitive or complete analyses of the significance of the relative authority account in each of these fields.

Chapter 10 argues that the relative authority account clarifies some of the puzzles of international and transnational legal theory, including conceptions of international law as law, the identity of international law's subjects, conceptions of sovereignty, and the value of dualism and monism as theories of international-domestic law relations. It then argues that some of the complexities of transnational law, particularly its hybrid public-private character, might also be explained through an account of relative authority.

Chapter 11 suggests that relative authority offers a 'fourth way' of understanding inter-authority relationships in the European Union, and an advance upon the so-called 'third way' of constitutional pluralism. In particular, its combination of procedural and substantive elements and its rejection of independent assessments of legitimate authority distinguish it from otherwise similar offerings from Kumm and Maduro.

Chapter 12 sets up an analysis of inter-authority relationships within the state, including relations between branches of government, relationships of federalism, and relations between state and indigenous authorities. The brief set-up is critical to, and is intended to support, the full-scale case study offered in Chapter 13.

Chapter 13 explores the example of indigenous and state authority relationships in New Zealand; offering one fully worked-out case study in order to show the potential of the relative authority account as a tool for assessing inter-authority relationships anywhere. It draws upon insights from theorists of self-determination and minority rights, both in general and in the specific context of New Zealand's constitutional relationships, in order to assess the values and characteristics of indigenous and state authority. Some of the chapter's insights may be comparatively useful, but it does not engage in comparison; rather, it isolates the precise features of indigenous-state relationships in New Zealand in order to show how they generate relative authority and to assess their resulting legitimacy. Chapter 13 is both long and detailed, because that detail is necessary to demonstrate and defend the view that the relationship is one of relative authority. In addition, while the choice of example here may be thought too specialized or too local to be of interest to those readers who are interested in the abstract or theoretical analysis of relative authority, it has to be both of these things if it is to work as a worthwhile illustration of both the theory and its usefulness.

4. Preliminary Objections and Clarifications

Several clarifications are important to this project, and there are some preliminary objections to face. One simple but important clarification is that relative authority does not entail that relationships between authorities are themselves relationships *of* authority. This discussion of relative authority and inter-authority relationships is not intended to imply that appropriate relationships between authorities are necessarily themselves relationships *of* authority—although sometimes this will be the case.

Other clarifications concern the concepts surrounding authority—concepts which are broadly within the family of concepts of control. This family of concepts includes, among others, notions of coercion, influence, power, and sovereignty, and these have connections with a set of expressly evaluative concepts, including legitimacy, justification, and validity. The distinctions and connections between these concepts will be examined at appropriate stages of this study, but as a preliminary matter it may be necessary to say something about the connections and distinctions between authority, sovereignty, and jurisdiction.

a. Authority or sovereignty?

Analyses of the array of overlapping regimes that characterize transnational law typically take one of two paths. The first focuses upon the abstract concept of sovereignty, arguing that sovereignty is being modified by all this transnationalism, and/or that sovereignty continues to constrain its extent. The second path focuses upon the technical question of jurisdiction, pondering how to manage jurisdictional conflicts or double-ups and so maintain a sense of *legal* order among normative disorder. Both are important and illuminating paths, but the former, I think, is too broad and the latter too narrow. This book carves a third path which engages in a deeper normative account than the one offered by emphasizing jurisdiction, but with a more specific target than can be offered through a normative account of sovereignty.

The centrality of states in many examples of plurality and inter-authority relationships immediately raises the suggestion that the real issue here is not authority, but sovereignty. I want to resist this suggestion for several reasons. The primary point is that questions of who has legitimate authority and who is legitimately sovereign are separate questions, which will frequently have different answers. Authority is the more specific type of power, but it exists in a wider range of locations and relationships, and generates more instances of plurality.

First, it is clear that sovereignty is a broader concept than authority; indeed, sovereignty is often described as a bundle of powers, rights, and obligations. Although these powers typically include having de facto and perhaps legitimate authority over subjects, sovereignty also includes powers relating to the use of coercion, jurisdiction over territory, property rights, the protection of subjects against outside influences, freedom from external control, and the right to be recognized by other sovereigns and represent the community at the inter-sovereign level of interaction.[11] Debates among theorists of sovereignty centre upon the precise character of these powers in the current global order, debating their location and the extent to which they are exclusive or can be overlapping.[12] Focusing on authority, separately from these other powers, allows a narrower and more precise focus, although there remains much to be learnt from those theories of sovereignty which have explicitly or implicitly emphasized the authority power within the sovereignty 'bundle'.

A second reason to examine authority rather than sovereignty is the extent of division over what sovereignty itself entails. Traditionally, the idea of sovereignty includes conceptions of supremacy and exclusivity, if not absolutism.[13] In the Westphalian international system, for instance, the classical account of sovereignty attributes supremacy and finality to states over internal authorities or competitors, and establishes independence from external authorities or competitors (evidenced by the formal international legal principles of sovereign equality and non-intervention). Using this conception of sovereignty would beg the answer to my question of relativity—indeed, it would end my enquiry, as the sovereign state would have supreme authority internally and independent authority externally. It is more illuminating to examine the state as an authority without begging the question of its supremacy or its separateness from other authorities (both internally and externally). Sovereignty theorists may respond that the conception of sovereignty in a post-Westphalian

---

[11] Different formulations of the sovereign powers abound; it is a complex and, perhaps, essentially contested concept. For a concise survey of different approaches to sovereignty, see S Besson, 'Sovereignty in Conflict' (2004) 8(15) *European Integration online Papers* § 2, 3. In the political theory literature, Krasner explains that there are not only different sovereign powers, but different kinds of sovereignty with different arrangements of powers: Stephen D Krasner, *Sovereignty: Organized Hypocrisy* (Princeton University Press, 1999), Ch 1.

[12] The literature in this field is vast, and spans work in international law, international relations, and constitutional and political theory. No footnote can represent the breadth of this literature, but a very selective list of major contributions includes: Neil Walker, *Sovereignty in Transition* (Hart Publishing, 2003); Neil MacCormick, *Questioning Sovereignty* (Oxford University Press, 1999); T Jacobsen et al., *Re-Envisioning Sovereignty: The End of Westphalia?* (Ashgate Publishing, 2008).

[13] On absolute sovereignty, see Jean Bodin, *Six Books of the Commonwealth* (MJ Tooley trans, B Blackwell, 1955); Bertrand De Jouvenel, *Sovereignty: An Inquiry into the Political Good* (Cambridge University Press, 1957); T Hobbes, *Leviathan* (JCA Gaskin (ed), Oxford University Press 1998).

international system can recognize such divided or partial or shared sovereignty; is no longer the absolute power that its traditional defenders have claimed; and perhaps is no longer the primary concept for understanding international organization or even domestic citizenship.[14] These arguments could assuage the previous worry, because if sovereignty can be divided, or has less significance than its classical form suggested, then the concept of sovereignty no longer begs the question of supremacy and exclusivity of authority, or rules out relativity. The important point, however, is that these very arguments generate new reasons to favour placing authority at the centre of analysis. If sovereignty can be shared and less than absolute, then it is again most usefully analysed through its constituent powers—one of which is authority—and if sovereignty need no longer be analytically central, there is good reason to target the more specific concepts that enable us to better understand the current arrangements of international power. Sovereignty and authority can, in this sense, come apart.

Third, sovereignty captures only a narrow range of relationships. Although sovereign states are central to many inter-authority relationships, both within and outside the state's borders, the idea of sovereignty captures only some of those relationships, and does not capture at all relationships among non-state authorities that are not themselves sovereign. To adequately capture the diversity of inter-authority relationships, and the extent of plurality, these non-sovereign actors ought not to be ruled out a priori.

Finally, and perhaps most importantly, my work's emphasis on authority rather than sovereignty shifts the focus away from what is often called 'popular' sovereignty; that is the right, power, or freedom of a polity to determine its own direction free from outside interference. Popular sovereignty is interesting and controversial not only for the opacity of its relationship to 'legal' sovereignty—which is best understood as a legal status of internal and external autonomy—but because, in a transnational and pluralist context, popular sovereignty seems to butt heads with cosmopolitan values and practices. Although I think the resulting debates are both interesting and important, I hope to leave them out of this study by focusing upon authority as a matter of the organization of moral reasons and obligations, rather than popular sovereignty with its invocations of politics and identity.

---

[14] Saskia Sassen, *Losing Control?: Sovereignty in an Age of Globalization* (Columbia University Press, 1996). For analysis and critique of post-sovereignty arguments, see Jacobsen *et al.*, *Re-Envisioning Sovereignty*.

b. Legitimate or de facto authority?

Throughout this work, I am interested in legitimate authority more than de facto authority. Although the two are clearly entwined within any conceptual or theoretical account, I use the language of authority here to mean legitimate rather than de facto authority—unless the contrary is specified. This usage and interest reflects the wider normative approach of this book.

c. Methodological objections

Conceptual analysis in jurisprudence has come under recent criticism as theorists devote sustained attention to issues of jurisprudential methodology.[15] Analysis of a concept (say, of law, or of authority) risks leading to endless debates about which elements of that concept are necessary or contingent; which are universal or particular. It is important to emphasize here that my analysis of authority is designed to better account for pluralist practices of authority that exist in empirical experience. If authority is something for philosophers to worry about, then working conceptions of authority need to capture what it is, wherever it is. In turn, if theorists of law then seek to engage a concept of authority in the course of explaining aspects of the nature of law, they must have available a concept of authority that might help them explain law in all its variant locations.

What is offered here might be considered a revisionist conception of authority. As Coleman argues, 'normally, revision of a concept is justified when the ordinary concept is misleading and confusing or when it does not serve theoretical or practical purposes well'.[16] The obvious objection, then, is that there is no need for such revision, and that the existing conception of authority is both clear and useful. Parts I and II of this work aim to show that it is not, and that some revision is needed. The problems with the existing concept not only reveal the need for revision of the concept itself but also, I think, the need for fresh conceptual analysis.

This work, however, is not only engaged in conceptual analysis. It also offers a new theory of legitimate authority that is matched to the revised concept. There are thus two steps to the work, and it should be read as such. The first step argues that authority should be conceived as relative, shared, and interdependent, not binary, monist, or independent. The second argues that the legitimacy of such relative authority depends directly upon inter-relationships between authorities.

---

[15] Halpin, 'Conceptual Collisions'; Andrei Marmor, 'Farewell to Conceptual Analysis (in Jurisprudence)', in Waluchow and Stefan (eds), *Philosophical Foundations of the Nature of Law*.
[16] JL Coleman, 'The Architecture of Jurisprudence' (2011) 121 *Yale Law Journal* 14.

PART I

AUTHORITY AND PLURALITY

2
Understanding Authority

Understanding authority involves answers to two questions: *what is authority* and *when is it legitimate?* Both are the subject of rich scholarly traditions rife with distinctions, debates, and refinements more detailed than can be given full attention here. Instead, this chapter sets out the key distinctions and focusing points that will turn out to be most important for my interest in inter-authority relationships and plurality of authority.[1]

1. What is Authority?

Practical authority is a 'normative power to change another's normative relations'.[2] This orthodox statement of the nature of practical authority summarizes three key ideas. First, practical authority is a power. It is a kind of capability *to do something*. Second, practical authority has both a normative character and potential. It can introduce or remove obligations, including both personal and inter-personal obligations, for its subjects. This normative character distinguishes authority from powers that are (merely) coercive, influential, or persuasive. Third, practical authority involves a tripartite relationship: *A has authority over B with respect to C*; where C refers to the domain of activity within which a practical authority can impose requirements upon B, the subject(s).[3] Each of these features is best elaborated in turn.

---

[1] Friedman attributes the persistence of debates about authority to the elusive but indispensable character of the concept of authority for work in political philosophy: Richard B Friedman, 'On the Concept of Authority in Political Philosophy', in Richard E Flathman (ed), *Concepts in Social and Political Philosophy* (Macmillan Publishing, 1973).

[2] Scott J Shapiro, 'Authority', in Scott J Shapiro and Jules L Coleman (eds), *Oxford Handbook of Jurisprudence and Philosophy of Law* (Oxford University Press, 2002), 398. This core idea is well supported in the literature, although given different formulations. See, eg Robert Paul Wolff, 'The Conflict between Authority and Autonomy', in Joseph Raz (ed), *Authority* (New York University Press, 1990), 20: 'the right to command and correlatively the right to be obeyed'. It can be more simply stated as 'the right to rule' (see Joseph Raz, 'Introduction', in Raz, *Authority*, 2–3); or according to Anscombe, 'a regular right to be obeyed in a domain of decision': GEM Anscombe, 'On the Source of the Authority of the State' (1978) 20 *Ratio* 1.

[3] Dudley Knowles, 'The Domain of Authority' (2007) 82 *Philosophy* 23, 29. See also Richard E Flathman, *The Practice of Political Authority* (University of Chicago Press, 1980).

a. Authority as power

Practical authority as a power is more precisely elaborated as a *power over* others. This contrasts with epistemic authority, or expertise, which denotes the superior knowledge or ability of an expert who is 'an authority' on an empirical subject, but who does not thereby have 'authority over' particular individuals as subjects.[4] This distinction, though not universally accepted, provides a basis for distinguishing between the (practical) authority exercised by a parent over a child, or a government over its subjects, and the (epistemic) authority held by a doctor in relation to her patient, or an emeritus professor of architecture in relation to those who know little of his subject. The two types of authority can exist together in the same office-holder, and sometimes the justification for the practical authority might depend on the presence of the epistemic.[5] On some justifications of governmental authority, for instance, a government has practical authority over its population if it has expertise on matters that its subjects know little about. In other accounts, the two are distinct: my doctor knows far more about medicine than I do, but decisions about my treatment are ultimately mine to make, not hers. An expert on architecture can try to teach me and persuade me of his theories, but I am not obligated to act in accordance with them.

This distinction is important here because I will use it to compartmentalize my interest. I am interested in the plurality of practical authority, and throughout this work will use the term 'authority' to refer to practical authority only. Theoretical authority drops out of this study, except when necessary for explicating ideas about practical authority, particularly in relation to those justifications that link the two types of authority together.

b. Authority's normativity

The second key dimension of authority is its distinction from other kinds of practical power that are non-normative and, most importantly, from coercive power. This distinction turns upon the character and content of authority's normativity—the link between authority and reasons, duties, and rights. Authority theorists broadly agree that the normative force of authority is 'content-independent', meaning that the obligatory force of directives from

---

[4] For a summary of the distinction, see Tom Christiano, 'Authority', in Edward N Zalta (ed), *The Stanford Encyclopedia of Philosophy* (Spring 2013 edn), <http://plato.stanford.edu/archives/spr2013/entries/authority/>.

[5] See, eg Heidi M Hurd, 'Challenging Authority' (1991) 100 *Yale Law Journal* 1611, 1667–1677. For objections to this view, including that practical authority binds even if it is known to be incorrect, while theoretical authority cannot, see Shapiro, 'Authority', 399.

a legitimate authority have their force because they come from the authority, not because of their particular content.[6] This does not mean that authority is considered to be content-irrelevant. In many theories the content of an authoritative order plays some part in the justificatory story, and its content must still be within legitimate limits, but the normativity of authority is independent of content.

The exact character of that normativity is then a matter of much contention. On one side is the idea that the normativity of authority is 'relational', ie a matter of duties and rights pertaining between persons. On the other, the normativity of authority is a matter of moral reasons, not relationships. These ideas compete for dominance in different accounts offered to explain authority, although, as contemporary theory reveals, the two are not strictly incompatible.

Relational approaches treat authority as a relationship between persons—a duty to govern others or a right to rule over them. Any relational account characterizes the normativity of authority as a relationship between persons, not between persons and reasons, so that the justification of the authority becomes a justification of the accountability relationship itself, not its outputs. Some relational accounts separate authority's force from moral reasons in general by giving an intervening role to consent. For instance, a Hobbesian approach explains authority as a hierarchical relationship between persons, in which the right to rule is grounded upon its acceptance by those subject to it.[7] There, the fact of acceptance (whether express or tacit) is what generates the normativity of authority.

The Hobbesian direct consent theory, where consent does all the work of conferring a right to rule, is out of favour among contemporary relational theorists, who reframe the relational element of authority so that it is sensitive to reason. A leading example is Stephen Darwall's 'second-personal' account, which regards authority as a standing to demand of others or hold others to account.[8] Like the Hobbesian accounts, what needs to be justified is one person having a right to rule, while another has an obligation to obey.[9] However, in contrast to

---

[6] Analysis of authority's content-independent character appears in HLA Hart, 'Commands and Authoritative Legal Reasons', in Raz, *Authority*, 92–114; Joseph Raz, *The Morality of Freedom* (Clarendon Press, 1986), 35–37.

[7] This right to rule is accompanied by an entitlement to coercive enforcement of commands. See discussion in Jean Hampton, *Hobbes and the Social Contract Tradition* (Cambridge University Press, 1988).

[8] Stephen Darwall, 'Authority and Second-Personal Reasons for Acting', in David Wall and Steven Sobel (eds), *Reasons for Action* (Cambridge University Press, 2009), 134. Raz has recently responded to Darwall's account, and relational views of authority in general, in Joseph Raz, 'On Respect, Authority, and Neutrality: A Response' (2010) 120 *Ethics* 279. For a concise analysis of the response, see Mark McBride, 'Darwall Versus Raz on Practical Authority' (2011) 3 *Public Reason* 73.

[9] As Hershovitz has put it, 'an account of authority must address the normative status of both ruler and ruled': Scott Hershovitz, 'The Role of Authority' (2011) 7 *Philosophers' Imprint* 10.

Hobbesian accounts, Darwallian authority has non-hierarchical foundations. All persons have an equal second-personal authority arising from human dignity, which both entitles them to demand actions of others and requires them to conform to valid demands posed by others and by the moral community.[10] In Darwall's view, all moral obligations are explained in this second-personal sense, using second-personal concepts of valid (authoritative) demand, reason, and accountability. The key element here is the notion of validity, which makes authority reflective to reason by making the relationship of standing reflective to reason. The legitimate content of second-personal demands is determined by morality; we are only bound by valid demands. Legitimate authority exists only where there is a 'background accountability relation' that gives authoritative directives their second-personal standing, and therefore their authoritative force.[11] Importantly, the content of the accountability relationship between persons is not simply determined by those individuals' preferences about their relationship, but by what is morally valid.

The relational approaches stand in contrast to the second kind of theory, which treats authority as a mediator between persons and the reasons that apply to them, so that authority's normative force is grounded not in a valid relationship but in an authority's service of subjects' conformity to right reason. Joseph Raz, the leading advocate of this approach, has generated considerable discussion and support for this idea and its ability to resolve the supposed paradox between autonomy and authority.[12] Raz argues that the exercise of authority changes the structure of reasons applying to the subject, providing the subject with a reason not to act upon some of the reasons that would otherwise have applied to him.[13] More precisely, Raz argues that the exercise of

---

[10] Darwall, 'Authority and Second-Personal Reasons for Acting', 24.

[11] Stephen Darwall, *The Second-Person Standpoint: Morality, Respect, and Accountability* (Harvard University Press, 2006), Ch 3. This view of authority has been picked up by others who, without committing to Darwall's extensive project of conceiving all moral obligations as second-personal, emphasize that a full explanation of authority must include an account of standing to demand and to hold the demandee accountable for failures. As Hershovitz explains, 'a full justification of the state's authority requires an explanation of why the state has the standing to hold its subject to account for wrongdoing': Scott Hershovitz, 'Accountability and Political Authority' (2006) *Minn Law Review* 1012. For a critical reply to Darwall, see Raz, 'On Respect, Authority and Neutrality'.

[12] The paradox of authority and autonomy is concisely formulated in Wolff, 'The Conflict between Authority and Autonomy'. Descriptions of Raz's account as the most influential account of authority appear in Jules L Coleman, *The Practice of Principle: In Defence of a Pragmatist Approach to Legal Theory* (Oxford University Press, 2001), 124; Scott Hershovitz, 'Legitimacy, Democracy, and Razian Authority' (2003) 9 *Legal Theory* 201; WJ Waluchow, 'Authority and the Practical Difference Thesis' (2000) 6 *Legal Theory* 45. As each of these and other authors' criticisms show, this influence does not equate to universal acceptance.

[13] Raz's analysis explores the structure of practical reasoning without being committed to any account of what good reasons are. But like all of Raz's writing in legal and political philosophy, his account of practical reasoning is deeply embedded in moral philosophy and, specifically, the objectivity

legitimate authority 'pre-empts' or 'excludes' some of the reasons on which a subject should act.[14] Raz reaches this 'preemption thesis' through an analysis of practical reasoning in which he distinguishes between primary reasons for action and secondary reasons (defined as reasons to act or not act for the primary reasons).[15] Raz regards authoritative commands as second-order reasons; they are reasons to act (or not act) upon primary reasons. He then specifies further, indicating that second-order reasons can be positive (reasons to act for a reason) or negative (reasons not to act for a reason). This second type of reason is called an exclusionary reason; it is a reason to exclude a set of primary reasons from factoring into the subject's practical judgment.[16] An exclusionary reason is a reason not to act on some of the reasons against obedience; in the case of authority, it excludes those reasons which already form part of the authority's decision or should be expected to form part of the authority's decision, and which tell against doing what the authority commands.

There is more: Raz explains that some exclusionary reasons are also 'protected reasons', meaning that in addition to excluding a set of first-order reasons for action, the exclusionary reasons themselves function as first order reasons for action.[17] The commands of a legitimate authority are the best examples, and the ones of most importance to this study. Raz indicates that the commands of a legitimate authority are exclusionary reasons to refrain from acting on the balance of first-order reasons, while also providing primary reasons for action

---

of reason. This becomes crucial to Raz's views on the justification of authority, discussed in the following chapters.

[14] See Raz, The Morality of Freedom, 57–63. The pre-emption thesis is central to Raz's positivist legal theory, but causes problems for his account of authority. For analysis of tensions between Raz's pre-emption thesis and his normal justification thesis, see Margaret Martin, 'Raz's the Morality of Freedom: Two Models of Authority' (2010) Jurisprudence 63. A common argument against the pre-emption thesis itself is that authoritative directives do not pre-empt reasons for decision; rather they either outweigh reasons against doing what the directive requires or provide reasons to treat these contradictory reasons as being outweighed. That is, they treat authoritative directives as reasons to be balanced against other reasons for action in the ordinary fashion. Authority then provides a particularly strong (and often overriding) reason to act one way and not another, but there is no special magic in authority's impact on practical reasoning. See, eg Michael S Moore, 'Authority, Law and Razian Reasons' (1988) 62 California Law Review 827, 846. That debate is not critical here, but the recurring tensions between the pre-emption thesis and the normal justification include strains of the problems raised by plurality of law, explored in Chapters 5 and 6.

[15] Joseph Raz, Practical Reason and Norms (2nd edn, Oxford University Press, 1999), 40–44.

[16] 'A second-order reason is any reason to act or to refrain from acting for a reason. An exclusionary reason is a second-order reason to refrain from acting for some reason': Raz, Authority, 39. This aspect of Raz's work has received extensive comment and criticism. See analysis in Shapiro, 'Authority', 402–420; Michael S Moore, Educating Oneself in Public: Critical Essays in Jurisprudence (Oxford University Press, 2000); Stephen R Perry, 'The Works of Joseph Raz: Second-Order Reasons, Uncertainty and Legal Theory' (1989) 62 Southern California Law Review 913.

[17] Raz, Practical Reason and Norms; Joseph Raz, 'Reasoning with Rules' (2001) 54 Current Legal Problems 1.

because people ought to obey legitimate authorities. Thus, to have authority is to have a 'normative power to change protected reasons'.[18] If the authority is legitimate, the subject is under an obligation to try to act as the authority demands, and this obligation applies even if the authority is mistaken on that particular matter, so long as it is generally successful at helping that subject conform to reason.[19]

Whatever the character of authority's normativity, whether or not relational, that normativity distinguishes authority from other types of power. The distinction between authority and coercion, for instance, draws attention to a special example of the distinction between a mere power and a normative power.[20] Conceptually, one can differentiate between authority as a normative power, and coercion as the use or threat of force. Yet in practice, authority and coercion are often exercised together or blurred. Coercion looks like a technique at the disposal of an authority, and authorities sometimes claim a *right* to use coercion to back up authoritative directives, or will simply use coercion as a tool for reinforcing those directives. In respect of governmental authorities, coercive force is commonly applied to those who do not comply with obligations created by the exercise of authority. The frequent co-existence of authority and coercion raises the question of the relationship between them, and in particular the question whether the justification of coercion is dependent upon the justification of authority, or vice versa.

On either the relational or the reason-based accounts of authority, it seems clear that the justifications for authority and coercion are separate; one can be justified in coercing someone over whom one lacks authority, while one might have authority over someone yet not be justified in coercing them.[21] Whether or not the justification of authority depends upon acceptance/relationships or upon reason, a justification for authority is not a justification for coercion, although having justified authority may be a part of a justification for coercion. They can be added together as separate features of a complex

---

[18] Joseph Raz, *The Authority of Law* (2nd edn, Oxford University Press, 2009), 18. Similarly, a promise can function as a protected reason: it excludes a set of reasons not to act on the promise, and because promises ought to be kept, a promise provides a primary reason of its own in favour of the action. When there is moral weight in favour of meeting the second-order reason, it becomes protected in the contest against competing reasons.

[19] Raz, *The Morality of Freedom*, 41.

[20] Jean Hampton usefully distinguishes 'mastery' from authority, suggesting that anarchists confuse coercion and authority, and that the response to anarchism is to show how political authority is different from just coercion: Jean Hampton, *Political Philosophy* (Westview Press, 1997).

[21] In contrast, Robert Ladenson defends an authority-coercion nexus in Robert Ladenson, 'In Defense of a Hobbesian Conception of Law' (1980) 9 *Philosophy and Public Affairs* 134. For Raz's dismissal of the justified coercion account of authority, see Raz, *The Morality of Freedom*, 25–27; Raz, 'Authority and Justification' in Raz (ed), *Authority* (New York University Press, 1990) 115–117. Compare A John Simmons, *Justification and Legitimacy: Essays on Rights and Obligations* (Cambridge University Press, 2001). David Estlund also separates authority from legitimate coercion, and offers

account of legitimacy, but their separate contributions to that overall account underscore their different normative characteristics.[22] They need not go together, and the conditions under which legitimate authority and legitimate coercion are justified might be quite different.[23] In the context of political authority, one can imagine circumstances in which a state would be justified in coercing someone over whom it does not have authority; for example, during a just war a state may be entitled forcibly to remove an occupying group but not be entitled to rule over them.[24]

These arguments are disputed by a third set of theories, which insist that an explanation and justification of authority is less important than a justification of coercive force. Such theories seek to subsume the explanation of authority within an account of justified coercion, or make the justification of authority secondary to that of coercion. Recent and rich analyses of this kind have been offered by Arthur Ripstein and Ronald Dworkin, who both treat the problem of justified coercion as the more urgent problem of political and/or legal philosophy.[25] On Dworkin's view, the existence of state institutions generates a special problem of justifying coercive force, as well as special political values applying to a social community. His interest is therefore not in legitimate authority, but in what, in modern political life, in any particular situation, justifies the use of the state's coercive power. He then develops a theory of law as an answer to that question, insofar as law carries the value of integrity—the coherent and consistent justification of coercion.[26] Ripstein similarly makes the question of the legitimacy of coercion primary, by using a Kantian notion of private right to justify the conditions of legitimate coercion first, and a state's claim to authority second. Ripstein's theory starts with the interaction of private persons, then asks 'how they may legitimately be *forced* to treat each other'.[27] According to Ripstein, a state may legitimately coerce people and rightfully tell them what

different conditions for their justification, in David M Estlund, *Democratic Authority: A Philosophical Framework* (Princeton University Press, 2008), 41–42.

[22] For one description of a 'dominant philosophical view' in which legitimacy combines justifications of both authority and coercive enforcement of authority, see Allen Buchanan, *The Legitimacy of International Law*, in Samantha Besson and John Tasioulas (eds), *The Philosophy of International Law* (Oxford University Press, 2010), 82.

[23] Tom Christiano, 'Justice and Disagreement at the Foundations of Political Authority' (1999) 110 *Ethics* 165, 170: 'justified coercion in pursuit of justice is not sufficient for a right to rule.'

[24] The example is from Christiano, 'Justice and Disagreement', 170. Similarly, in the context of parental authority there may be situations where a parent is justified in coercing another person's child without having authority over that child. See Leslie Green, *The Authority of the State* (Clarendon Press, 1988), 243.

[25] Arthur Ripstein, 'Authority and Coercion' (2004) 32 *Philosophy and Public Affairs* 2. Among legal theorists, the most prominent is Ronald Dworkin. See Ronald Dworkin, *Justice in Robes* (Belknap Press, 2006); Ronald Dworkin, *Law's Empire* (Belknap Press, 1986).

[26] Dworkin, *Law's Empire,* see especially Chs 3 and 7.

[27] Ripstein, 'Authority and Coercion', 6.

to do, in order to create 'a regime of equal freedom' enabling people to have rightful private relations.[28]

For purposes of this work, I will leave open the possibility that, when we have said all there is to say about plurality of authority and relationships between authorities, we should then ask about the legitimacy of coercion, and the possible explanations for plurality of legitimate coercive power. The question about the justification of coercion will be kept separate from my discussion of authority here, but it does not disappear.

c. Authority's subjects and domains

The third key element of authority is its tripartite character. If *A has authority over B with respect to C*, we need to consider what it is to be a subject of an authority, and what it means to have a domain of authority. Plurality clouds these aspects of authority wherever authorities share subjects or activities, ie wherever the domains of authorities shade into each other in important (and often controversial) grey areas.

To be a subject of an authority is to be susceptible to having one's normative relations altered by what the authority does (or omits to do). The subject has some kind of reason (many think an obligation, but at least a content-independent reason of some force) to comply (or try to comply) with the authority's directives within a certain domain of activity. The limits of the domain, or the boundaries of what an authority can or cannot require of its subjects, is then a matter of crucial importance, whose specification will depend on the type of authority at issue and the particular conditions of its legitimacy.[29] Importantly, the limits of an authority's domain are not determined simply by asking what domain an authority claims. An authority's domain will be determined by whatever it is that makes that authority legitimate. To speak of the domain of an authority, therefore, is to speak of its sphere of legitimate authority.

Subjects and domains can, however, be separated for descriptive purposes. For instance, and for reasons of descriptive simplicity, it is possible to conceptualize an authority acting outside its domain by trying to command non-subjects to act in ways that it could only legitimately require of subjects; or trying to direct purported subjects to do things that are not properly the concern of the authority, thus freeing them from any obligations of subject-hood. Yet the elements of the domain and the subject are not really conceptually distinct.[30] A person

---

[28] Ripstein, 'Authority and Coercion', 35.
[29] Knowles, 'The Domain of Authority', 30: 'The specification of intra-/ultra vires (boundary) conditions to authority is a parochial exercise which varies from authority to authority as states, religions, armed forces, schools and families differ in the content and stringency of their particular rules'.
[30] Knowles, 'The Domain of Authority', 30: 'Strictly speaking the domain of a particular authority encompasses both specified subjects and a limited range of actions. The variables in the schema

is only subject to an authority within a particular range of action; outside that range of action, a person is not a subject of that authority. Equally, a domain of action is only a domain in respect of certain persons—the subjects. We do not achieve much by trying to separate out the set of subjects from the domain of activity in which they are subjects, in part because both the domain of activity and the set of subjects are constituted by whatever makes the authority legitimate. It seems clearer then to think of authority as a normative power that exists over certain persons in respect of certain actions, so that both elements constitute the legitimate range of the authority.

2. 'Public' Authority—General or Special Justification?

Authority is a power that features in many human interactions, from familial to professional, from co-member to co-national. As a result, it is plausible that there are many distinct 'types' of authority to be conceptualized, explained, and justified independently, rather than one concept of authority and one general justificatory test. Among those arguing for the latter view, Joseph Raz states that there is one concept of authority, whose justification is normally a matter of securing a subject's better conformity to reason. In Raz's view, while the existence or exercise of political authority might raise additional and specific questions that parental or employer authority does not, at base the justification for authority does not change between the contexts in which it is exercised.[31] Many have disagreed with Raz on this point, arguing that the special characteristics of political authority (including its generality, its relationship to coercive power, and its impersonality) require special justification.[32] Raz in turn accepts that political authority such as that exercised by a state may require supplementary justification, but insists that no supplementary justification can justify an authority that is not first justified by helping subjects act in closer conformity with the reasons that apply to them.[33] In my work here, that debate will be left open by concentrating on 'public' authority while leaving open the possibility that whatever justifies the exercise of public authority might also be (or might even necessarily be) a justification for practical authority in general. It also leaves open the possibility that 'public'

---

are not independent of each other'. Note also that terminological variations here can add to the confusion.

[31] Joseph Raz, *Ethics in the Public Domain* (Oxford University Press, 1994).
[32] Samantha Besson, 'Review Article: Democracy, Law and Authority' (2005) 2 *Journal of Moral Philosophy* 89; Hershovitz, 'Accountability and Political Authority'.
[33] Joseph Raz, 'Authority, Law and Morality' (1985) 68 *The Monist* 295 (1985).

authority can be exercised by actors that are not as clearly 'public' as a state or a branch of government.

By 'public' authority, I mean to capture the authority of governing bodies/institutions, including both legal and political institutions, and across state and non-/supra-/intra-/inter-state locations.[34] The nature of authority does not change whether it is exercised by legal or political institutions, or whether it is located in local, national, transnational, or international communities. Wherever authority is located, it remains a normative power over subjects. This approach has the advantage of enabling an initial analysis of authority (and relationships between authorities) free from the characteristics that are associated with the particular (and contingent) institutionalization of such authority in modern state legal systems, as well as maintaining the ability to assess the mutually constitutive and constraining roles of legal and political, state-level, and other-level authority. The key feature of public authority in this sense is that it is institutionalized in some way, and to some degree.[35] The institutionalization attaches authority to an office rather than a natural person or a role (such as a parent) that natural persons fulfil. A public office of authority will of course be occupied by natural persons (either alone or in complex arrangements with others), but it is the *official*, rather than the person, who holds public authority.

The distinction between a public office and a private role is parasitic upon a distinction between public and private authority. For present purposes I take this to be a distinction of context, without committing either to a conceptual or justificatory distinction. My distinction is drawn by examining three contextual features of any particular authority: (i) its formal basis or constitutive foundations; (ii) the nature of its connection to its subjects; and (iii) its interactions with other authorities. The basis of authority might be

---

[34] Explanations of political authority often entwine legal and political authority in order to distinguish political authority from political power. See, eg Edmundson: 'Political authority consists in the state's (purported) moral power to place us under obligations to obey its commands, particularly its laws': William A Edmundson, 'Political Authority, Moral Powers and the Intrinsic Value of Obedience' (2010) 30 *OJLS* 179. See Leslie Green, 'The Duty to Govern' (2007) 13 *Legal Theory* 165, 169. Compare theorists who treat legal authority as akin to jurisdiction, where such authority/jurisdiction is conferred by law. Later in this work, I will ask whether there is anything distinctive about the authority of law which renders it necessary to isolate legal authority in the final analysis of plurality of authority. For instance, does the exclusivity and supremacy of law's claim to authority, which some legal theorists insist upon, preclude plurality or relationships among legal authorities? These and other concerns about relative authority and the authority of law are addressed in Chapter 9.

[35] For a detailed analysis of the idea of an institution, see Keith Charles Culver and Michael Giudice, *Legality's Borders: An Essay in General Jurisprudence* (Oxford University Press, 2010); and for its significance for understanding authority, see Andrei Marmor, 'An Institutional Conception of Authority' (2011) 39 *Philosophy and Public Affairs* 238.

clearly public (as are state institutions constituted under public law) or clearly private (as are authorities constituted under private law), but the likelihood of boundary or hybrid cases, and cases without any clear formal basis at all, means the first contextual feature is not sufficient to distinguish public from private authority. Adding the second feature reveals that a public authority has an impersonal connection with a general set of subjects, while private authority involves inter-personal connections between authorities and subjects based on a familial, voluntary, or contractual status.[36] Even with the addition of this second element, however, it is still possible to conceive of borderline examples such as small-scale public authorities that do in fact operate with the individual and personal consent of their subjects. The third contextual element therefore offers an additional framing device, by looking at relationships between authorities to identify what kind of authority (public or private) each exercises. Religious authority presents a tricky but illuminating case; it is sometimes a type of public authority, sometimes purely private. The characterization depends upon the relationships between the relevant religious authorities and more clearly public authorities such as a state government. Where religious authority is located within, at the head of, or in formal cooperation with an official, publicly constituted structure of governance, then it is best regarded as a kind of public authority. Where religious authority is isolated from such official structures of governance, it is more sensibly thought of as private authority. For this work I do not need to make any particular characterization of religious or any other kind of authority as public or private; but I am excluding from consideration any types of authority which on this analysis are clearly private, such as the authority held by parents over their children.

3. Legitimate Authority

Perhaps the key distinction within any account of authority is the distinction between legitimate and de facto authority. Indeed, confusion can arise when an account of authority consistently fails to specify whether de facto or legitimate authority is being explained. For this study, I will use the term 'authority' to

---

[36] This distinction may not satisfy advocates of associative political obligations, some of whom do explain political obligations precisely by analogy with such private associative obligations. For an analysis and rejection of theories of associative political obligations, in part because they simply do not fit our large-scale societies which are impersonal in the way I describe, see A John Simmons, 'Associative Political Obligations' (1996) 106 *Ethics* 247, 247. Even if we accept associative political obligations, the public-private distinction would remain descriptively useful as a way of differentiating the contexts in which authority is exercised.

refer to authority that is legitimate, and use the full term 'de facto authority' to describe authority that is not legitimate.[37] When it is necessary to distinguish between legitimate authority and de facto authority, I will specify as such.

A de facto authority claims legitimacy, but does not necessarily have it. Thus, put simply, legitimate authority is distinguished from de facto authority by reference to whatever criteria determine legitimacy.[38] It is important not to over-simplify this distinction, for one point on which all theories of authority seem to converge is that authority can exist only where it is effective—that is, only where some person or body actually has the capacity to direct and/or coordinate subjects. Effectiveness is often made an express condition of legitimacy, so that part of establishing that a person or body has legitimate authority is to show that it actually has de facto authority.[39] An authority cannot be legitimate, on these theories, if it cannot effectively exercise authority over subjects in its domain. With this in mind, the distinction between de facto and legitimate authority remains critical to both analytical and normative analyses of authority. If legitimate authority is authority that carries whatever normative weight is given to it by a justificatory theory, and de facto authority describes a factual situation without any direct normative consequences, then to get to the normative, one has to add a justificatory story that gives value to the fact of an authority's existence.

The exact details of a justification for authority are the key points of dispute between theorists of authority. The task of justification is driven by the desire to explain the conditions under which the apparent interference in a subject's autonomy is justified. The question becomes: *what makes it true of X that she has legitimate (public) authority?*[40] Answers then roughly divide into two structures of justification: justification *to* the subjects of authority; or justification *simpliciter*, in accordance with reason.

In the first category are a range of 'procedural', 'non-instrumental', or 'input' theories, which all require some form of participation from the subject(s) of an authority in order for that authority to be legitimate. On these accounts,

---

[37] This usage follows Raz. See Raz, *The Authority of Law* (2nd edn, Oxford University Press, 2009, 8–11).

[38] Hampton, *Political Philosophy*, 70: 'de facto political authority can be exercised in all sorts of unjust and morally unacceptable ways; so there is a difference between de facto political authority and political authority that is just and morally legitimate'.

[39] For discussion of this 'de facto condition' see Chapter 7.2.a. For an elaboration of 'task-efficacy' theories of authority, see Green, 'The Duty to Govern'.

[40] In some accounts this justificatory question is framed to ask not when authority is legitimate, but instead under what conditions it is rational for someone to accept an authority over them, consistently with their autonomy. It is then debated whether these two questions ask the same thing. For my purposes it does not matter, because both the existence and the rational acceptance of legitimate authority will be challenged by plurality in the same way. See Chapters 5 and 6.

authority is legitimate only if autonomous individuals have in some way accepted that authority over them or have at least participated in a process that binds them to abide by the outcome.[41] These are non-instrumental theories because authority is legitimated by the intrinsic value of its inputs—ie procedures such as democratic election, or actual consent, or affiliation. In the second category are 'substantive', 'instrumental', or 'output' theories, which offer an account of moral or political value(s) and consider authority to be instrumentally justified in so far as it serves that (or those) values. Justification on these theories is reflexive to reason, not to people, so that the justification of an authority depends upon whether it can promote subjects' conformity with reason, regardless of what its subjects have to say about it or of how it came to power.

The distinction can be illustrated through theories that insist that public authority can only be legitimate if it is democratic. These can diverge along the two basic approaches. On the procedural view, democratic processes justify a resulting authority because they reflect a majority's consent, or are the result of a contest of opinion on equal terms, or empower subjects to express and contest views while arriving at a firm decision.[42] The authority that has been successfully *justified to* a majority of a population via a legitimate democratic process is legitimized by passing through that process. In contrast, the substantive view argues that democratic processes actually produce good outcomes and the outcomes are what justify the authority.[43] The difference lies in the structure of justification; arguing from procedure and participation in the first case; or service of reason and substantive value(s) in the second.

a. Justification to subjects

Procedural justifications typically begin from liberal commitments to the equal value or autonomy of individuals. They range from theories requiring the actual consent of the subject, to theories of democratic participation or deliberation or discourse, to agonistic approaches which legitimize authority only if a subject has the ability to contest the structures of authority that exist over them. Arguments from consent are the most familiar of these procedural theories of legitimate authority, as well as others that require voluntaristic

---

[41] Shapiro calls this the dominant model in modern liberal theory: Shapiro, 'Authority', 431–433.
[42] For an account of democracy that grounds its force on its promotion of equality, see Christiano, 'The Authority of Democracy', 182. Note, however, that many theorists deny that democracy adequately captures the value of equality, at least not without adding substantive protections to prevent discrimination or to remedy systemic disadvantages between persons. See, eg TRS Allan, *Law, Liberty, and Justice: The Legal Foundations of British Constitutionalism* (Clarendon Press, 1993).
[43] Estlund, *Democratic Authority*.

conduct short of consent. The basic argument (that authority is legitimate only if it is consented to by its subjects) underscores classical accounts from Hobbes and Locke through to modern, convention-based variants proposed by Hampton and Gauthier.[44] Consent matters because it legitimizes what would otherwise be illegitimate—in the context of political authority it legitimizes the imposition of obligations by a collective's representative over autonomous individuals who give their consent. As Green describes the supposed force of consent, 'the fact that an individual has consented is a sufficient if defeasible reason for holding him to be under [a] duty'.[45] On the most pure of these accounts, the authority's legitimacy depends only upon the fact of its subjects' individual agreement; the rationality or reasonableness of that agreement is not relevant.[46]

Consent accounts have come under sustained criticism, including from Raz who concludes that consent can be a way of reinforcing the legitimacy of a government that is already justified, but cannot confer legitimacy upon one which is not.[47] Raz's argument is that consent is only normatively significant in circumstances where there is a non-will-dependent reason to treat it as such. In other words, consent to a political authority 'is binding only if there are good reasons to enable people to subject themselves to political authorities by their consent.'[48] Raz further argues that consent is not necessary to establishing a just government, so the reason to value political consent cannot be that it is necessary to secure justice. The fact that one has consented has normative significance by creating an additional reason to obey a government, but it does not alone suffice to justify its authority. There are also costs involved in giving consent any general validity; so that the best we can say about consent is that (instrumentally) it plays a supplementary role in justification. Non-instrumentally, it is a valuable constituent element in a relationship between a citizen and a reasonably just society represented by authorities, but has no value if the society is not reasonably just.[49] It is therefore problematic to attribute justificatory power to consent alone, for if a purported authority acts contrary to reason or justice, then consent in such circumstances would be irrational and devoid of the requisite normative value.

---

[44] As Estlund explains, 'the nub of consent theory, its controversial element, then, is the libertarian clause: if A does not consent to B's authority, then, for that reason B has no authority over A. Roughly, *no authority without consent*': Estlund, *Democratic Authority*, 119 (emphasis in original). See also David P Gauthier, *Morals by Agreement* (Clarendon Press, 1986).

[45] Green, 'The Duty to Govern', 160.

[46] Green, 'The Duty to Govern', 162.

[47] Raz, *The Morality of Freedom*, 88–94.

[48] Raz, *The Morality of Freedom*, 89.

[49] Raz, *The Morality of Freedom*, 92.

There are two further persistent problems with consent theories.[50] The first is that the accounts must show why consent matters: does it protect some form of natural autonomy, or some type of independence of judgment and belief? Is there some special force in consent itself so that the mere act of voluntarily committing to obedience is a sufficient explanation for the legitimacy of the one being obeyed? Or is it simply valuable as a pragmatic method of legitimizing some form of necessary authority, in the face of public disagreement? If consent has normative value, then we have to look to the source of its normative value, not consent itself, to explain why consent might justify authority.[51]

Secondly, a consent account offers an individualized justification, which leaves little room for social or interactive concerns. To the extent that social concerns clash with the preservation of individual autonomy, a justification based on consent prioritizes individual autonomy above other values, and so must make a case for doing so. A consent theory of public authority also needs to explain the move from individual consent to general public authority—the idea that an authority can be legitimate for a whole community including some who have not or could not have consented.[52] Even if a subject can legitimize an authority over himself by consenting, he obviously cannot consent to authority over others or confer community-wide legitimacy on a body that purports to have such authority.

These concerns have prompted modifications which integrate the consent condition with a condition of justice. Modified consent theories use justice as a measure of the normative power of consent: consent to an unjust authority is not normatively valuable consent. Critics of these views can respond that the addition of a condition of justice, even a minimal condition, suggests that consent itself is no longer doing sufficient normative work towards justifying authority. Yet the two prongs of the justification do not totally align so as to make one redundant: on a consent-based approach, an authority cannot be legitimate simply by virtue of being just; it must, necessarily, receive the voluntary consent of its subjects. Unfortunately this does not help us much, but simply reverts back to the first concern, which is to identify the normative value of consent and thus show how it can justify an authority.

---

[50] There are of course other difficulties associated with consent theory. For a detailed account of the criticisms, see A John Simmons, *Moral Principles and Political Obligations* (Princeton University Press, 1979).

[51] Raz argues convincingly along these lines in Joseph Raz, *Between Authority and Interpretation: On the Theory of Law and Practical Reason* (Oxford University Press, 2009), 159–162. He concludes that as consent binds us only when there is reason for it to do so, it is reason, not consent, which provides the key justification for authority.

[52] On the problem of authority over non-consenters, see Edmundson, 'Political Authority, Moral Powers and the Intrinsic Value of Obedience'.

The second concern about the individualized justification is raised by contractualist theories, which move further towards integrating the justificatory force of consent and justice. Contractualist approaches socialize the account of authority so that the significance of consent is not simply due to individuals consenting to authority over themselves; it is due to members of communities settling upon principles and institutions to structure and manage their interaction with other members. The justificatory force comes not from individual consent, but from social and reasonable consensus, which provides evidence of the content of just relations for that community. In this approach, individuals only have an obligation to obey just institutions; therefore, only just institutions can have legitimate authority.

The justificatory task then lies in specifying the conditions of justice upon which legitimate authority depends. Most famously, Rawls and other contractualists argue that the basic structure of society must be organized in such a way that reasonable people would/could agree to; while specifying that reasonable consensus is itself limited to views that are in accordance with public reason.[53] In Scanlon's version of contractualism, the normative role of consensus is reversed; morality consists in principles that reasonable people could not reject, based on their relationships of mutual respect.[54] Rejectable principles are those that cannot be justified to others. Though there are a number of differences between the variants of contractualism, the effect of both moves is to insist that public authority must be *justifiable* to those over whom it is exercised. It does not require that authority is actually consented to by subjects, but it preserves the idea that the subjects' opinions matter to the question of justification by requiring that authority be reasonably acceptable (or not reasonably rejectable). On Scanlon's version, the effect is much the same as a theory of justification simpliciter: what is reasonably rejectable will depend on principles of morality, while consensus itself does not seem to do much if any moral work. Rawls' own version rests closer to the side of justification to the subject by requiring reasonable consensus, and according legitimacy only to authority which is grounded in principles on which there is an overlapping consensus among reasonable views.

These contractualist approaches occupy an intermediate category between the procedural and the substantive structures of justification. They link justification with the content of justice, by requiring that subjects have some involvement in the selection of any authority over them, while limiting the

---

[53] For example, see John Rawls, *Political Liberalism* (Columbia University Press, 1993), 100–101: 'since justification is addressed to others, it proceeds from what is, or can be, held in common; and so we begin from shared fundamental ideas implicit in the public political culture in the hope of developing from them a political conception that can gain free and reasoned agreement in judgment'.

[54] Thomas Scanlon, *What We Owe to Each Other* (Belknap Press of Harvard University Press, 1998).

justifiable outcomes of subjects' participation to outcomes that are consistent with public/right reason. In this respect they measure the justification of political authority by both its substantive and procedural qualities.[55]

An alternative intermediate point between procedural and substantive justification appears in David Estlund's justification of democratic authority by way of 'normative consent'.[56] Estlund's approach is intermediate in that legitimacy does not require that a justification of authority be actually accepted by everyone subject to it, but nor is conformity to rightness or justness, by itself, sufficient to confer legitimate authority. Estlund argues that there is a moral obligation to consent to the authority of an 'epistemic proceduralist' democratic political system, and that because non-consent to such a system would be invalid, it does not matter whether the opportunity to consent is actually given. This notion of normative consent is a kind of hypothetical consent, which is 'morally equivalent to a promise to obey'.[57] Estlund establishes this moral obligation by arguing: (i) that there is value in having laws that are substantively just; (ii) that a proper democratic procedure can be demographically neutral and is fair and acceptable to qualified points of view; (iii) that a democracy's involvement of many participants can potentially achieve epistemic benefits; and (iv) that there are no non-democratic arrangements that all qualifying points of view could agree would serve justice better. In light of the urgent task of committing people to obey a system which provides them with protection, Estlund finds there is a 'duty to promise to obey', if asked.[58]

Importantly, the contractualist theories and Estlund's epistemic proceduralist account both rely upon the interplay of two key elements—the participatory and the reasonable—to do the work of justifying authority. The social participation element links contractualist approaches not only with the consent tradition, but also with other accounts that require the participation of subjects in the constitution of legitimate authority. The type of participation required in order to legitimize authority varies across different theories. According to aggregative democratic approaches, consensus is not necessary (and is highly unlikely); instead, the common opinions of the majority determine legitimate authority within a community. According to deliberative approaches, in contrast, majorities can rule only if they justify their practices and policies under fair conditions in which all can participate. According to agonistic approaches,

---

[55] For an analysis of the substantive and procedural democratic credentials of contractualism, and a response to those who reject contractualism for being too outcome-focused, see PJ Weithman, 'Contractualist Liberalism and Deliberative Democracy' (1995) 24 *Philosophy and Public Affairs* 314.
[56] Estlund, *Democratic Authority*. On normative consent, see Ch 8.
[57] Estlund, *Democratic Authority*, 152.
[58] Estlund, *Democratic Authority*, Ch 8.

consensus is not possible without illegitimately overriding some contending views or limiting some members' abilities to participate; so we should look instead to processes of contestation and opportunities for adversarial engagement that can test the legitimacy of public authority.[59] These accounts suggest that commonality, consensus or contestation cannot legitimize authority if the terms of such participation are not themselves just.[60] The element of reason, then, links contractualist approaches to substantive theories which insist that what matters is justification simpliciter, where authority is justified only by reference to its support for individuals being able to realize particular values or reasons that apply to them, including reasons associated with justice and/or fairness.

b. Justification simpliciter

Justifications simpliciter are similarly concerned with an objective characterization of legitimacy, rather than what the subject perceives to be legitimate.[61] They can include both instrumental and intrinsic justifications, and reference to both procedural and substantive values. Their variety is evident among the leading contenders to be considered here: Raz's equation of legitimacy with the promotion of a subject's conformity to reason; Hershovitz, who, drawing upon Darwall's second-personal account, has built a justification of authority that depends upon whether the practices constituting the role of authority are sufficiently (intrinsically or instrumentally) valuable; and Finnis, who sees authority as legitimate only when it provides the social framework necessary for the individual pursuit of common human goods.[62]

In these accounts, the value of authority means that efficacy or effectiveness of authority is expressly made a condition of its legitimacy. In order to be justified by virtue of (for Raz) serving a subject's conformity to right reason, or (for Finnis) providing the social coordination necessary to allow individuals to pursue the objective goods, or (for Hershovitz) occupying a

---

[59] For agonistic accounts, see William E. Connolly, *Identity/Difference: Democratic Negotiations of Political Paradox* (University Of Minnesota Press, 2002); Ernesto Laclau and Chantal Mouffe, *Hegemony and Socialist Strategy: Towards a Radical Democratic Politics* (2nd edn, Verso, 2001); Chantal Mouffe, *On the Political* (Routledge, 2005).

[60] Allen Buchanan, *Secession: The Morality of Political Divorce from Fort Sumter to Lithuania and Quebec* (Westview Press, 1991).

[61] Put another way, this is the difference between a sociological account of legitimacy and a normative account. See Samantha Besson, 'The Authority of International Law—Lifting the State Veil' (2009) 31 *Sydney Law Review* 343, 345.

[62] On the distinctiveness of Finnis' account of duties of governance, see Green, 'The Duty to Govern'.

role (either voluntarily or mandatorily), in which rights and obligations are established by a justified practice, an authority must be effective.[63]

From that point of similarity, the justifications diverge in two key respects. First, they diverge over the range of justification. For Raz, justification is individualistic and can be piecemeal—justification differs between individuals so that authority can be justified over some members of a community but not others. For Hershovitz, the justification is specific to particular practices, which might, it seems, admit either a checkerboard pattern or a community-wide justification depending upon the view we take of political authority. For Finnis, justification of authority is a social matter; authority is justified over all those persons within the community whose common good it serves (those for which it establishes the conditions necessary to enable individual flourishing).

Second, and relatedly, theories give different accounts of the value of authority. For Finnis and Raz, authority has instrumental value; for Hershovitz, value depends upon the specific practice in which authority is located. In Hershovitz' approach, we need to look at whether reason justifies the existence of Darwallian second-personal authority-rights and obligations, not in isolation but as part of a justified practice of allocating such rights and obligations.[64] In the case of political or public authority, that practice might be intrinsically and/or instrumentally justified.

For Finnis, authority is legitimate when it enables individuals to pursue the realization of those basic 'goods' that have objective and self-evident value for all humans.[65] Finnis argues that in order for people in communities to pursue these goods through their own objectives and following their own life plans, a community needs an authority to solve coordination problems.[66] The authority provides a 'common good' of a special kind, that is, the 'set of conditions which enables the members of a community to attain for themselves reasonable objectives, or to obtain for themselves the value(s), for the sake of

---

[63] Raz expressly makes effectiveness a necessary condition: 'only bodies that enjoy de facto authority (i.e., that are in fact followed or at least conformed with by considerable segments of the population) can have legitimate authority': Joseph Raz, 'The Problem of Authority: Revisiting the Service Conception' (2006) 90 *Minn Law Review* 1003, 1036. Finnis, in contrast, gives efficacy 'fundamental' but 'defeasible' importance: 'the conjunction of the principle [that authority is good] with the opportunity [for its exercise] is only presumptively sufficient to justify the claim to and recognition of authority': John Finnis, *Natural Law and Natural Rights* (Clarendon Press, 1980), 246.

[64] Hershovitz himself notes that more work needs to be done to flesh out the implications of this account for the question of the justification of political authority, but the groundwork is here to do so, and, importantly for my study, the structure of justification that he lays out is clear and plausible: Hershovitz, 'The Role of Authority', 25.

[65] Finnis, *Natural Law and Natural Rights*, 155. Finnis' list of the human goods includes life, sociability, play, religion, knowledge, and aesthetic experience.

[66] Finnis, *Natural Law and Natural Rights*, 231–233.

which they have reason to collaborate with each other'.⁶⁷ Importantly, this argument suggests that legitimate authority is limited to the establishment of such order as is necessary for this sort of human flourishing to occur, without doing violence to any one of the basic goods.⁶⁸

Raz's instrumental account, in contrast, leaves the requirements of reason open to be determined in particular situations. This seems to leave more room for legitimate authority to operate beyond what is merely necessary to help individuals achieve Finnisian basic goods. Rather than arguing that authority must serve certain values that are essential for all human flourishing, Raz claims that what is valuable to people is to conform to the reasons that apply to them.⁶⁹ For Raz, all reasons are facts of various kinds, and the normatively significant facts are facts about what is valuable.⁷⁰ Raz's account aims to make authority consistent with autonomy by showing how legitimate authority provides the service of mediating between people and the reasons that apply to them.⁷¹ Thus, the ultimate aim an authority must serve is to promote the subject's conformity to reason; and where it does so, the subject's obedience is consistent with her autonomy.

The centrality of Raz's account in contemporary work on authority means his justificatory story needs extra attention. Using the explanatory account of authority outlined earlier, where authority provides content-independent and exclusionary reasons for action, Raz argues that a legitimate authority must make decisions on the basis of the same reasons that would apply to the subject.⁷² He then offers a 'normal justification' for authority (the 'normal justification thesis' (NJT)). According to the NJT, it is a condition of legitimate authority:⁷³

> [t]hat the subject would better conform to reasons that apply to him anyway (that is, to reasons other than the directives of the authority) if he intends to be guided by the authority's directives than if he does not.

---

⁶⁷ Finnis, *Natural Law and Natural Rights*, 155. The goods are common not in any aggregate sense, but because they are 'good for each and every person', and because they can be enjoyed by any number of persons in numerous ways.

⁶⁸ Finnis then goes on to argue that legal authority provides the best possible solution for coordinating social activity while still allowing for individual self-determination of goals and plans, by providing constraints on discretion and arbitrary power and thereby securing cooperation on terms that are not only stable, but also fair. Finnis uses this argument to ground a general obligation to obey the law, as a requirement of practical reasonableness: Finnis, *Natural Law and Natural Rights*, Ch 10.

⁶⁹ This includes all the reasons that apply to their relationships with others: Raz, *The Morality of Freedom*, 72.

⁷⁰ Raz, *Practical Reason and Norms*, 22–23.

⁷¹ Raz, 'Authority, Law and Morality', 300.

⁷² Raz calls this the 'Dependence Thesis', which holds that 'authorities do not have the right to impose completely independent duties on people... their directives should reflect dependent reasons which are binding on those people in any case': Raz, *Morality of Freedom*, 47–53.

⁷³ Raz, *Between Authority and Interpretation*, 136–137.

Or, as Raz explained in an earlier version:[74]

> The normal way to establish that a person should be acknowledged to have authority over another person involves showing that the alleged subject is likely better to comply with reasons which apply to him (other than the alleged authoritative directives) if he accepts the directives of the alleged authority as authoritatively binding and tries to follow them, rather than by trying to follow the reasons which apply to him directly.

Raz is careful not to elevate conformity to reason to an imperative standard. He adds an 'independence' condition to sit alongside the NJT in the task of justifying authority, which clarifies that not all matters of practical action are matters where conformity to reason is the most important aim.[75] This second condition stipulates:[76]

> The matters regarding which the first condition is met are such that with respect to them it is better to conform to reason than to decide for oneself, unaided by authority.

Raz gives the examples of choosing one's friends or partners to illustrate that it is sometimes more important for individuals to decide a question for themselves, rather than to decide correctly. 'Conformity to reason is not everything: how we decide what to do is, sometimes, of independent value.'[77] Referring specifically to the case of political authority, Raz confirms that 'governments can have legitimate authority only over matters regarding which acting according to right reason is more important than deciding for oneself how to act'.[78]

Raz's account indicates that the two conditions operate independently: he does not argue that reason recommends individual decision-making on some matters—so that it is reason itself that excludes the operation of an authority—rather, that on some matters, individual choice is more important than conformity to reason. That is, there are other types of reasons which weigh in favour or against having an authoritative determination at all. However, Raz argues that these reasons behind deciding for oneself, and the reasons for action

---

[74] Raz, *The Morality of Freedom*, 53–57. In developing his theory, Raz changed the requirement from 'compliance' to 'conformity' with reason. The difference is not significant for my purposes here, but for discussion, see Bruno Celano, 'Are Reasons for Action Beliefs?', in Lukas H Meyer, *et al.* (eds), *Rights, Culture and the Law: Themes from the Legal and Political Philosophy of Joseph Raz* (Oxford University Press, 2003), 40 *ff*.

[75] According to Raz, the NJT and the independence condition (appearing in earlier work as a 'jurisdiction condition') provide 'the two conditions of legitimacy': see Joseph Raz, 'Government by Consent', in J Rowland Pennock and John W Chapman (eds), *Authority Revisited* (1987), 350; and for other discussions of the independence condition, see Joseph Raz, 'Comments and Responses', in Lukas H Meyer (ed), *Rights, Culture and the Law* (2003), 261; Raz, *Between Authority and Interpretation*, 137, 149–150.

[76] Raz, 'The Problem of Authority: Revisiting the Service Conception', 1014.

[77] Raz, 'Government by Consent', 349.

[78] Raz, 'Government by Consent', 349.

with which we should conform, need not be incommensurable and can be interwoven. For instance, reasons favouring self-reliance might be instrumental to right reason, for example when self-reliance today will enable greater conformity with reason in the long run by improving one's ability to make good decisions.[79] Yet Raz accepts that in some situations, the reasons for independence or conformity will not be clear-cut, or will be incommensurate, leaving it unclear whether independent action or obedience to authority is required.[80]

As the leading contribution to this field, Raz's work has attracted much elaboration, amendment, and criticism. Although there are too many responses to Raz's account to assess here, three points on which Raz has faced criticism will continue to be important for my own account of relative authority. The first is perhaps the most generally powerful objection to Raz's account. Darwall, among others, has argued that Raz's normal justification for authority shows when it would be rational for someone to treat another person as having authority; not that that person actually has such authority. On According to this view, authority is not simply a power to create pre-emptive reasons for action, as Raz suggests; instead, authority (and what must be justified) is a right to create those pre-emptive reasons, and an obligation (not just a reason) for subjects to obey.[81]

A second criticism references a debate about the kind of theory Raz offers. As Hershovitz has indicated, Raz's theory could be interpreted as a kind of sponge theory, which absorbs all those other theories of justification in which authority serves values that happen to be in accordance with reason.[82] For example, if democratic authority serves equality and autonomy in some combination that right reason does in fact recommend, then such authority would be justified on Raz's account.[83] Or, if Finnis were right about the list of human values that authority can serve, then his account would be consistent with Raz's. Hershovitz argues, however, that such an interpretation 'make[s] the normal justification thesis empty...hence it ceases to be a competitor with other candidate theories of legitimacy'.[84] He explains that Raz's theory is supposed to be substantive: it asks whether conformity with authority enables

---

[79] Raz, *Between Authority and Interpretation*, 138. Raz gives the convincing example of children who are allowed to practice making their own decisions being more capable of becoming reason-conforming adults.

[80] Raz, *Between Authority and Interpretation*, 139. I return to problems associated with this independence condition, and its significance for my account of relative authority, in Ch 6.

[81] Stephen Darwall, 'Authority and Reasons: Exclusionary and Second-Personal' (2010) 120 *Ethics* 257; see also Hershovitz, 'The Role of Authority'.

[82] Hershovitz, 'Legitimacy, Democracy and Razian Authority', 219–220.

[83] For a counter-argument which seeks to modify the normal justification condition to include democratic requirements without rendering the normal justification empty, see Besson, 'The Authority of International Law—Lifting the State Veil'.

[84] Hershovitz, 'Legitimacy, Democracy and Razian Authority' 219.

an individual to better conform to the reasons that apply to them to do X or Y, not about the reasons an individual has to make the decision between doing-X or doing-Y in a certain way, using a certain process (eg by following or not following an authority). If Hershovitz is right about the kind of account Raz offers, then Raz's theory does not simply absorb Finnis' account, or others that link the justification of authority with the service of particular values that happen to be in accordance with reason.

A third persistent question is whether the normal justification thesis might work as a justification for some forms of practical authority, particularly parental authority, but fail to capture the justification of public authority. There are two related themes in this challenge: first, that the normal justification ignores some important values associated with public authority; second, that it does not accord with our social practice of public authority. In the first theme, critics have argued that political/legal authority serves or instantiates values other than simply mediating between people and the reasons that apply to them. In particular, authority may be instrumentally justified by its role in providing dispute settlement services to its subjects; or it may carry intrinsic value as a process enabling subjects to contest and control political arrangements in a manner that preserves their ability to disagree and respects their autonomy.[85] It is worth reiterating here that Raz insists that he offers only a normal justification for authority, not a complete justification, and that other theories of legitimate authority may be important as supplements to the normal justification, including theories that capture intrinsic values or other instrumental values. Raz has expressly accepted that 'an ability to identify with one's political community is...intrinsically valuable' and concedes that an exclusively instrumental account of legal authority would be incomplete.[86] Raz thus suggests that we can build many other combinations of theories on top of the normal justification, provided their role as supplements is clearly understood—they cannot legitimize authority that does not already meet the normal justification.

The second theme of the criticism responds to Raz's claim to provide a 'normative explanatory' account of the practice of authority.[87] There are many elements of Raz's work that might be regarded as surprising from a practical perspective. For instance, Raz's account makes justification particular to individuals, so that an authority that is justified for one person may not be

---

[85] See Shapiro, 'Authority', on the 'arbitration' model of authority; Jeremy Waldron, *Law and Disagreement* (Clarendon Press, 1998); and see Besson, 'Review Article: Democracy, Law and Authority', 89–99.
[86] Joseph Raz, 'Multiculturalism' (1998) 11 *Ratio Juris* 193.
[87] Raz, *The Morality of Freedom*, 64.

justified for her neighbour. This sits uneasily with any sense that the range of a political authority extends over members of a political community in a blanket rather than patchwork fashion. More generally, Raz's account sets such a high standard for justification that it seems likely that very few of the bodies that claim legitimate authority actually have it. The criticism is then that the theory departs too far from the widespread social practice of treating much public authority, particularly democratically elected authority, as legitimate. This is by no means fatal; indeed, it may simply reflect the distinction between a 'sociological' conception of legitimacy, which conceives of legitimacy as what people think is legitimate, rather than a conception of normative legitimacy, or what actually is legitimate.[88] Furthermore, even if the result of applying Raz's test is that there is very little legitimate authority out there, we can either live with this radical result, or make other arguments about reasons to respect even illegitimate authority.

The arguments presented in the following chapters present distinctive versions of these two themes: first, that there is something special about public authorities—namely that there is a plurality of them and as a result they are engaged in relationships with one another—and, second, that Raz's theory does not seem to explain the practice of plurality and relationships between authorities. My questions are a challenge to the conception of singular or independent authority that is assumed in all of these accounts of what authority is and when it is justified. To make that challenge, it is first necessary to elaborate the phenomena of plurality and inter-authority relationships, which, I argue, a theory of authority should be able to explain.

---

[88] See Besson, 'The Authority of International Law—Lifting the State Veil'.

3
Plural Authorities and Inter-Authority Relationships

There is nothing new in the observation that contemporary arrangements of legal and political order feature a complex web of overlapping and conflicting powers, norms, and regimes, spread across local, federal, regional, international, supra-national, and non-state hosts. A whole field of scholarship pursues interests in such transnational, 'post-Westphalian', 'post-sovereign', or 'post-national' arrangements of power, giving a new lease of life to the study of legal pluralism.[1] This chapter presents these arrangements as complex arrangements of authority. I aim to show that what has been described as an 'endemic overlap' of powers is not simply an overlap between the places in which power is exercised, or the people over whom it is exercised, or even the jurisdictions that are implicated; rather, it is an overlap in the domains of different authorities.[2] I make authority central to the study of the transnational sphere in order to better understand its various types of arrangements and assess their legitimacy.

This chapter does not add another full description of this complex order of dispersed or integrated institutions with authority. The work that has been done elsewhere suggests that most if not all authorities operate inside networks or webs of relationships which include others with which they share or contest subjects and/or arenas of activity.[3] Instead, the task here is to set up the conceptual tools that will be necessary to establishing later whether,

---

[1] Nicholas Barber writes that 'legal pluralism has become fashionable', especially in Europe, where the complexity of systems 'demands a pluralist interpretation': NW Barber, 'Legal Pluralism and the European Union' (2006) 12 *European Law Journal* 306. For discussion of the terminology, see Neil Walker, 'Flexibility within a Metaconstitutional Frame: Reflections on the Future of Legal Authority in Europe', in Grainne De Búrca and Joanne Scott (eds), *Constitutional Change in the EU: From Uniformity to Flexibility?* (Hart Publishing, 2000), 26–27, n 58.

[2] Neil Walker, symposium presentation transcribed in *Four Visions of Constitutional Pluralism* (European University Institute, 2008). See also symposium summary in Matej Avbelj and Jan Komárek, 'Four Visions of Constitutional Pluralism' (2008) 4 *European Constitutional Law Review* 524.

[3] On networks, see Walker, 'Flexibility within a Metaconstitutional Frame'; Anne-Marie Slaughter, *A New World Order* (Princeton University Press, 2004). For a comprehensive assessment of the prevalence of plurality see Paul Schiff Berman, 'Global Legal Pluralism' (2007) 80 *Southern California Law Review* 1155.

and then how, authority can be located among these different actors in a way that is sensitive to the relationships between them. Section 1 begins by examining the phenomena of plurality and inter-authority relationships, and introducing two key distinctions between different types of each. Section 2 then examines different types of relationships in detail, using a typology to demarcate compatible, coordinated, and conflicting relationships. Section 3 examines existing work in legal and constitutional pluralist literature to seek tools for understanding plurality and relationships, and suggests that more in-depth and accurate insight can be gained through the lens of authority.

1. Introducing Plurality and Inter-Authority Relationships

Throughout this study I use the term *plurality* in a descriptive/explanatory sense to refer to the fact of multiplicity of authority, or what Walker has elegantly described as the 'fragmented, fluid and contested configuration of authority of a multi-dimensional order'.[4] Plurality simply describes the existence of multiple locations of public authority. It is a synonym for multiplicity, with no implied normative position about its desirability or otherwise. In contrast, the term *pluralism* is used here to capture the normative position that responds to the fact of plurality by embracing it; and by rejecting attempts to consolidate plural authorities or organize them into centralized or coordinated hierarchies.[5]

Plurality in this descriptive sense is sometimes treated as a consequence or facet of the proliferation of rule-systems to deal with global interactions. That, of course, simplifies too much—any student aware of the tradition of scholarship on legal pluralism knows that the phenomenon is easily traced back to pre-Westphalian eras where multiple overlapping legal systems were

---

[4] Neil Walker, 'The Idea of Constitutional Pluralism' (2002) 65 *MLR* 317, 337, 347. Walker himself calls this the explanatory dimension of pluralism, but I will use the term 'plurality' to avoid confusing this explanatory dimension with the normative case for pluralism.
[5] Walker, 'The Idea of Constitutional Pluralism', 337. Walker specifically links pluralism with the normative requirement of 'mutual recognition and respect between national and supranational authorities'. Both the observation of plurality and a commitment to pluralism can be driven by adopting a particular lens on public authority, which 'implies an incommensurability of the knowledge and authority (or sovereignty) claims' emanating from different locations of authority: Walker, 'The Idea of Constitutional Pluralism', 338. It seems most useful to see the study of plurality and pluralism not as a distinct field of study, but rather a particular representation of the legal world, and a particular approach to legal thinking. For example, Ruth Buchanan considers legal plurality a 'metaphor', a frame, or a style of legal thinking, which 'might provide a more productive avenue through which to approach the pressing issues of law's inclusivity and legitimacy in the transnational realm': Ruth Buchanan, 'Reconceptualizing Law and Politics in the Transnational: Constitutional and Legal Pluralist Approaches' (2008) 5 *Socio-Legal Review*, § 3.

endemic and unremarkable. Yet the influence of globalization seems to have given interest in plurality a new impetus, to attract not only predominantly sociological or anthropological theorists, but also interest from general jurisprudents and doctrinal scholars in those fields which must confront the facts of plurality, or which advocate pluralism in their doctrinal and normative debates.

Plurality is most obvious within the international order, where authority is exercised by supra-national or international organizations, regional organizations, specialist bureaucracies, courts and tribunals, and states themselves. Yet it is also found within state systems: it is obvious in federal or composite nation states which seek to divide authority between different entities; or where authority is exercised by sub-state entities arranged geographically or even along ethnic, religious, or cultural divides. Plurality might exist along more or less formal lines of division, whether drawn by legal rules or functional/practical necessity, and can exist in any combination of arrangements that generate multiple 'levels' or 'networks' of authority.[6] Although the broadest sense of plurality would include the plurality of authorities that have nothing to do with one another, which I call 'parallel' authorities, these authorities fall outside of my interest in inter-authority relationships. As an empirical matter, there might be very few authorities that have nothing to do with any other authority; even states with seemingly independent sovereign status must often interact with each other when exercising their authority.[7] Insofar as there are authorities operating in parallel, they are not the concern of this study as their authority is simply subject to the ordinary and independent assessments of legitimacy.

Even setting aside parallel authorities, plurality of authority encompasses a large and diverse set of inter-authority relationships. To impose a sense of order, I will introduce two types of plurality, and two categories of interrelated authorities.

a. 'Same-domain' and 'interactive-domain' plurality

There are two types of plurality of authority. The first exists where there are two or more authorities in the same domain ('same-domain plurality'); the second where two or more authorities with separate domains interact with

---

[6] For an analysis of the ideas of 'levels' and 'networks' of authority in political and legal theory, see Armin Bogdandy and Philipp Dann, 'International Composite Administration' (2008) 9 *German Law Journal* 2013, 2015–2020.

[7] As Delmas-Marty puts it, 'interdependency renders isolation impossible': Mireille Delmas-Marty, *Ordering Pluralism: A Conceptual Framework for Understanding the Transnational Legal World* (Hart Publishing, 2009), 19.

one another ('interactive-domain plurality'). Same-domain plurality exists when more than one person/body is authoritative for the same subjects in relation to the same field of activity. This occurs both when there is a complete overlap or identity of subjects/activities between the authorities, and when there is only a partial overlap, such that one authority purports to govern in only part of the other's domain (over some fields of action and/or some subjects). Setting aside for now questions of legitimacy, examples of purportedly same-domain authority include instances of concurrent powers between federal and state legislatures, or concurrent jurisdictions between national and supra-national judicial institutions.

Interactive-domain plurality, in contrast, exists where the domains of the authorities are separate but come into contact, either through the interaction of their respective subjects or the interconnectedness of the activities they seek to regulate. That is, one authority might be legitimate over a defined set of subjects, who then interact with subjects of another legitimate authority in ways that bring their respective authorities into contact. Alternatively, an authority might govern in domains of activity which engage the domains of a different authority, either deliberately or simply as a result of the activities themselves being connected. For example, subjects engaged in cross-border commercial activities may require the interaction of authorities in order to pursue their plans or resolve cross-jurisdictional disputes that arise with subjects of another authority. Similarly, states working together to combat transboundary problems have interactive domains with respect to such activities. For instance, State A's domain interacts with State B's domain where States A and B make a joint commitment to such projects as reciprocal environmental obligations, trade access, shared regulatory standards, or mutual defence. Where both states undertake such commitments on behalf of their subjects, their domains of authority are interactive.

An inter-authority relationship then arises out of either (i) the overlap or (ii) the interaction of the domains. These relationships might be passive, that is, authorities that come into contact through the interaction or overlap of their domains may choose to ignore each other's operations rather than seek to work with or against the other authority in any way. Often, however, the nature of the interaction or overlap means that authorities cannot ignore each other, at least not for long, for doing so would lead to some failure to fully act in authority over their respective subjects, or to fall short of meeting their standards of legitimacy or effectiveness. If an authority is to succeed in securing social coordination or pursuing other goods for its subjects, it may be necessary to engage actively with other authorities. In both same-domain and interactive-domain situations, for instance, the presence of multiple authorities may defeat or limit the ability of each authority to successfully coordinate subjects or achieve other goals, which would be better served if the authorities either found a way to work together, or established working hierarchies or exclusive spheres of operation. This, in a nutshell, is the core idea of relative authority upon which the later chapters of this book will elaborate.

b. Integrated and disjunctive authorities

For greater clarity, it is useful to categorize interrelated authorities as either *integrated* or *disjunctive*. Integrated authorities are arranged or organized by common rules and principles applying to their relationship, while disjunctive authorities are separate; their relationships are not governed by organizing rules or principles. Straightforward examples of integrated relationships include relationships between branches of government (courts, legislatures, and executives) and levels of government (federal, state, local) ordered by a shared constitution; between states and particular supra-national institutions whose formal authority is agreed by treaty; and between self-governing territories within a state whose autonomy is protected by treaty or constitutional provisions. Disjunctive relationships, in contrast, include relationships between states (outside of matters on which they are committed to one another under international law); between international institutions with distinct sources of authority and areas of competence; and between state governments and internal authorities which exercise an autonomy that is not formally recognized or protected.

The distinction between integrated and disjunctive authorities will be important both for understanding and evaluating authorities in light of their relationships, and for evaluating the relationships themselves. For integrated authorities, integration under norms means that each authority's conformity with the relationship-governing norms can be analysed and evaluated; while on their face, disjunctive authorities look to be free from constraints or commitments to each other against which their interactions can be evaluated. Yet there are complicating factors which mean that we cannot always differentiate easily between integrated and disjunctive authorities. For a number of reasons, it might be difficult to establish whether a particular relationship is governed by norms or simply exists de facto. Rules governing a relationship might not always be easy to locate; they might be customary or informal rules, or they might be contained in many separate arrangements rather than being neatly laid out in a formal constitution or similar superior arrangement. Perspective might also prove critical in assessing whether interaction generates customary rules rather than just regular habits of conduct, or whether different authorities are separate or are actually subsidiaries of an overarching system. Alternatively, a particular relationship might be partially governed by rules and partially left to de facto arrangements, in which case it would be misleading to characterize those authorities as either integrated or disjunctive. Similarly, the lack of a normative framework applying between disjunctive authorities may not mean that there are no rules in place whatsoever, for in the case of institutional authorities, the internal constitutional rules of each institution will often include constraints upon that institution's relationships with other authorities.[8] Even where there are integrated authorities, the integrating normative framework is likely to be complicated by the internal rules of each constitutional order, which might contradict the rules applying to their relationship and/or each other.

2. Types of Inter-Authority Relationships

Although the complexity of many inter-authority relationships makes it difficult to situate any particular relationship in any one category, a basic typology can indicate the different arrangements of powers distributed between authorities. One possible way of cataloguing types of relationships would be to position relationships along a social dimension ranging from cooperative to competitive. That social dimension, made up of the preferences and conduct of the authorities towards one another, is important as an outward manifestation of their relationship, but it does not help us understand arrangements of powers or their implications, as cooperation and competition can occur between authorities in all sorts of different normative or de facto arrangements.[9] To get to a more precise typology, we therefore need to examine the distribution of powers within inter-authority relationships, and consider their effects upon the obligations or reasons applying to their subjects. The typology offered here makes a distinction between relationships that are compatible, coordinated, and conflicting—a distinction drawn by examining different impacts upon the reasons applying to the respective or shared subjects of interrelated authorities.

a. Compatible authorities: deference and toleration

Plural authorities will be compatible if their directives to subjects are either identical or are non-contradictory, but remain separate and uncoordinated. In

---

[8] These constitutional constraints are key to Raz's explanation for multiplicity of legitimate authority, as discussed in Ch 5.

[9] As Shapiro suggests, authorities of equal or unequal powers may compete with one another to have the greatest influence on policy: Scott J Shapiro, 'Law, Plans, and Practical Reason' (2002) 8 *Legal Theory* 415.

other words, authorities are compatible if their (shared or interacting) subjects could comply with each of their directives simultaneously, but the authorities are not intentionally working together. Compatibility therefore refers not to the mere existence of the authorities, but to their exercise of authority. This compatibility can occur between authorities within a single domain or across interactive domains, and can be a product of coincidence or the result of a deliberate attempt by one authority to align itself with another. Deliberate compatibility can arise in an overlapping domain through a practice of deference or toleration in which one authority chooses not to exercise its authority in order to avoid conflict with another; while between interactive domains, compatibility might be due to an authority's respect for another's domain, as evident in the practice of comity between sovereign states.

Practices of deference/toleration and respect/comity entail similar arrangements of powers and identical effects on the reasons applying to the subject. Both practices entail that the deferring/respecting authority has the power to decide the matter itself, but also the power to choose not to decide, or to decide differently.[10] Both therefore avoid creating practical conflict for the subjects. Deference and comity can (but need not) involve normative restraints upon the conduct of either or both authorities, and characteristically, when there are internal normative constraints upon the decision to defer, they leave plenty of discretionary space to the authority making that choice.

Examples of deferential relationships are most easily found within integrated relationships (such as judicial powers to review executive action within a common constitutional framework), and may be indistinguishable from the types of coordinated relationships that are discussed in the following section. Yet deference can also be found in disjunctive relationships, where it is perhaps better described as a kind of toleration in which one authority simply allows another authority space to operate, without interfering in the exercise of its authority. A relationship of toleration entails that one authority has the capacity to interfere in some way with another authority that partially shares its domain—for instance by disrupting or undermining the exercise of the other's authority—but it chooses not to. Importantly, toleration of another authority involves more than simply being indifferent towards or ignoring that other authority's operation. It involves some recognition or at least awareness that there is another authority out there with an overlapping or interacting domain, and tolerating that situation. It is, in this respect, a kind of basic

---

[10] It only makes sense to speak of deferential relationships when there is this element of choice involved, to distinguish it from an obligation to apply another's decisions (as occurs in authority relationships) or a simple inability to deny the application of another's decision in favour of one's own.

or passive support for a compatible authority's operation.[11] Perhaps the most interesting examples of toleration include relationships between official legal systems and other normative systems that operate at least partially within the official system. A legal authority—legislative or judicial—might tolerate the operation of normative arrangements that empower other compatible authorities to exercise authority over the law's subjects.[12] For instance, without being required to do so by constitutional or other legal rules, a legislature might leave room for the operation of a semi-autonomous region or population with its own legal arrangements.[13]

Comity is also a relationship between disjunctive authorities in interactive domains. It is the archetypal relationship between sovereign states that interact with one another through their own or their subjects' activities, and is therefore found in examples from both public and private international law. National judiciaries sit in horizontal relationships to one another, but their domains of authority interact through their jurisdictional arrangements, when a particular dispute between subjects of their separate authority might be heard in more than one jurisdiction.[14] When this occurs, each legal system's own doctrines of private international law control the application of jurisdiction, as well as the choice of which law to apply, which can lead to situations of concurrent proceedings regarding the same or related subject matter.[15] Many judicial systems have responded to such phenomena by unilaterally developing legal doctrines (including stays of proceedings and

---

[11] Toleration between authorities is not necessarily linked to the political ideal of toleration for reasonable views or the ethical principle of toleration for persons with whom one disagrees (although both ideals might motivate a particular authority to tolerate the operation of another).

[12] This account of toleration might be interpreted as a more passive version of Raz's claim that legal systems are characteristically supportive of other normative systems. See Joseph Raz, *The Authority of Law* (2nd edn, Oxford University Press, 2009), 119–120.

[13] Examples might include religious or ethnic populations located in relatively autonomous areas, which do not threaten the state's existence or the basic peaceful order of society. This is just an approximation. The exact question of the conditions under which a semi-autonomous or self-determining group should be tolerated is a more detailed matter. For analysis, see Avishai Margalit and Joseph Raz, 'National Self-Determination' (1990) 87 *The Journal of Philosophy* 439.

[14] This scenario generates what one common law judge has described as 'a jungle of separate, broadly based, jurisdictions all over the world': Lord Goff in *Airbus Industries GIE v Patel* [1999] 1 AC 199. This fact leads to the much-discussed topic of 'forum-shopping' by plaintiffs seeking to get the best substantive outcome. See, eg Andreas F Lowenfeld, 'Forum Shopping, Antisuit Injunctions, Negative Declarations, and Related Tools of International Litigation' (1997) *American Journal of International Law* 314.

[15] For detailed analysis of the problem of *lis pendens*, the doctrines developing to address it in both civil and common law systems, and the principles on which such doctrines are based, see Campbell McLachlan, *Lis Pendens in International Litigation* (Martinus Nijhoff, 2009).

anti-suit injunctions) that decline jurisdiction in order to give effect to relationships of comity and respect for a foreign court's authority.[16]

b. Complementary authorities: cooperation and coordination

Strictly speaking, complementarity is a species of compatibility because it entails no eventual practical conflict for the shared or interactive subjects. Yet complementarity is distinct from other types of compatibility because it involves bilateral arrangements of cooperation or coordination between authorities. Like compatible relationships, complementary relationships between authorities can occur within shared domains or across interactive domains. They can occur between authorities that are either hierarchically structured with distributions of powers to supervise, overrule, or obligate one another, or through 'dialogical' practices in which both authorities' conduct is responsive to each other.

There are two basic types of complementary relationships: cooperative and coordinated. Cooperative relationships entail an intention held by two or more agents to work together towards common goals, either through the pursuit of a single shared activity or different but complementary activities that are part of a shared plan of 'joint action'.[17] As with cooperation among individuals, cooperation among authorities can be explained as a kind of joint action which is either fully cooperative, when agents work together towards a single shared goal, or coordinative, where agents have 'compatible private goals' which, if they are to be achieved optimally, are dependent upon taking into account each other's actions; along with the intention to pursue their private goals without upsetting the others'.[18] Such cooperation is, importantly, compatible with conflicting beliefs and desires among the participants, so long as these do not alter their intentions to work together.

---

[16] McLachlan suggests that comity is a vague and unprincipled basis upon which to explain or limit the practice of courts' renouncing their own jurisdiction in favour of waiting to see what happens in another's. Although the practice may generate more predictability, the concern is that a court having jurisdiction should not decline it, as this might lead to denial of justice. See McLachlan, *Lis Pendens in International Litigation*, Ch 2.

[17] For the conception of cooperation as an activity determined by participants' mutually responsive and interlocking intentions, see Michael E Bratman, 'Shared Cooperative Activity' (1992) 101 *The Philosophical Review* 327. A more precise analysis would use Bratman's distinction between 'joint intentional action', which is cooperative only in the sense of participants intending to act together and 'mesh' their sub-plans, and 'shared cooperative activity', in which participants also intend to mutually support one another. For my purposes here, the broader categorization is sufficient.

[18] Here, when referring to cooperation of institutional authorities, I intend to invoke the same concept that applies to individual agent authorities. Institutions are to be understood as corporate agents with the capacity to act, including cooperatively.

Examples of cooperation between disjunctive authorities can be found in the lead-up to treaties, contracts, or other arrangements which turn disjunctive authorities into integrated authorities in respect of the matters subject to those arrangements. They can also occur informally in circumstances in which formal cooperation is either undesirable or unachievable. Examples include the political cooperation that occurs between states in order to influence policy and affect outcomes in multilateral decision-making processes.[19] Indeed, wherever there is a need for or an advantage in joint international decision-making, states can be expected to cooperate to greater or lesser degrees with others who seek the same goals.[20] Cooperation might also occur between state and non-state authorities, such as collaborative efforts between governments and religious leaders or leaders of cultural/ethnic minority communities, or between these non-state entities. There are also many examples of direct but informal cooperation between regulatory and administrative agencies from separate states which cooperate with their foreign counterparts in order to achieve ends more effectively, including through collection of information, improving efficiency or delivery of services, or enforcing regulations.[21] Although in the current era of treaty-making these relationships are often formalized by inter-state agreements, they can also occur prior to such formalization, or deliberately off the radar of official commitments.

Where there are integrated authorities, we can more easily identify the distinctive normative arrangements within the relationship, including the rights, powers, obligations, and liabilities distributed between the interacting authorities.[22] For example, formal partnership relationships entail a rule-governed division of contributions, competencies, and responsibilities that are agreed

---

[19] Within multilateral organizations, for example, informal groups and particularly strong political alliances work to influence the agenda, share information, or act as voting blocks. For example, in the United Nations Security Council, informal 'Groups of Friends', 'Contact Groups', and 'Core Groups' cooperate to influence Council decisions and are sometimes informally responsible for certain decisions being taken. See analysis in Jochen Prantl, 'Informal Groups of States and the U.N. Security Council' (2005) 59 *International Organization* 559. Outside of the UN, cooperation occurs in particular subject-specific international settings: from whaling to trade liberation to climate change or financial regulation.

[20] The reasons for which states cooperate are, of course, much more complicated than this. For my purposes the fact of cooperation is important, the motivating reasons for it are not.

[21] Cooperation is common in pursuit of transboundary activities, from crime to anti-competitive practices to communications and transport. Increasingly, such cooperation is being standardized and formalized into treaties and more or less formal working arrangements. Such arrangements, in my terminology, transform the type of relationship from a disjunctive into an integrated one, although in practice little may change in the daily interaction between authorities.

[22] Rights and liabilities within relationships can include any of the types of rights as classified by Hohfeld, or combinations of such rights. For Hohfeld's system, see Wesley Newcomb Hohfeld, *Fundamental Legal Conceptions* (Yale University Press, 1964).

upon by the interacting authorities. The rules can establish obligations between parties and may empower each authority to call the other to account for any breaches. Many international treaties are best understood as such partnership agreements, which commit the states parties to cooperate with one another by (for example) sharing information, undertaking internal policies which will effect international changes, or making joint contributions to a common project.[23] Such commitments are particularly common in the international economic and financial systems, where transnational regulatory cooperation, harmonization of commercial law, and trade liberalization commitments are evidence of complex networks of cooperation among states and specialized agencies therein.[24] Joint commitments to common goals can also be found in other fields, including environmental treaties, which assign joint responsibility for management of a resource or area to coalitions of states.[25] Mutual defence arrangements such as NATO provide another familiar example. At other times, partnership is designed to enable an authority to enforce or give effect to private ends that require some degree of assistance from an external authority, such as treaties of extradition or mutual assistance, which enable the more effective operation of national criminal laws. Alternatively, partnerships with other authorities might be needed to provide efficient processes for dealing with the prevalence of cross-border activities by the authorities' subjects, such as treaties establishing mutual recognition for foreign judgments, family status, or consumer safety standards.

Alternatively to all these forms of cooperation, complementarity can be achieved through coordination. Coordination involves a link between authorities, which either places them within hierarchical networks or engages them in dialogical processes that incrementally bring them into alignment. Hierarchical coordination can include relationships of authority, supervision, or delegation/agency. Authority relationships exist where one authority can obligate another to act or refrain from acting. Relationships of supervision entail a power to reverse or nullify a lower authority's decision. Delegation and relationships of agency involve transfers of power in which one authority

---

[23] Such cooperation can occur multilaterally or bilaterally, but is particularly obvious in bilateral settings where states commit to specific mechanisms of cooperation.

[24] On regulatory cooperation, see GA Bermann *et al.*, *Transatlantic Regulatory Cooperation: Legal Problems and Political Prospects* (Oxford University Press, 2000); Elliot Posner, 'Making Rules for Global Finance: Transatlantic Regulatory Cooperation at the Turn of the Millennium' (2009) 63 *International Organization* 665.

[25] One of the most interesting examples is the Antarctic Treaty System, which sets aside any questions of sovereignty over the continent while permitting existing territorial claims to be maintained and, in a 1991 protocol, designated the continent 'as a natural reserve, devoted to peace and science': Protocol on Environmental Protection to the Antarctic Treaty 1991, Art 2.

conditionally gives powers to another, usually with a residual power to withdraw the transfer or at least supervise the exercise of the power.[26] A key feature of all these hierarchical relationships is that they involve two layers of subjects: first is the authority that is subject to the authority/supervision/direction of another authority (the 'subject-authority'); and second are the 'ultimate subjects', being the individual subjects of the subject-authority.[27]

It is easy to find examples of such hierarchically coordinated relationships, but harder to differentiate clearly between specific relationships of authority, supervision, delegation, and agency without engaging in detailed analyses of particular constitutional systems. The most obvious examples appear within the complex (and composite) structures of administration in modern states—often including layers of administration at sub-state or supra-state levels—where detailed constitutional, administrative, and public laws arrange specific relationships between branches and levels of government.[28] The most complex examples of integrated authority relationships occur in federated systems, which typically involve hierarchical relationships in combination with relationships of compatibility and conflict.[29] In the international sphere, states that are themselves authorities have become subjects of international authorities, most obviously judicial or other rule-applying authorities.[30] These juridical authorities, as well as the quasi-legislative, executive authority located in the United Nations Security Council, all have powers to impose obligations upon those states subject to their jurisdiction (or all states in the case of the Security Council).[31] Indeed, all the seminal examples of institutional authorities in

---

[26] David A Lake, 'Delegating Divisible Sovereignty: Sweeping a Conceptual Minefield' (2007) 2 *The Review of International Organizations* 219. According to Lake, delegation involves 'a hierarchical relationship in which an agent receives a conditional grant of authority to act for a principal under some specified conditions'. As Lake explains at 7: 'The grant of authority from the principal to the agent must be conditional and revocable, and the principal retains all residual rights of control including the right to veto actions by the agent either directly or indirectly'.

[27] Samantha Besson argues that international legal obligations apply in this way to states as subjects, and in turn their subjects as ultimate or possibly derivative subjects: Samantha Besson, 'The Authority of International Law—Lifting the State Veil' (2009) 31 *Sydney Law Review* 343.

[28] See examples in Bogdandy and Dann, 'International Composite Administration'.

[29] Again, the precise character of the authority relationship will depend on a particular system's arrangements, but commonly a federal structure provides for federal supremacy on the matters within the sovereign's traditional prerogative such as national defence and foreign policy. In the case of the United States, the relationship is made more complex by (among other principles) constitutional provisions which clarify that the powers vested in the federal government are delegated by the states. Nevertheless, the delegation of authority can involve a transfer of power over oneself.

[30] A synoptic chart of courts and tribunals produced by the Project on International Courts and Tribunals is available at <http://www.pict-pcti.org/publications/synoptic_chart/synoptic_chart2.pdf>. For analysis of examples and the implications of proliferation, see Yuval Shany, *The Competing Jurisdictions of International Courts and Tribunals* (Oxford University Press, 2004).

[31] For a recent examination of the manner, form, and content of the public authority exercised by international institutions, as well as detailed essays examining particular authoritative regimes, see

the international system are authorities over other authorities (mostly but not exclusively states), while the direct authority of international institutions over private or individual subjects is a more recent development. In some cases, this picture is complicated by the fact that a subject-authority also sits as part of the higher authority, such as a state that sits as a member of the UN Security Council or within a conference of states parties to a particular treaty-enforcement body. In such cases we can still understand an authority relationship persisting between the authorities—the office of authority can still be differentiated from the office of the subject—although this may have important implications for how we analyse the relationship and the legitimacy of those engaged within it.

Care must be taken in characterizing an authority relationship, particularly in the international system, where it must not be confused with mere influence or coercive power. Some international relations literature obscures this difference either by ignoring or avoiding the key element of obligation, and so finding authority relations wherever there are power hierarchies brought about by economic or military disparities.[32] Many relationships of influence might look like relationships of authority, insofar as one authority purports to control another, but unless there is a normative relation of an obligation to obey and a right to rule, the relationship remains one of coercion or influence.

In contrast to the normative arrangements that hierarchically coordinate authorities, dialogical coordination is a process of authorities making decisions with one eye upon how other authorities have treated similar issues in the past, and another attuned to influencing how other authorities treat those issues in the future. Dialogical relationships of coordination have attracted a large amount of attention from scholars seeking to explain relationships between institutions that are not organized into clear hierarchies yet seem to be responsive to one another. Dialogue between courts and legislatures, national and supra-national courts, and different supra-national courts or tribunals, have all been the subjects of in-depth analyses exploring empirical examples, their effect on legitimacy, and the drivers of dialogue.[33] Whatever

---

Armin von Bogdandy *et al.*, *The Exercise of Public Authority by International Institutions: Advancing International Institutional Law* (Springer, 2009).

[32] For instance, David Lake has argued that obligation, although central to authority relationships, is 'inherently unobservable' and so we must locate authority relationships by the presence of consent by the subordinate state, including tacit or implied consent. Such an analysis imports all the problems plaguing consent theories of authority, and more, for implied consent here looks like no more than a submission to coercive or other forms of influential power. Lake's interpretation does not exemplify relationships of authority as they are conceived here. See David A Lake, 'Escape from the State of Nature: Authority and Hierarchy in World Politics' (2007) 32 *International Security* 47, 61–65.

[33] Ricardo Lorenzetti, *Global Governance: Dialogue between Courts* (European University Institute, 2010); Alec Stone Sweet, 'A Cosmopolitan Legal Order: Constitutional Pluralism and Rights Adjudication

explains dialogue, it generates incremental coordination whenever authorities self-consciously make decisions in line with their peers. Dialogue itself, of course, does not guarantee coordination. It is possible for dialogue to generate competitive rather than coordinated results, in which 'exceptionalist' authorities make a point of sticking to their own decisions even in the face of weighty or numerous contrary decisions. When dialogue does generate coordination, however, the long-term effect is much the same as having hierarchical structures through which decisions get made and re-made; with similar methods of revisiting existing reasoning and verifying or revising established positions, and similar practical results in which complementary reasons apply to the interacting or overlapping subjects. The major difference is that coordination through dialogue does not involve a distribution of normative powers between the interacting authorities.

c. Conflict: actual and 'false' conflict

The third category of relationships between authorities is relationships of conflict. As in the previous categories, this categorization is drawn by examining the existence of reasons and obligations facing the relevant subjects. Thus, conflict need not involve outward manifestations of hostility or even competition. Conflict exists in two distinct circumstances. First, conflict exists when two or more legitimate authorities with overlapping domains establish incompatible obligations for their shared subjects. In other words, shared subjects of the multiple authorities face single-agent practical conflict; each agent cannot comply with both obligations. Secondly, a relationship of conflict exists between authorities in interactive domains if the directives each authority issues to its subjects are incompatible because of their interaction. Although the individual subjects of each authority do not face single-agent practical conflicts, there are conflicts between their obligations as interacting subjects, which I call 'inter-subject practical conflicts'.

It is important first to distinguish 'actual conflicts' from 'false conflicts', which arise when there are two or more purported authorities each claiming to obligate their subjects but in fact only one is authoritative in that domain. False conflicts are either resolved into situations of singular authority when one

---

in Europe' (2012) 1 *Journal of Global Constitutionalism* 53. For critical analysis, see Luc B Tremblay, 'The Legitimacy of Judicial Review: The Limits of Dialogue between Courts and Legislatures' (2005) 3 *International Journal of Constitutional Law* 617; Jeremy Waldron, 'Some Models of Dialogue between Judges and Legislators', in Grant Huscroft and Ian Brodie (eds), *Constitutionalism in the Charter Era* (LexisNexis Butterworths, 2004), 617–648. On supra-national dialogue, see Lech Garlicki, 'Cooperation of Courts: The Role of Supranational Jurisdictions in Europe' (2008) 6 *International Journal of Constitutional Law* 509, 509–530.

purported authority's claim turns out to be unjustified, or into hierarchies of authority when a rule, principle, or procedure operates to give one authority power or precedence over the other.[34] False conflicts of the first kind are simply relationships between an actual authority and an agent who claims but does not have authority. False conflicts of the second kind are actually instances of coordinated authority relationships, but the rules, principles, or procedures which coordinate the authorities are so complex or obscure that to the casual observer the authorities appear to be in conflict.

Thus, conflict is by no means limited to relationships between disjunctive authorities; integrated authorities provide us with just as many, and often more interesting examples. Importantly, the opacity of some coordinated relationships can work in reverse, to generate actual conflict out of supposedly coordinated authorities. Where the rules coordinating authorities into partnerships or hierarchies are vague or internally contradictory, they can leave open the possibility of conflict. Indeed, many relationships organized by principles are vague by design, or deliberately create the potential for conflict; and even the clearest of organizational rules can generate unintentional conflicts when authorities follow their own interpretations of them.[35] Wherever complementarity between authorities has a dialogical character, (as is common in judiciary-legislature or federal-state relationships), the in-built potential for conflict is also potential for innovation and progression.

A detailed thought experiment might help to illustrate types of actual conflict and their distinction from false conflicts. Imagine two authorities within a state: one the official state government (S) with authority over the entire group of residents/citizens in the territory; the other a tribal authority (T) with more limited authority over matters of real property and private law between tribe

---

[34] Examples include jurisdictional rules that allocate final competence to one level of government, or give priority to one level over others. The European Union presents a suitably complex example in which areas of 'shared competence' are either areas in which the Union is given priority, so that Member States can act only if the Union has not, or areas in which the Union is treated as the benchmark, so that Member States can establish standards above but not below those set by the Union. On shared competence, see Paul P Craig and Grainne De Búrca, *EU Law: Text, Cases, and Materials* (Oxford University Press, 2008); Peter Orebech, 'E.U. Competency Confusion: Limits, Extension Mechanisms, Split Power, Subsidiarity, and Institutional Clashes' (2003) 13 *Journal of Transnational Law and Policy* 99.

[35] The European Union is again an instructive example, with some national courts (most famously the German Constitutional Court) rejecting the European Court of Justice's claims to have the final interpretative power over European law. See, eg *Brunner v The European Treaty* [1994] CMLR 57. See also Mattias Kumm, 'The Jurisprudence of Constitutional Conflict: Constitutional Supremacy in Europe before and after the Constitutional Treaty' (2005) 11 *European Law Journal* 262; Mattias Kumm, 'Who Is the Final Arbiter of Constitutionality in Europe?: Three Conceptions of the Relationship between the German Federal Constitutional Court and the European Court of Justice' (1999) 36 *Common Market Law Review* 351.

members within a part of the state's territory. Imagine, first, that S enacts a statute declaring all marine life to be a public resource, and requiring landowners in all coastal areas to permit public access across their property to the coast for purposes of recreational fishing. T, wishing to restrict harvesting of shellfish in its coastal territory which, under tribal property law, belong to the tribe and are subject to internal allocatory rules, directs members to restrict access to passers-by by building fences and erecting signs to indicate that the land is tribal land and there is to be no trespassing.

There may be actual conflict caused by either overlap or interaction between these authorities' domains, or it may be a case of false conflict. There will be overlap if the members of the tribe are legitimately subjects of both S and T, in regard to the same activities. For example, there may be tribal authority over members of the tribe in respect of property and resources located within the defined tribal territory, but state authority to manage all public resources and matters of national interest concerning the entire state territory. That overlap generates single-agent practical conflict when the two legitimate authorities issue conflicting directives pertaining to activities within the area of overlap. The subjects now have an obligation to obey both conflicting directives. In contrast, there will be interaction between the domains if subjects of T are non-subjects of S regarding their real property and activities under private law (ie there is exclusive tribal jurisdiction) but subjects interact across the jurisdictional divide, or activities of T and S require engagement with each other. That interaction generates inter-subject practical conflict if the directives issued by one or both authorities are incompatible with the interaction of the subjects or impede the engagement of the authorities. Finally, the bare facts given might prove, upon further investigation, to be a case of false conflict if either of the contenders turns out to be illegitimate, or it turns out that there are legitimate rules giving priority to one authority over the other.

In later chapters I address the implications of both actual and false conflicts for the practice of authority and the practical obligations of subjects. At the outset, however, it is important to establish that conflict need not be seen as a problem to be resolved, or as something unfortunate, in either the single-agent case or the inter-subject case. There is nothing particularly problematic about a subject facing a practical conflict; a subject in such a position will simply make a choice and fail in conforming to one obligation to the extent that it is inconsistent with the course of action they have chosen.[36] In the case of inter-subject practical conflicts, there are important questions to be asked

---

[36] Joseph Raz, 'Personal Practical Conflicts', in Peter Baumann and Monika Betzler (eds), *Practical Conflicts: New Philosophical Essays* (Cambridge University Press, 2004).

about the implications of conflict, but these need not treat conflict as necessarily threatening to social order. The responses to conflict are a matter for separate evaluation.

However benign or otherwise conflicts might be, relationships of conflict between authorities result in the sort of normative messiness that attracts interest among theorists in a number of fields. This literature provides a starting point for bringing the accounts of authority and plurality together.

4
Plurality of Authority in Legal/Constitutional Theory

An interest in plurality and relationships between authorities is by no means new. Some of the great works in jurisprudence and political theory have been at least sensitive to the possibility of authority being shared or divided between locations; others have examined such divisions in the course of arguing for or against a particular kind of authority.[1] Plurality of authority is also a core feature of research in public and private international law, transnational law, federalism and administrative law, European (or other regional) law, commercial law, environmental law, indigenous law, and constitutional law. The shared interests of all these fields however, remain underexplored. Scholars of authority have been insufficiently attentive to its contemporary fragmentation, while scholars of legal pluralism (broadly conceived) have been insufficiently willing to integrate detailed analytical or normative accounts of authority into their work. Even within each field, theorists offer a multitude of conceptions of the exact phenomena being examined, and an array of terminologies which can make for difficult reading.[2] The starting premise of this chapter is that a pluralist analysis of authority provides a tool to enable each strand of literature to engage more fruitfully with one another, and be internally more consistent, in order to better understand the actual practices of plurality of authority with which they are all concerned.

This chapter begins by considering existing theoretical contributions that relate, more or less directly, to my interest in plurality of authority. Those contributions come from a range of disciplines and approaches, and will be familiar to scholars from these disciplines, but the aim here is to take them out of their disciplinary borders in order to examine what they may reveal about plurality of authority. The brevity of my treatment of these contending or complementary ideas will, I hope, be excusable in light of that aim, as well as the broader aim of bringing disparate theories into the common focus offered by the idea of plurality of authority.

---

[1] Most famously, see T Hobbes, *Leviathan* (JCA Gaskin (ed), Oxford University Press 1998).
[2] Ralf Michaels, 'Global Legal Pluralism' (2009) 5 *Annual Review of Law and Social Science* 243.

To make my task manageable, this chapter isolates the key concepts that have dominated relevant literature on legal/constitutional pluralism, broadly conceived. It is obviously artificial to separate concepts that are often treated together in the literature; but by grouping together work on the same concept rather than adhering to disciplinary groupings, it should be easier to shed light on that work's relevance to my own. In section 1, I examine work on constitutionalism, pluralism, and constitutional pluralism. Section 2 then analyses conceptions of sovereignty; section 3, accounts of law, with a sub-section on transnational legality; and section 4, accounts of authority. I argue that none of the work on these concepts has adequately captured the idea of plurality of authority, and that it leaves open a number of analytical and normative puzzles.

1. Constitutionalism, Pluralism, and Constitutional Pluralism

Scholarship on 'constitutional pluralism' emerged as an attempt to explain the structural arrangements of European and Member States' legal regime(s) and now features an illustrious set of theorists both within and outside Europe, producing work in all the major European languages.[3] Scholars' interests span a search for the best way to describe, explain, and/or evaluate the increasingly complex interaction of legal norms between the European legal order and the legal orders of its members. In the course of debates, a set of fine distinctions have been drawn between constitutionalist and pluralist approaches to inter-order relationships, between types of constitutionalism and pluralism, and around the coherence of the very idea of 'constitutional pluralism'.

These debates echo, and sometimes directly engage, analyses in international legal theory where there is a similar divide between accounts of (and arguments for) the fragmentation versus constitutionalization of international legal authority.[4] Contemporary international legal theory is full of analyses of the

---

[3] The body of Anglophone literature has its foundations in the influential work of Joseph Weiler and Neil MacCormick, including: Joseph Weiler and Marlene Wind, *European Constitutionalism Beyond the State* (Cambridge University Press, 2003); Joseph HH Weiler, 'The Transformation of Europe' (1991) 100 *Yale Law Journal*; Joseph Weiler, *The Constitution of Europe: 'Do the New Clothes Have an Emperor?' And Other Essays on European Integration* (Cambridge University Press, 1999); and Neil MacCormick, 'Liberalism, Nationalism and the Post-Sovereign State' (1996) 44 *Political Studies* 553; Neil MacCormick, 'The Maastricht-Urteil: Sovereignty Now' (1995) 1 *European Law Journal* 259; Neil MacCormick, 'Beyond the Sovereign State' (1993) 56 *MLR* 1.

[4] A rich collection of essays on these subjects appears in Tomer Broude and Yuval Shany, *The Shifting Allocation of Authority in International Law* (Hart Publishing, 2008). See also Jeffrey L Dunoff and Joel P Trachtman, *Ruling the World?: Constitutionalism, International Law, and Global Governance*

fragmentation of international law into myriad specialized and sometimes 'colliding' regimes, on the one hand, and analyses of international law's constitutional moments, constitutional norms, constitutionalizing processes, or constitutionalism, on the other.[5] Research on international courts, tribunals, and administrative institutions further details particular relationships between specific international bodies, exploring the extent of systemic integration and the norms which might generate or obstruct it, and discussing the implications of the proliferation of institutions and norm-regimes for the practice and study of international law.[6] The fragmentation/constitutionalism debate continues to be divided over the matter of relative normativity and the absence of formal norm hierarchies in international law. Some continue to echo Weil's original concern that relative normativity would become a pathology of the international system, in which conflict between norms and norm-regimes cannot be resolved by reference to common or superior norms. Others see it as benign or at least an inescapable structural characteristic, in which material or substantive hierarchies between norms are sufficient for dealing with their conflicts.[7]

In both the European and the international contexts (which are themselves problematically related to one another), plurality of law generates division among proponents of different normative responses to that plurality. In simplified form, 'constitutionalist' approaches seek to order multiplicity within a common framework of norms or principles, while 'pluralist' approaches see value in heterarchy and fragmentation. Koskenniemi describes the difference:[8]

(Cambridge University Press, 2009); and International Law Association, 'Conclusions of the Work of the Study Group on the Fragmentation of International Law: Difficulties Arising from the Diversification and Expansion of International Law' (2006) 2 *Yearbook of the International Law Commission* 2

[5] Jean D'Aspremont, 'The Foundations of the International Legal Order' (2007) 18 *Finnish Yearbook of International Law* 219; A Fischer-Lescano and G Teubner, 'Regime-Collisions: The Vain Search for Legal Unity in the Fragmentation of Global Law' (2003) 25 *Michigan Journal of International Law*. See also Jeffrey L Dunoff, 'A New Approach to Regime Interaction', in Margaret A Young (ed), *Regime Interaction in International Law: Facing Fragmentation* (Cambridge University Press, 2012).

[6] Much of this literature embraces the insights of global administrative law. See Benedict Kingsbury *et al.*, 'The Emergence of Global Administrative Law' (2005) 68 *Law of Contemporary Problems*; see also essays in Margaret A Young, *Regime Interaction in International Law: Facing Fragmentation* (Cambridge University Press, 2012).

[7] A powerful argument against relative normativity is offered by Prosper Weil, 'Towards Relative Normativity in International Law?' (1983) 77 *The American Journal of International Law* 413. The opposing view is represented by Dinah Shelton, 'Normative Hierarchy in International Law' (2006) 100 *The American Journal of International Law* 291. On the inadequacy of material hierarchies, see Samantha Besson, 'Whose Constitution(S)? International Law, Constitutionalism and Democracy', in Jeffrey L Dunoff and Joel P Trachtman (eds), *Ruling the World?: Constitutionalism, International Law, and Global Governance* (Cambridge University Press, 2009).

[8] Marti Koskenniemi, 'The Fate of Public International Law: Between Technique and Politics' (2007) 70 *MLR* 1.

…constitutionalism and pluralism are abstract responses to the emergence of multiple legal regimes. Each comes with a disciplinary tradition—one associated with law, the other with political science—split against itself. In its self-confident, ruling mode constitutionalism appears as centralism, rights and order, supported by histories of State-building. From a pluralism perspective, however, it often means bureaucratic authoritarianism and rule by the ancien regime. By contrast, pluralism's major mode highlights diversity and freedom, spontaneous development. But that is surely vulnerable to the constitutionalist retort: it accepts de facto rule merely because it is there.

Others have identified that constitutionalism itself pulls in two different directions and embodies competing values. As Maduro argues, one direction pulls 'towards pluralism, linked to the values of freedom and private autonomy. The other, towards unity or hierarchy, linked with the ideals of equality, the rule of law and universality'.[9] This leads into a debate over the very possibility of constitutional pluralism, which challenges the coherence of substantive and/or methodological constitutional principles being shared between pluralistic systems without a unifying institutional structure.[10] At the very least, many argue, constitutionalism itself must be radically reconceived if it is to be pursued pluralistically.[11]

Another approach rejects any descriptively sound distinction between elements of pluralism and constitutionalism, arguing that most if not all orders will include dimensions of both pluralist heterarchy and constitutional hierarchy.[12] Or, in normative terms, they offer justifications for both types of arrangements within any single order, or for a combination of arrangements into some form of 'ordered pluralism' or fragmented constitutionalism.[13] Some maintain that the distinction can capture an important differentiation,

---

[9] MP Maduro, 'Three Claims of Constitutional Pluralism', in M Avbelj and J Komárek (eds), *Constitutional Pluralism in the European Union and Beyond* (Hart Publishing, 2012).

[10] Compare the pluralist principles favoured by Maduro in Miguel Maduro, 'Contrapunctual Law: Europe's Constitutional Pluralism in Action', in Neil Walker (ed), *Sovereignty in Transition* (Hart Publishing, 2003), with Pavlos Eleftheriadis, 'Pluralism and Integrity' (2010) 23 *Ratio Juris* 365, 387, arguing that pluralist principles fail to promote the value of political integrity. For a sceptical and critical view of the contribution of constitutional pluralism, see J Weiler, *Prologue: Global and Pluralist Constitutionalism—Some Doubts*, in The Worlds of European Constitutionalism (G De Búrca and J Weiler (eds), 2012).

[11] See M Avbelj and J Komárek, *Constitutional Pluralism in the European Union and Beyond* (Hart Publishing, 2012); Nico Krisch, *Beyond Constitutionalism: The Pluralist Structure of Postnational Law* (1st edn, Oxford University Press, 2010).

[12] Alec Stone Sweet argues that the two are 'separate variables with the potential to interact with one another': Alec Stone Sweet, 'Constitutionalism, Legal Pluralism, and International Regimes' (2009) 16 *Indiana Journal of Global Legal Studies* 621.

[13] On ordered pluralism, see Mireille Delmas-Marty, *Ordering Pluralism: A Conceptual Framework for Understanding the Transnational Legal World* (Hart Publishing, 2009).

but might be more helpfully conceived as a spectrum along which both descriptive plurality and normative responses to plurality can be situated.[14]

These debates all generate further refined discussion about what exactly constitutionalism and pluralism represent, on their own terms. Constitutionalism, first, typically refers to the ordering of different kinds of legal or political authority, but this includes both authority's allocation between different authorities and its constraint by rules or principles such as substantive human rights norms or procedural requirements. Both functions of constitutionalism are thought to carry value, and to be worth preserving, for the role they play in ordering communities and respecting the individuals within them. Constitutionalism can then vary by degree and type. It can be weak or strong, rule-based or principle-based, formal or informal. The differences between these degrees and types of constitutionalism are reflected, in part, in the extent to which they are compatible with, or at least not hostile to, pluralism.

A particularly important and persistent distinction is also made between different categories of plurality. These can be categorized according to degree, using variations upon Griffiths' classic discussion of 'strong' versus 'weak' legal pluralism.[15] Or, by type: MacCormick, for instance, offered a distinction between 'radical pluralism' in which constitutional orders are separate, with each having internal competence; and 'pluralism under international law', in which separateness is retained but there are international legal obligations pertaining between orders.[16] Similarly, Krisch explains a differentiation between 'systemic pluralism'—a true multiplicity and competition between orders in the absence of integrating or ordering principles and rules—and 'institutional pluralism'—a plurality of institutions which remain ordered by principles or rules governing their interaction.[17]

Within all these distinctions lies a sub-text of plurality of authority. For instance, a spectrum between pluralism and constitutionalism must have a spectrum line—some common factor over which approaches can differ. There must also be a core feature that separates 'institutional' from 'systemic' types of plurality. A candidate for both roles must be the existence and organization

---

[14] Both Kumm's and Walker's accounts have this character. For their direct exchange on this point see the symposium transcript: Matej Avbelj and Jan Komárek (eds), 'Four Visions of Constitutional Pluralism' (2008) 1 *European Journal of Legal Studies* 325; or symposium summary in Matej Avbelj and Jan Komárek, 'Four Visions of Constitutional Pluralism' (2008) 4 *European Constitutional Law Review* 524.

[15] Griffiths' original distinction appears in John Griffiths, 'What Is Legal Pluralism' (1986) 24 *Journal of Legal Pluralism and Unofficial Law* 1, 5.

[16] Neil MacCormick, *Questioning Sovereignty: Law, State, and Nation in the European Commonwealth* (Oxford University Press, 1999), 117–121.

[17] Krisch, *Beyond Constitutionalism*, 71–75. In my terminology the descriptive distinction is between 'institutional plurality' and 'systemic plurality'.

of legitimate authority. The descriptive distinctions from MacCormick and Krisch broadly correspond to my own demarcation of integrated and disjunctive authorities, although my narrower emphasis on authority brings into focus the kind of power that exists between the different relevant institutions. The difference between institutional and systemic pluralism is not the existence or lack of any sort of power whatsoever; it is the existence or lack of normative powers accompanied by rules establishing and/or regulating their distribution across different locations. Similarly, along the normative spectrum between constitutionalism and pluralism, the power that requires justification is a normative power. Both normative positions try to justify arrangements of authority and the limits and legitimacy of those arrangements; they simply occupy different positions along a spectrum of authority arrangements, disagreeing over the details of where it should be located and how it should be organized. The constitutionalist end of the spectrum favours ultimate and exclusive authority, with an apex of decisional and interpretive authority that gives final say to a particular institution. At the pluralist extreme, authority can be justifiably fragmented and divided between competing institutions without the need for lexical or hierarchical ordering.

The upshot of all this work on constitutional pluralism is that it becomes critical to examine the character of the authority power which is the subject of so much dispute. Section 4 will examine the extent to which constitutional pluralism has engaged that task, but first there are two other key discussions of plurality that dominate the existing literature.

2. Conceptions of Sovereignty

Many studies of plurality within legal and constitutional scholarship frame their interest as a matter of sovereignty, which is often conceived as 'post',[18] 'late',[19] 'shared',[20] and 'interdependent'[21] sovereignty.[22] This is true of work in

---

[18] Richard Bellamy, 'Sovereignty, Post-Sovereignty and Pre-Sovereignty: Three Models of the State, Democracy and Rights within the E.U.', in Neil Walker (ed), *Sovereignty in Transition* (Hart Publishing, 2003).

[19] Neil Walker, 'Late Sovereignty in the E.U.', in Walker, *Sovereignty in Transition*, 19–25.

[20] Stephen D Krasner, 'The Hole in the Whole: Sovereignty, Shared Sovereignty, and International Law' (2003) 25 *Michigan Journal of International Law* 1075.

[21] This terminology has currency in the domestic context, as between courts and legislatures in the UK; see, eg TRS Allan, 'Constitutional Dialogue and the Justification of Judicial Review' (2003) 23 *OJLS* 563.

[22] For a full analysis of contemporary conceptions of sovereignty, see Jens Bartelson, 'The Concept of Sovereignty Revisited' (2006) 17 *European Journal of International Law* 463 (2006); Krasner, 'The Hole in the Whole', 160.

both the European and international law literature in which there is wide recognition that the contemporary practice of sovereignty features some degree of dilution, limitation, or other alteration due to the presence of international or regional authorities, yet must still play a significant role.[23] However, it is often unclear which aspect of sovereignty is subject to such dilution or at least modification. Where there is discussion of the alteration of a sovereign's authority power, it is squarely within my topic and should contain important insights.

Perhaps the leading analytic account of pluralistic sovereign authority is Besson's series of analyses of the European and international legal orders.[24] Besson has offered a conception of 'cooperative sovereignty' in which multiple sovereigns work together to achieve their tasks and to realize their 'shared sovereign values' by applying the same rules and principles.[25] Sovereignty is thought to be exercised in common and cooperatively, especially where there is overlap in territory or in the community of sovereigns' subjects. This conception of sovereignty expressly relies upon the important role of a subsidiarity principle, particularly within the EU realm, but also, Besson argues, for determining the proper locations of sovereignty. If the tasks of multiple sovereigns are entwined, and their values are shared, then subsidiarity requires that sovereignty is located between them rather than finally in one or other.

Besson then offers a normative defence for this conception of cooperative sovereignty:[26]

Sovereignty should be conceived as a reflexive concept whose correct use is to reflect on and disagree over the values protected by sovereignty, ie mainly democracy and fundamental rights.... The protection of the values underlying those contestable concepts would therefore benefit more from cooperation between different competent authorities and entities and how best to protect their common values and hence on when to give up sovereignty to others, than from the mere declaration of primacy of one sovereign over the other.

---

[23] In the case of international law, sovereignty still seems central to explaining the very possibility of international law; while for European law, sovereignty is still thought normatively important for its potential affiliation with individual or community/state identity. Timothy A Endicott, 'The Logic of Freedom and Power', in S Besson and J Tasioulas (eds), *The Philosophy of International Law* (Oxford University Press, 2010) offers a discussion of the paradox of classical sovereignty—it is necessary to make international law possible, but is itself impossible if there is to be international law.

[24] S Besson, 'Sovereignty in Conflict' (2004) 8(15) *European Integration online Papers* 01; S Besson, 'European Legal Pluralism after Kadi' (2009) 5 *European Constitutional Law Review* 237; S Besson, *The Morality of Conflict: Reasonable Disagreement and the Law* (Hart Publishing, 2005).

[25] Besson, 'Sovereignty in Conflict' 13.

[26] Besson, *The Morality of Conflict*, 535.

For all this richness, persuasiveness, and complexity, Besson's account remains an account of sovereignty which does not break it down into its constituent parts. Her discussion of the interrelationship of sovereign authorities argues that it is their sovereignty which is shared, including the competencies and functions that go with it. Cooperative sovereignty engages 'competent' authorities in a practical discourse, but we do not know, within this account, whether these must be legitimate authorities or whether/how their cooperation might impact upon that legitimacy. Besson's work links the subsidiarity principle to the location of sovereignty, which must be understood as something different from (although encompassing) authority. As I indicated in my introduction and will elaborate in the discussion of international law in Chapter 10, it seems conceptually and analytically clearer to isolate the authority power in order to consider its operation in circumstances of plurality.

3. Law and Legality

Until very recently, the study of plurality's implications was outside the canon of Anglo-American jurisprudential enquiry.[27] Theoretical work on legal pluralism was dominated by sociological and anthropological ontologies and methodologies, while the dominant works in contemporary analytical and normative jurisprudence were mostly uninterested in any direct exchange with legal pluralists.[28] Instead, 'general' jurisprudents have mostly analysed the features of law, and the concept of law, by focusing on the central case of official state law without worrying (much) about other or borderline instances of law.[29] On the other hand, theorists of 'legal pluralism' have either avoided a direct confrontation over the nature of law by offering stipulative and sometimes idiosyncratic

---

[27] On the reasons for this isolation of 'legal pluralists', see WL Twining, *General Jurisprudence* (Cambridge University Press, 2009).

[28] One example is the synthesis of legal pluralism offered by Brian Tamanaha, which adopts a sociological concept of law: Brian Z Tamanaha, 'Understanding Legal Pluralism: Past to Present, Local to Global' (2008) 30 *Sydney Law Review* 375. Paul Schiff Berman, 'Global Legal Pluralism' (2007) 80 *Southern California Law Review* 1155, 1178 describes the dominance of sociological theories which 'aim to study empirically which statements of authority tend to be treated as binding in actual practice and by whom'.

[29] For instance, Raz's account of the authority of law is explicitly a theory about municipal law: Joseph Raz, *The Authority of Law* (2nd edn, Oxford University Press, 2009), 44, 104–105. On this marginalization of legal pluralist interests, see Twining, *General Jurisprudence*. There are exceptions: key works in jurisprudence that have considered the 'legality' of other normative systems (notably customary, international, and customary international law) include HLA Hart, *The Concept of Law* (2nd edn, Clarendon Press, 1994), Ch X; Finnis, *Natural Law and Natural Rights* (Clarendon Press, 1980); Lon L Fuller, 'Human Interaction and the Law' (1969) 14 *American Journal of Jurisprudence* 1.

explanations of law, or have preferred to analyse normative systems (including customary, religious, or tribal systems) free from any attempt to fit them within canonical jurisprudential accounts of the concept of law.[30]

Theorists of legal pluralism emphasize multiplicity of law(s) and relations between legal systems through accounts of 'global legal pluralism',[31] inter-legality,[32] 'legal polycentricity',[33] and 'postnational law'.[34] Some are focused upon relationships between the legal orders or systems that make up transnational law; others are most interested in jurisdiction, exploring both formal and informal boundaries between institutionalized normative systems and the ways in which they are traversed, while still others focus on federalism but give it a wider and more varied meaning than the orthodox focus of federalism within the state.[35] Together these present a tangle of terminologies, distinctions, and syntheses, with conflicting uses of concepts,[36] and a spread across the full spectrum of theoretical approaches to law—from the dominant contributions in sociology and anthropology of law,[37] to some representation in critical and postmodern legal theory,[38] through to very occasional interest in analytical jurisprudence.[39] The fields feature a range of methodological interests: some aim to contribute to conceptual questions about sovereignty or law or jurisdiction and the like; others make political arguments for or

---

[30] The debate is discussed in Franz von Benda-Beckmann, 'Who's Afraid of Legal Pluralism' (2002) 47 *Journal of Legal Pluralism and Unofficial Law* 37, which also offers an example of a particular conceptual framework while acknowledging that this may be fit for comparative but not other purposes. Similarly, Twining offering a particular account of law for the limited purposes of examining global law: Twining, *General Jurisprudence*.

[31] Berman, 'Global Legal Pluralism'; Boaventura de Sousa Santos, 'Law: A Map of Misreading. Toward a Postmodern Conception of Law' (1987) 14 *Journal of Law and Society* 279.

[32] de Sousa Santos, 'Law: A Map of Misreading'.

[33] Hanne Petersen, *Legal Polycentricity. Consequences of Pluralism in Law* (Ashgate, 1995).

[34] Krisch, *Beyond Constitutionalism*.

[35] For work on both federalism and jurisdiction, see Robert B Ahdieh, 'From Federalism to Intersystemic Governance: The Changing Nature of Modern Jurisdiction' (2007) 57 *Emory Law Journal* 1; Judith Resnik, 'Foreign as Domestic Affairs: Rethinking Horizontal Federalism and Foreign Affairs Preemption in Light of Translocal Internationalism' (2007) 57 *Emory Law Journal* 31; Robert A Schapiro, 'Federalism as Intersystemic Governance: Legitimacy in a Post-Westphalian World' (2007) 57 *Emory Law Journal* 115, and other essays in that symposium issue of the *Emory Law Journal*.

[36] For a summary of the range and disparities of work on plurality, see Michaels, 'Global Legal Pluralism'. On different concepts of pluralism, see Tamanaha, 'Understanding Legal Pluralism', 26–27.

[37] See, eg Sally Engle Merry, 'Legal Pluralism' (1988) 22 *Law and Society Review* 869.

[38] See, eg Margaret Davies, 'Pluralism and Legal Philosophy' (2006) 57 *Northern Ireland Legal Quarterly* 577.

[39] Twining, *General Jurisprudence*; Jeremy Waldron, 'Legal Pluralism and the Contrast between Hart's Jurisprudence and Fuller's,' in Peter Cane (ed), *The Hart-Fuller Debate in the 21st Century* (Hart Publishing, 2010). Going further back, see Hans Kelsen, *General Theory of Law and State* (Harvard University Press, 1945). These categorizations are suggestions for exemplary reading, and not to be regarded as conclusive categorizing of the author's work, nor an exhaustive list of contributions.

against particular normative arrangements; while others address particular political or legal regimes. Sometimes these aims are unclear owing to a lack of distinction between descriptive and normative goals, and a mingling of the descriptive terminology (what I call plurality) with the normative language of pluralism.[40]

Recent developments in theoretical interests suggest the end of a division between legal pluralism and general jurisprudence, and greater clarity in the analysis of pluralistic concepts of law. This change can be put down to changes in the practice of law that jurisprudence seeks to explain. The expansion of international and supra-state law and even transnational law—in scope and in impact—means that the practice of law is no longer just about state law, if indeed it ever was. International law—both public and private—and regional legal systems (of which Europe is the most developed but not the only example) are now the well-established, low-hanging fruits of legal pluralism, obvious to even the most sceptical monists, and the need to make sense of their content, to give them concrete application and/or to challenge their normativity places plurality back within the cross-fires of doctrinal legal argument. These developments in the phenomena that jurisprudence seeks to explain have ignited the need for a robust 'pluralist jurisprudence'.[41]

Today, such pluralist jurisprudence could be considered fashionable.[42] Most obviously, there has been a resurgence of work on the philosophy of international law, which seeks to understand the structure, character, legitimacy, content, and organization of the international legal system, as well as its relationship to other (mostly state) legal systems. Apart from the international legal philosophy renaissance, much of the jurisprudential analysis of plurality accompanies or is inspired by those theories of constitutional pluralism discussed in section 1, particularly European constitutional theory. For instance, European plurality has inspired work that interrogates the possibilities of interacting and overlapping legal systems using the tools of positivist legal theory, including the multiplicity of rules of recognition, the necessity of claims to supremacy, and the conditions of systemic identity.[43] Others, such as Kumm, have expressly

---

[40] Many scholars use the term 'pluralism' both descriptively and normatively. This is unproblematic where the writers then go on to make it clear which sense they intend, but some do not. For an express account of the normative implications of pluralism, see Paul Schiff Berman, 'Towards a Jurisprudence of Hybridity' (2010) *Utah Law Review* 11.

[41] Nicole Roughan, 'The Relative Authority of Law: A Contribution to "Pluralist Jurisprudence"', in M Del Mar (ed), *New Waves in Philosophy of Law* (Palgrave Macmillan, 2011). I am grateful to Palgrave Macmillan for permission to reprint parts of that chapter in this work.

[42] NW Barber, 'Legal Pluralism and the European Union' (2006) 12 *European Law Journal* 306, 306.

[43] Julie Dickson, 'How Many Legal Systems? Some Puzzles Regarding the Identity Conditions of, and Relations between, Legal Systems in the European Union' (2008) 2 *Problema* 9. That work

adapted Dworkinian and Alexian jurisprudential models to explore the normativity of constitutional pluralism and the relationship between international and national law.[44]

To date, the most substantial line of inquiry into pluralist jurisprudence has focused upon the institutional dimension of legality. The appeal of an institutional theory of law, and its suitability for explaining the features of pluralist legal practice between or among institutions, lies in its potential to capture legal phenomena beyond the standard case of state law, and to include law 'across legal orders, jurisdictions, levels, traditions, and cultures'.[45] Foundational work in this field was offered by MacCormick, whose institutional theory of law included 'an inherently pluralistic conception of legal system' that is opposed to 'centralizing theories about sovereignty, its absoluteness and its essential quality for securely established law'.[46] Although MacCormick's own work never explored the full pluralist potential of his institutionalist theory, later work within the same tradition has sought to do so directly.[47] Culver and Giudice, for instance, build upon MacCormick in order to offer an 'inter-institutional' theory, which focuses upon the combinations, matrixes, or interactions of normative powers that occur between institutions, rather than upon the practices of particular institutions or (especially) officials.[48] Legality is then tied to the distinctive role played by 'institutions of law'—conceived as clusters of norms having legal functions—in generating obligations upon law-subjects, and, in turn, the connection that these institutions of law

---

reinvigorates the contributions of Hart and Kelsen to identifying the status of international law and its relationship to legal systems. Kelsen's conclusions were monist; he denied the possibility of multiple legal systems over the same actors, viewing international and national law as part of a single legal order grounded on a single grundnorm: Kelsen, *General Theory of Law and State*, 325–380. Hart's account of the rule of recognition, in contrast, leaves open the possibility of plurality, even the possibility of plurality of rules of recognition. See analysis in Raz, *The Authority of Law*, 98, fn 32.

[44] See, eg Mattias Kumm, 'Democratic Constitutionalism', in Sujit Choudhry (ed), *The Migration of Constitutional Ideas* (Cambridge University Press, 2005). Kumm's body of work will be considered directly in Ch 11.

[45] Twining, *General Jurisprudence*, 24, 39.

[46] MacCormick, *Questioning Sovereignty*, 75, 78. On the institutional theory of law, see MacCormick, *Institutions of Law: an essay in legal theory* (Oxford University Press, 2007). Not all of MacCormick's work on sovereignty emphasizes the authority power—he has also examined at length a sovereign's power to determine the limits of its own competence, which, properly understood, is not the same thing as its domain of authority.

[47] Twining expressly challenges this centrality and suggests the pluralist implications of MacCormick's work in William L Twining, 'Institutions of Law from a Global Perspective', in Maksymilian Del Mar and Zenon Bankowski (eds), *Law as Institutional Normative Order* (Ashgate Publishing Co, 2009).

[48] Keith Charles Culver and Michael Giudice, *Legality's Borders: An Essay in General Jurisprudence* (Oxford University Press, 2010), 113–120.

have to organized 'legal institutions'. Culver and Giudice conceive of legality as measured by different degrees of 'legal-normative interaction' among subjects—high intensity in the municipal state, low intensity in other types of sub-state, supra-state, or trans-state legal orders.[49] The interactions of institutions, rather than their status within a system of law, are then presented as the core of legality.

None of these variants of institutionalist theory re-examine the kind of authority that law might claim, or the kind of authority that law might have. The central feature of law under MacCormick's institutional theory is its institutionality, not its authority or claim to authority. MacCormick argued that in order to make a conceptual divide between law and state, and so open the possibility for pluralism, we need to differentiate authority ('the normative form of power') from political power ('non-normative social power, human power in its factual sense'), but did not go on to explain how such authority might encompass 'subsidiarity, negotiation, [and] balance' as the central pluralist ideas.[50] Indeed, the focus of MacCormick's last works was to advocate his institutional theory as an explanation for state law—as the central and most significant type of legal order. The implications of Culver and Giuduce's work suggest that somehow bound up in inter-institutionality might be a different sense of the authority that the institutions can have, or can claim, but this is not the target of their work.

Other work has focused upon the actual rules or practices that serve to link legal orders, systems, or regimes together. In Von Daniels' work, for instance, legal systems of different kinds can be linked together through 'linkage rules'—which either 'purport to validate, delegate or influence other systems, or recognise validation, receive, or complete demands "from outside" '.[51] Importantly, one legal system cannot determine how it will be received or respected outside, or whether its own other-regarding linkage rules will succeed. Linkage rules cannot obligate or empower on their own.[52] Rather, the practice of the linkage rules 'depends upon the response and possible mutual correspondence between the systems involved'.[53] Von Daniels argues that any descriptive theory of law must account for these linkage rules, which are part of the practice of all systems, and so cannot conceive of any single legal system in isolation from at least one

---

[49] Culver and Giudice, *Legality's Borders*, 110–115. This idea of variable-intensity legality echoes a suggestion offered in Roger Cotterrell, 'Transnational Communities and the Concept of Law' (2008) 21 *Ratio Juris* 1, that legality itself might be a matter of degree. Cotterrell does not explain what implications that might have for law's authority.

[50] MacCormick, *Questioning Sovereignty*, 76.

[51] D Von Daniels, The Concept of Law from a Transnational Perspective (Ashgate Publishing Co, 2010), 161.

[52] Von Daniels, *The Concept of Law from a Transnational Perspective*, 162.

[53] Von Daniels, *The Concept of Law from a Transnational Perspective*, 161.

other. In arguing for the strength of a descriptive theory of law in explaining the diversity of contemporary legal phenomena, Von Daniels is not seeking to establish the authority that these rules and the relationships they establish can have; rather, he is seeking to fit them within a richer descriptive theory of law.

Nor is authority one of the concepts expressly identified for revision from Twining's global perspective.[54] Although there are elements of authority implied within the conceptual frameworks that Twining does discuss, these are buried within the broader ideas of order, normative relations, and legal systems. Twining himself argues that, from a global perspective, it is 'illuminating to conceive of law as a species of *institutionalised social practice* that is oriented to ordering relations between subjects at one or more levels of relations and of ordering'.[55] However, if jurisprudence is to do as Twining suggests and examine 'different levels of normative and legal relations and ordering', some conception of authority will be needed to explain both the normativity and the ordering— even if the resulting analyses go on to emphasize other normative or social concepts in their analysis of legal relations. The remaining chapters of this work take up Twining's broad suggestion of the need for conceptual revision, but apply it to the notion of authority; to consider whether a global perspective makes any difference to an account of what authority is and when it is legitimate; and to see what that analysis contributes for understanding plurality and pluralism.

a. 'Transnational' law

It seems worth singling out, from all this scholarship on legal pluralism, a significant body of legal practice, which breaks away from the elements of sovereignty and constitutionalism that continue to attach to other analyses of pluralistic jurisprudence, and indeed can challenge the boundaries of legality. This is the idea that some law is transnational, meaning it is not sourced in, legitimated by, or emanating from a state. Rather, in Jessup's definitive account, transnational law is 'all law which regulates actions or events that transcend

---

[54] Twining, *General Jurisprudence*, 63–4. Twining's chosen concepts for revision include 'legal relations, legal subjects (persons), social practice, rule (norm), institution and system'; 'normative order, legal order, legal system, group, community and society'; and 'levels of law, social arena, surface law, interlegality, and invisible or unnoticed legal orders'. Importantly, Twining is sympathetic to a naturalist turn which emphasizes continuity between conceptual and empirical analysis. He suggests a form of moderate naturalism, wherein the elucidation of concepts is important as long as it is sensitive to knowledge of the real world (pp 55–56).

[55] Twining, *General Jurisprudence*, 117 (emphasis in original). Twining is careful to explicate each of the concepts relied upon within this formula, and to clarify that this is a limited-purpose, not general, conception of law.

national frontiers. Both public and private international law are included, as are other rules which do not wholly fit into such standard categories'.[56]

Extensive bodies of work have been devoted to the analysis of non-standard transnational legal phenomena, from the long-practiced but now globally significant *lex mercatoria*, to transnational private regulatory governance, from transnational human rights law to transnational public law.[57] Many accounts of transnational law focus upon its strongest manifestation, in the cross-border regulatory systems that are sometimes private, sometimes quasi-public, and can include both state and non-state or even hybrid actors.[58] Others argue that understanding transnational law requires understanding 'transnational legal process'—the use of legal processes, whether domestic or international, to blend transnational and domestic legal norms.[59] These exchanges may be still less formal, occurring beyond ordinary legal process and featuring, in Resnik's terms, 'precepts and influences [that] transcend the boundaries of the nation-state through myriad exchanges not always codified as formally shared legal regimes'.[60]

Other scholars emphasize the methodological shift that is required both to identify transnational law and its relationship with other instances of law, and to explain it in relation to other social or normative practices.[61] That methodological shift requires an openness to insights from sociological approaches, systems theory, critical legal scholarship, and interdisciplinary studies (including, notably, work in economics, politics, and business). The best theoretical work on transnational law is conscious of the methodological difficulties, but nevertheless the necessity, of drawing an account of transnational law that integrates insights from these distinctive fields and approaches.[62]

Through all of this work, transnational law attracts a great deal of theoretical care, and some suspicion, over its status as law, its relationship to kinds of

---

[56] Philip C Jessup, *Transnational Law* (Yale University Press, 1956), 2.
[57] For analysis of the different instances of transnational law, and their relationships, see Peer Zumbansen, 'Transnational Legal Pluralism' (2010) 1 *Transnational Legal Theory* 141. See also specific essays and detailed contextual studies in Günther Handl and Joachim Zekoll, *Beyond Territoriality: Transnational Legal Authority in an Age of Globalization* (Martinus Nijhoff Publishers, 2012).
[58] Harold Hongju Koh, 'Why Transnational Law Matters' (2005) 24 *Penn St. International Law Review* 745.
[59] Harold Hongju Koh, 'Transnational Legal Process' (1996) 75 *Neb Law Review* 75.
[60] J Resnik, 'Law as Affiliation: "Foreign" Law, Democratic Federalism, and the Sovereigntism of the Nation-State' (2008) 6 *International Journal of Constitutional Law* 33.
[61] As Zumbansen sees it, transnational law emerges 'as a methodological lens through which we can study the particular transformation of legal institutions in the context of an evolving complex society': Peer Zumbansen, 'Defining the Space of Transnational Law: Legal Theory, Global Governance and Legal Pluralism' (2011) 15 *Law of Contemporary Problems* 5.
[62] See, eg Peer Zumbansen, 'Transnational Legal Pluralism'; A Claire Cutler, *Private Power and Global Authority* (Cambridge University Press, 2003).

official (eg state and international) law, and its implications for thinking about the concept of law.[63] Contemporary theoretical work, however, appears more interested in examining the processes that transnational law generates, and is generated by, than in debating its independence or autonomy from the state, or its true legal status.[64] This all means that, having left legal theory facing an 'identity crisis', and having generated no plausible 'legal theory of globalization', at the same time as revealing the deficiencies of standard conceptual tools, the expansion of transnational legal phenomena raises serious problems for any truly pluralist jurisprudence.[65]

One of the key problems is the question of whether, and under what conditions, transnational legal phenomena (or indeed processes) can have legitimate authority. Much of this debate then turns upon further analysis of a distinction between public, private, or hybrid regulation (and authority), and as both Zumbansen's and Cutler's work reveals, these questions are embedded within a much deeper divide between the social and the official, between society (and/or the market) and the state. As Cutler notes, the trend towards juridification of commercial, political, and economic practice—in which law is used to legitimize diverse claims to authority, only makes it more difficult to proceed with a conception of public, state-focused authority that does not include various forms of hybrid or even fully private authority.[66] The richness of both Cutler's and Zumbansen's work goes beyond what can be addressed in this study. However, insofar as both challenge the idea that analytic and normative conceptions of legitimate public authority can be used to explain pluralist and indeed transnational practices of authority, their work invites the response that will be offered by my relative authority theory in Chapter 10.

4. Authority

Mainstream approaches to authority in legal and political theory have concentrated their explanations on the authority that is held (or at least claimed by) single actors, albeit sometimes complex actors such as governments or states.

---

[63] Many scholars treat the *lex mercatoria* as the most far-reaching and well-supported example of transnational law. For a discussion of its legal character, see Thomas Schultz, 'Some Critical Comments on the Juridicity of the Lex Mercatoria' (2008) 10 *Yearbook of Private International Law* 667; and Emmanuel Gaillard, *Legal Theory of International Arbitration* (Martinus Nijhoff Publishers, 2010).

[64] Zumbansen; 'Transnational Private Regulatory Governance: Ambiguities of Public Authority and Private Power', in *Law and Contemporary Problems* (2013, forthcoming), available at: <http://ssrn.com/abstract=2185031> (OHLS CLPE Research Paper 45/2012), 1–4.

[65] Zumbansen, 'Transnational Private Regulatory Governance', 1–6.

[66] Cutler, *Private Power and Global Authority*, Ch 3. Cutler argues that merchant law, for instance, merges both public and private authority.

Although there are plenty of accounts of authority that insist upon explaining authority and the conditions of its justification without reference to any particular holder of authority, and so are not, strictly speaking, 'state-centric', they nevertheless do not explore the coherence of authority that is shared, divided, or in other respects pluralistic. This shortcoming is paralleled in pluralistic legal theoretical accounts, for even those which expressly or implicitly focus upon authority do not explore the analytic coherence of plural authority or sufficiently engage the leading contenders for its justification. Both then skip too quickly over my interest in whether, as a conceptual and/or a normative matter, the ideas of exclusivity and supremacy that are antithetical to any rich practice of plurality of authority can be disposed of quite so easily.

Sociological approaches to legal pluralism (such as Tamanaha's) are often vague about the notions of authority they employ. Tamanaha's own account is committed to the plurality of law, identifying six sources of normative ordering that typically claim to possess authority to bind, normative supremacy, legitimacy, and existing or justified control over matters within their scope.[67] Tamanaha argues that, as a matter of social fact, all systems that are considered 'manifestations of law' have in common 'the claim to represent legitimate normative authority'.[68] He then goes on to examine the range of relationships—both cooperative and conflicting—that such claims generate, noting that these inter-systemic relationships raise the question of 'the relative power of the competing systems'.[69] This explanation is revealing, but it is where my interest begins. If what each of these manifestations of law has in common is a claim to legitimate authority, then we should ask the further question of what would make those claims true; and where there are relationships between authorities, we should ask not only how those relationships reflect arrangements of relative power, but how they reflect, and may themselves influence, authority.

Other expressly pluralist approaches consider authority itself more directly, and seek to be sociologically informed while also committed to a more robust

---

[67] Tamanaha, 'Understanding Legal Pluralism', 42. Compare Galligan, who denies that non-state normative systems make any claim to final authority: DJ Galligan, *Law in Modern Society* (Oxford University Press, 2007). For Tamanaha, law is a 'folk concept', whose content shifts between time and place, so that although state law is today considered paradigmatic, that will not be the case always or everywhere. Regardless of what one makes of Tamanaha's account of law and its manifestations, he is right to note that there are many analyses we can fruitfully pursue without solving the issue of what conceptual tools pluralism needs from legal theory. That includes important work on the doctrinal and political responses to pluralism; on the normative implications of different inter-systemic relationships; and on specific inter-systemic interactions.

[68] Tamanaha, 'Understanding Legal Pluralism', 35. Tamanaha's list of normative systems includes international law, customary law, religious law, natural law, and mercantile law.

[69] Tamanaha, 'Understanding Legal Pluralism', 51.

analytical or normative account. Paul Schiff Berman's work, for instance, challenges 'rigidly territorialist or positivist visions of legal authority', which he thinks are unsuited to the complex relationships between normative systems that characterize transnational law.[70] He suggests instead that transnational law generates 'spheres of complex overlapping legal authority' in which states must 'share legal authority', and which can lead to conflict that cannot be resolved by searching for 'a single relevant legal authority'.[71] Yet Berman does not pursue the analytical task of explaining shared or overlapping authority, or the implications of conflict for the very idea of authority; nor does he examine the justificatory implications of such authority.

Normative questions arising from plurality of authority are most richly engaged by theorists offering alternative normative theories of legitimate authority. Within the constitutional and international pluralist literature, Walker, Kumm, Krisch, and Besson have devoted the most sustained attention to arrangements of authority specifically, and to a shift away from understandings of ultimate authority towards an analysis of multiple sites of legal/constitutional authority and the complex relationships of hierarchy or heterarchy that pertain between them.[72] Walker expressly addresses the problem of boundary disputes between authorities, and the search for a metaprinciple or 'basic grid' of authority.[73] Most important for my account here is Walker's argument that even ultimate authority can be non-exclusive, and can 'allow the possibility of overlap without subsumption'.[74] Walker then separately ties the legitimacy of each constitutional authority to the collective self-legislation of sovereign polities, and requires that ultimate authority must be tied to polities where there is subjective acceptance by the key officials of the polity that it *is* a sovereign polity, and general obedience to the polity's laws. Thus, rather than locating a single metaprinciple to give order to all these different sites of authority, Walker claims that there is no 'Archimedean point—from which we can evaluate the strength and validity of the different, and in some respects

---

[70] Paul Schiff Berman, 'Federalism and International Law through the Lens of Legal Pluralism' (2008) 73 *Missouri Law Review* 1151, 1176.

[71] Berman, 'Federalism and International Law through the Lens of Legal Pluralism', 1179; Berman, *Global Legal Pluralism*, 9.

[72] Neil Walker, 'Flexibility within a Metaconstitutional Frame: Reflections on the Future of Legal Authority in Europe', in Grainne De Búrca and Joanne Scott (eds), *Constitutional Change in the EU: From Uniformity to Flexibility?* (Hart Publishing, 2000); Kumm, 'The Jurisprudence of Constitutional Conflict: Constitutional Supremacy in Europe before and after the Constitutional Treaty' (2005) 11 *European Law Journal* 262.

[73] Neil Walker, 'Beyond Boundary Disputes and Basic Grids: Mapping the Global Disorder of Normative Orders' (2008) 6 *International Journal of Constitutional Law* 373, 375–376.

[74] Walker, 'Idea of Constitutional Pluralism', 346.

contending, authority claims'.[75] He thus suggests that there are contending metaprinciples of authority—some favouring state sovereignty, others advocating its replacement—resulting in a '*dis*order of normative orders'.[76]

Walker's radically pluralist denial of any standpoint from which the validity of overlapping and competing claims to authority can be assessed does not, however, fully engage with theories of what makes authority legitimate. Walker argues that consent to fully coordinated inter-authority relationships will never be achievable, but then seems to give up on the possibility that an alternative theory might be used to examine when such inter-authority relationships are legitimate. As discussed in Chapter 2 of this work, consent, as a justification for authority (and, derivatively, of justified networks of coordinated authorities), is just one of many candidates for the justificatory side of the story, and one which has been widely challenged by theorists of authority. We must therefore look more closely at the idea of authority and its justification before giving up on the commensurability of different claims to it.

A promising engagement of this sort is suggested by Kumm, who has argued that an idea of 'graduated authority' might be used to explain the doctrinal practice in which courts, in particular, engage national law with international or regional law. Graduated authority embodies structures and doctrinal frameworks, which, Kumm thinks, generate questions about 'who needs to look at what and give what kind of consideration to what is being said and done'.[77] Kumm finds the answers to these questions by applying a constitutionalist model which assesses comparative legitimacy—between, for instance, international treaties and national law—by reference to principles of formal legality, subsidiarity, procedural propriety, and reasonable outcomes.[78] Kumm expressly offers this account as a model of 'cosmopolitan' constitutionalism, and as the best interpretation of constitutional pluralism.[79] In Kumm's words, 'constitutional pluralism allows us to reconceive legitimate authority and institutional practices in a way that makes sense without the ideas of the state, of sovereignty, of ultimate authority, and of "we the people" as the basic foundations of law and the reconstruction of legal practice'.[80] For Kumm, constitutional legitimacy is tied to reasons—any constitutional order,

---

[75] Neil Walker, 'The Idea of Constitutional Pluralism' (2002) 65 *MLR* 317, 338.
[76] Walker, 'Beyond Boundary Disputes', 376.
[77] Kumm, 'The Cosmopolitan Turn in Constitutionalism', in Jeffrey L Dunoff and Joel P Trachtmann (eds) *Ruling the World* (Cambridge University Press, 2009) 258, 289.
[78] Kumm, 'Democratic Constitutionalism', 261ff.
[79] Mattias Kumm, 'The Cosmopolitan Turn'; Kumm, *Conflicts of Authority* (unpublished 2012) (draft paper on file with author).
[80] Kumm, in symposium transcript. Matej Avbelj and Jan Komárek (eds), 'Four Visions of Constitutional Pluralism' (2008) 1 *European Journal of Legal Studies* 325, 360.

wherever located, must perform well in realizing, respecting and fulfilling liberal democratic constitutional principles. Taken together, Kumm's work suggests a promising way to test the legitimacy of authority, wherever it is located, and with sensitivity to the prospect of overlap between authorities. However, the relationship between graduated authority, comparative legitimacy, constitutionalism, and constitutional pluralism generates more questions than answers. Outstanding questions include whether comparative legitimacy determines the degree of graduated authority, or whether graduated authority instead refers to a doctrinal structure for the management of conflicts between different levels of law. More abstractly, it is unclear what role comparative legitimacy plays in a constitutional pluralist model—can comparative legitimacy apply to the assessment of different constitutionalist models as well as specific bodies of law? These questions, and the promise of this approach, will be revisited in Chapter 11. Most importantly for my account, however, is the implication from Kumm's work that, while assessments of legitimacy can be compared, and authority can be graduated, the legitimate authority that is being compared and graduated is held independently by those who hold it. Indeed, this independence seems necessary in order to make sense of the very ideas that legitimacy can be compared, and authority graduated.

In contrast to the constitutionalist model that Kumm prefers, Krisch makes a normative case for a pluralist model, in which authority is dispersed and conflicting.[81] Krisch's arguments for favouring a pluralist interpretation of post-national law include the concern that other frameworks of analysis struggle to integrate competing claims to ultimate or supreme authority.[82] Instead, Krisch offers the suggestion that authority be conceived as graduated, or gradated, and that even legal authority is (and should be conceived as) a matter of degree rather than as a binary matter.[83] Yet there is a degree of imprecision over what it means for authority to be gradated or graduated; indeed, the two terms suggest different ways of conceiving of authority—one where there are precise steps or degrees or levels of authority, the other where each level shades into the next. Even if Although both are helpful ways in which to view the pluralistic practice of authority, more needs to be said about what might justify such vaguely bounded authority if it is to be successful in integrating competing claims to supremacy. According to Krisch's broadly Habermasian account, legitimacy depends upon how citizens relate to different levels of post-national order, through their multiple, overlapping political identities

---

[81] Nico Krisch, *Beyond Constitutionalism: The Pluralist Structure of Postnational Law* (1st edn, Oxford University Press, 2010), esp 210–212.
[82] Krisch, *Beyond Constitutionalism*, 176.
[83] Krisch, *Beyond Constitutionalism*, 12, 305. Compare the use of 'Graduated' authority at 293 with 'gradated' authority at 294.

and loyalties. For Krisch, practices of public autonomy, not abstract moral principles, are the foundation of legitimate authority and he argues that, at the moment, these support a pluralist order that can accommodate and balance competing claims of 'inclusiveness and particularity'.[84] Specifically, Krisch argues that practices of public autonomy across different 'publics' are normatively valuable only when they are consistent with others' rights of self-legislation, and that this test must be applied to determine both the processes by which political associations are formed and the very make-up of the polity forming them. In this light, the legitimacy of public authority is a test that all these different political associations, polities, and publics must meet independently. Indeed, Krisch's view seems to insist upon the very independence and distinctness of legitimate orders in order to make pluralism both possible and defensible.

Another group of theories focuses on authority by itself, without express attempts to conceive of it in relation to constitutional, pluralist, or constitutional pluralist models. Some take broadly Razian ideas about the justification for authority, and turn them upon non-state authorities such as those in the international legal system.[85] For instance, Tasioulas has argued that the Razian account of authority is all one needs to explore the legitimate authority of international law, and that this can be applied to work out the authority of that law, for separate states as subjects.[86] The most detailed of these accounts is offered by Besson's modified Razian test for legitimate authority—modified to emphasize that coordinative and democratic credentials must accompany Raz's own normal justification for authority.[87] Besson's 're-interpretation' insists that in the context

---

[84] Krisch, *Beyond Constitutionalism*, 101 and 103: 'the plural, divided identities, loyalties and allegiances that characterise postnational society are better reflected in a multiplicity of orders than in an overarching framework that implies ultimate authority'.

[85] Studies of the legitimacy of international law sometimes use theories of authority to argue that international law has or lacks legitimacy. See, eg John Tasioulas, 'The Legitimacy of International Law', in Samantha Besson and John Tasioulas (eds), *The Philosophy of International Law* (Oxford University Press, 2010); Samantha Besson, 'The Authority of International Law—Lifting the State Veil' (2009) 31 *Sydney Law Review* 343; Allen Buchanan, 'The Legitimacy of International Law', in Besson and Tasioulas, *The Philosophy of International Law* treats authority as one element of legitimacy. More commonly, however, theorists analyse international law's legitimacy by its satisfaction of conditions of justice, efficacy, or fairness, as standards that can be applied to international legal powers other than its authority. On the distinction, see Allen Buchanan, *Justice, Legitimacy, and Self-Determination: Moral Foundations for International Law* (Oxford University Press, 2007). Examination of these other kinds of legitimacy is outside the scope of this study.

[86] Tasioulas, 'The Legitimacy of International Law', 97–100. In a similar vein, Krehoff argues that a Razian theory of authority can be used to locate legitimate authority in whichever actor best serves the reasons applying to the subjects: Bernd Krehoff, 'Legitimate Political Authority and Sovereignty: Why States Cannot Be the Whole Story' (2008) 14 *Res Publica* 283.

[87] Besson, 'The Authority of International Law', 357 argues, contra Tasioulas, that the normal justification 'needs to factor in our epistemic disagreements and the need for co-ordination by a public authority as its primary feature. This interpretation of the normal justification condition does not,

of public authority, the law provides reasons for whole communities of people to coordinate their action over matters of common concern. In Besson's own words, '[w]hat a legal authority does... is provide legal subjects with reasons to coordinate over an abstract set of reasons they share objectively even if they disagree about it'.[88] Besson then argues for an account of legitimate international authority in which there is democratic inclusion of individuals, states, and groups of states, at different levels of law-making processes.[89]

Besson's conception of authority, and her theory of its justification, are designed to enable an explanation of the authority of both state law and international law over the same subjects. Her solution to the conceptual and normative implications of plurality is to conceive of the subjects as identical— ie one subject is a subject of different authorities— then assess the authorities' legitimacy independently in respect of that subject. She explains that, while consent cannot be a source of legitimate authority in either the international or domestic contexts, it can be important as a source of recognition of an authority. In Besson's words: 'due to the plurality of subjects involved in international law making and their manifold roles, as is particularly clear from the role of states qua subjects and officials, consent can clarify the existence of justifications for the authority of international law for specific subjects'.[90] This is an important point, which will be discussed further in Chapter 10, but for present purposes the notable element of Besson's explanation of authority is the persistence of the idea that authority is a power held, and justified, independently. Even where persons are subjects of multiple authorities, Besson's test would justify the legitimacy of those authorities separately and in turn.

Among non-Razian approaches to authority itself, the closest to an explanation of pluralistic authority appears in Buchanan's work on legitimacy, which explains legitimacy as the existence of a right to govern and a duty of support for (or non-interference with) that right.[91] Buchanan's explanation of plurality of legitimate authority rests on a rejection of exclusivity of authority. He suggests that, even if the dominant view of state legitimacy includes a condition that only the state's institutions can legitimately govern (an 'exclusive justification condition'), that account is not appropriate for explaining

---

however, turn it into an empty requirement by condoning any co-ordination procedure that turns out to be effective. The democratic procedure is based on and protects individual autonomy in conditions of political equality and disagreement over matters of common concern'.

[88] Besson, 'The Authority of International Law', 356.
[89] For the full account of 'demoi-cracy', see Samantha Besson, 'Institutionalizing Global Demoi-Cracy', in Lukas H Meyer (ed), *Justice, Legitimacy and Public International Law* (Cambridge University Press, 2009), 58.
[90] Besson, 'Authority of International Law', 371–372.
[91] Buchanan, 'Legitimacy of International Law'.

the authority of international legal institutions, some of which do not claim exclusive authority.[92] This is an important step towards dismantling any link between authority and exclusivity, and Buchanan's precision makes for a very persuasive account, but it does not take the further step of considering the implications for a full conception of pluralistic authority, which encompasses both exclusivity and non-exclusivity, and resulting inter-authority relationships.

5. Outstanding Puzzles

Despite their varying theories of legitimacy, these normative theories of legitimate, pluralist authority share a conception of independently legitimate authority, and seek conditions for its existence. Although most make legitimacy open to contestation by different authorities, and embrace the facts of plurality of authority, they do not make the legitimacy of authority interdependent between authorities or between constitutional orders, or expressly make inter-authority relationships themselves a condition of legitimacy.

The upshot of the discussion in this chapter is that there is space left over for a conception of interdependent authority and its justification. There is much to learn from existing works' applications of ideas about pluralistic practices to complex problems in constitutional and international theory, as from similar accounts focusing on problems of federalism, administrative law, or other fields. Yet these accounts seldom ask whether such diverse practices of authority are problematic as matters *about authority*, or whether conceptions of authority might help to shed light on the practice of plurality and normative arguments about pluralism. They do not explore the plausibility or coherence of dispersed, gradated, graduated authority, nor processes of '"sharing", "pooling" "division", or "co-ordination," of authority'.[93] They do not indicate how arrangements between such entities might have implications for the legitimacy of their authority, because their tests treat legitimacy as a quality attaching (or not) to multiple but independent authorities. This leaves a series of questions to be asked if we are to explain what authority is, if it is not ultimate or exclusive; and when it is legitimate, if it is overlapping and shared.

---

[92] Buchanan, 'Legitimacy of International Law', 83–85; compare the argument that international law does claim authority, in Mattias Kumm, 'The Legitimacy of International Law: A Constitutionalist Framework of Analysis' (2004) 15 *European Journal of International Law* 907.

[93] Walker, 'The Idea of Constitutional Pluralism', 339.

Through the lens of authority theory, practices of plurality and arguments about pluralism generate three broad and related questions which will drive the remainder of this work.

(i) Under what conditions (if any) can multiple claims to legitimate authority be true?

It is a lot easier to talk about a plurality of claims to authority than it is to talk about plurality of authority itself, and it is understandable that much pluralist writing has focused upon empirical questions about the former. Yet claiming is irrelevant to the issues of whether authority exists and under what conditions it is justified. One can have authority without claiming it, and one can claim authority without having it. We need to ask instead what might make those claims true, and in circumstances of plurality this requires asking whether it is ever possible to have multiple true claims to legitimate authority and, if so, under what conditions. Specifically, we must ask whether it is possible to have multiple authorities, or whether multiple claims to authority simply end up as false conflicts where only one authority is truly legitimate, and/or whether such multiple claims themselves deny the possibility of any authority whatsoever. We can thus make the transition from the observation of multiple claims to authority, to asking whether there really is plural legitimate authority.

(ii) As a conceptual matter, (how) can authority be overlapping, shared, or non-exclusive?

The first question opens the door for many more precise questions. What exactly is an overlap of authority? Is it conceptually coherent? Does it mean an overlap of subjects? How do overlaps manifest in conflict, cooperation, or coordination? Do overlapping authorities necessarily have equal authority or can they be differentiated and ranked? If so, how can that differentiation occur? How does sharing or overlap affect or even effect the primary subject-authority relationship?

(iii) How does plurality of authority affect the justification of authority?

If the above enquiry reveals that it is possible to have multiple legitimate authorities, and that authority itself can be shared and arranged in relationships, the next step must ask how multiplicity affects authority's legitimacy. Can there/must there be an Archimedean point from which to evaluate each separate claim against one another, or is there another way of assessing their claims? Can the legitimacy of authorities be lexically ordered or will there be problems of incommensurability?

The challenge is to find an account of authority that can address these puzzles raised by plurality, and provide a tool for its evaluation.

PART II

THE PUZZLES OF PLURAL AUTHORITY

5
Compatible and Complementary Relationships

It should be easy to explain inter-authority relationships when authorities are compatible or complementary. These relationships are familiar in practice and are not obviously conceptually problematic; thus any worthwhile justification of authority should be able to explain when two or more authorities working together or in harmony are justified, as opposed to just one working alone. Yet the explanation of compatibility and complementarity between authorities is not as straightforward as it seems.

Substantive, procedural, and hybrid theories of legitimate authority have not devoted much attention to the question whether complementary/compatible inter-authority relationships can be explained within a justification of authority. The exception is an exchange between Jeremy Waldron and Joseph Raz, which specifically tackles this problem and reveals some of the key differences between explanations of inter-authority relationships. This chapter argues that there is more to it than either Waldron or Raz has elaborated, and that their explanations for even the most straightforward of inter-authority relationships are unconvincing. Waldron's solution fails to explain how priority is given to one authority over others, or to justify relationships between disjunctive (as opposed to integrated) authorities. Raz's response is similarly constrained by applying a monist lens that makes his account unsatisfactory. In sum, the debate between the two leaves outstanding questions about the legitimacy of inter-authority relationships, both complementary and compatible, and the effect they might have upon the legitimacy of the authorities engaged within them.

1. Procedural Justifications and Plurality

Raz's account of justified authority is substantive, and Waldron's is a hybrid with an emphasis on the procedural element.[1] To give a full picture, however,

---

[1] The substantive element of Waldron's theory, which will not be explored in detail here, favours a principle of institutional settlement which is not, in itself, a process of authorizing a particular

a brief assessment should first be made of the third category of justification—purely procedural theories—for their potential to explain compatible and complementary relationships between authorities.

As discussed in Chapter 2, there are a number of problems with purely procedural justifications for authority, making them less attractive starting candidates for an analysis of plurality. Nevertheless, there is residual attraction and normative appeal in an account based on the consent of the governed. This appeal is unlikely to disappear no matter how strident the non-proceduralist objections become. Thus, a consideration of their explanation for compatibility and complementarity between authorities is warranted. Unfortunately, that analysis only reveals further defects in the proceduralist case. The obvious difficulty is that a process of consenting or otherwise legitimating a particular authority seems to leave no room for that authority to work with others. The authority that is consented to is *the* legitimate authority for those subjects. If a subject's consent/participation matters to the justification of a particular authority, then there are no grounds for that authority cooperating with another authority to which those subjects have not consented, nor for its deference to another authority to bring about compatibility between their directives.

One way around this problem might be to argue that the consent process can be conducted so that inter-authority cooperation is included within the package to which subjects consent. There are ways in which a consent process can be made sensitive to the prospects of inter-authority cooperation and deference; indeed, this has become the norm in many EU Member States where national elections are contested partly on the question of pro-EU and anti-EU platforms. However, it seems that if consent is to do the normative work of legitimizing a particular authority, it also needs to do the work of managing that authority's relationships with other authorities that have not been legitimated by the same subjects. Given the array and prevalence of such relationships, as outlined in Chapter 3, it seems unlikely that procedures can be sufficiently sensitive to plurality to enable them to sustain legitimate authority.

A second way to avoid this problem would be to elevate the value of the process of consent itself, rather than focusing upon its role in legitimating particular authorities. Then we might say that as long as particular authorities are legitimated through a consent process, they can legitimately cooperate with or defer to others who are also (separately) legitimated. This, however, begs the question of the normative value of consent itself. If consent has

authority; rather it is a substantive commitment to prioritizing an already procedurally legitimate authority in order to avoid causing confusion. See Jeremy Waldron, 'Authority for Officials', in Lukas H Meyer, *et al.* (eds), *Rights, Culture and the Law* (2003).

normative value, surely it has that value as a carrier of something valuable about the person who has given it. If we remove the specific person and the specific object of their consent, it is hard to see how consent can have any value at all.

A third argument could maintain that subjects can consent to more than one authority, giving both legitimacy, and enabling them to relate to one another as they see fit. The problem with this result is that it leaves the content of the inter-authority relationship free from any legitimating test, and opens the possibility of separate consent-based authorities coming into conflict. That prospect will be explored in detail in Chapter 6.

2. The Waldron-Raz Exchange

Returning to the direct debate between Raz and Waldron, the question is whether an account of authority can explain relationships between authorities. Waldron argues that Raz's normal justification thesis (NJT) cannot explain relationships 'as between officials or institutions', particularly relationships of deference when two institutions have legitimate authority, but one defers to another.[2] Waldron argues that in order to explain these relationships, Raz needs a special justification for political authority, which prioritizes public settlement of questions of common concern.[3] Waldron's own preferred solution is a principle of institutional settlement, which prioritises settled institutions in the interests of public coordination. Raz rejects Waldron's arguments, responding that the NJT can apply between public institutions to determine when deference is justified, and that the details of any specific inter-authority relationship are determined by the de facto constitutions of those institutions.[4]

Waldron takes it to be a central part of the practice of public authority that sometimes one authority should defer to another, even when the deferring authority would make a better judgment than the authority to which it defers. Waldron argues that to explain such inter-authority deference, we need something outside of the NJT, because the NJT's sole focus upon helping subjects do better according to reason means that it cannot comprehend justifying an authority that would lead subjects towards less conformity with reason.

---

[2] Waldron, 'Authority for Officials', 45.
[3] Waldron's initial suggestion was less of a direct challenge to Raz's normal justification thesis than a question for Raz and others to consider in relation to a more general theory of authority. Waldron, 'Authority for Officials', 69. Importantly, the debate appears to have prompted Raz to offer the clarifications about multiplicity of authority that were discussed in Ch 4 and which appears in Joseph Raz, 'The Problem of Authority: Revisiting the Service Conception' (2006) 90 *Minn Law Review* 1003.
[4] Raz responds in the course of a general chapter addressing many of the volume's contributions, and is consequently fairly brief, but his responses must be read in conjunction with his more detailed

Waldron's central example is a relationship between public officials (A and B) within a single system, who both issue directives to the same subject (C). Waldron then evaluates three possible explanations for deference between A and B. First, he says we cannot simply apply the NJT 'comparatively' between A and B with regard to C, ie so that if C would do better following A than B, then B should defer to A. The whole idea of deference in inter-official relations is, according to Waldron, that B should defer even when it is the case that B's directive is (or could be) better.[5] Although Waldron hints that an application of Raz's NJT might be available to explain why this idea of deference as part of inter-official authority is misconceived, he suggests that we should not accept it 'unless we find there is no other way of adequately explicating the common understanding of authority in this area'.[6] It will not do to say that the NJT supplies the explanation that B should defer to A when C would do better following A than B.

Second, Waldron considers whether A's directive to C might implicitly be accompanied by a directive to B to refrain from making contradictory demands upon C. Could we then apply the NJT separately to that directive, to see if it was legitimately authoritative for B? If so, then B is a subject of A. Here the trouble, Waldron thinks, is that A might never have intended to issue the separate directive. Although Waldron does not elaborate upon this point, it seems convincing if we take the view that the exercise of authority can only occur if the authority intends to exercise its power to determine a subject's obligations.[7]

Third, Waldron suggests that we cannot simply look for other rules according to which B is a subject of A, without regard for A's better ability to enable subjects to conform to reason. Specifically, he argues that although a constitutional rule might direct B to follow A regardless of whether that would produce a better outcome, we cannot simply use this rule to assess the inter-authority relationship. Although a constitution might direct B to defer to A, the issue is how we can assess *that* directive; the constitution itself is not an answer to the question of evaluating inter-authority relationships.[8] The explanation of

---

explanations of his wider moral and political philosophy: Joseph Raz, 'Comments and Responses', in Lukas H Meyer (ed), *Rights, Culture and the Law* (Oxford University Press, 2003).

[5] Waldron also considers that 'it is part of our understanding of this sort of authority relation among officials that in some cases B should not even start off down the road of considering whether he could come up with a better directive': Waldron, 'Authority for Officials', 67.

[6] Waldron, 'Authority for Officials', 67.

[7] Estlund, among others, has argued that the exercise of political authority is necessarily aimed at creating duties, it is not an accidental power: David M Estlund, *Democratic Authority: A Philosophical Framework* (Princeton University Press, 2008), 143. In a recent account of authority Raz also describes authority as 'the power to impose duties on others simply by expressing an intention to do so': Joseph Raz, 'On Respect, Authority, and Neutrality: A Response' (2010) 120 *Ethics* 279 (2010).

[8] Waldron, 'Authority for Officials', 68.

inter-official authority cannot simply be that a constitution requires that a legislature disregard an international institution, or that a court defer to a legislature. When a constitution does provide rules for inter-authority relationships, we should still examine and explain whether those institutions are authoritative; we should still ask whether the constitutional rules are consistent with their legitimacy.

Waldron's fourth possibility is the one he prefers. He argues that to understand authority relations among officials we must focus on the primary relationship between A and C, then say that the requirement of deference applying to B is a requirement not to upset the A–C relationship. As a public authority, A is the coordinating director of a society; the one tasked with coordination over problems of common concern.[9] B must not interfere with that coordinating role by offering conflicting directives, if doing so would cause confusion about what the subjects should do. Waldron says that the 'usual story' requiring citizens to follow authority when it is important and obligatory to find a common solution has an analogy with officials.[10] An official ought to defer if the other official issues a directive that 'holds a fair chance of securing coordination among the citizens'.[11] Because these questions of common concern admit of multiple answers, and because the subjects all need to be able to look to an authority to quickly coordinate their activities, then once there is a directive out there which stands a good chance of coordinating action, other officials ought not interfere with that directive even if they think or even know that their own directive would do better. This prioritization of a particular authority to which others defer is justified, in Waldron's view, by the special task of public authority—the identification and then coordination of matters of common concern.[12]

Waldron illustrates the problem through a thought experiment which supposes that the US Congress would do better (in helping subjects conform to reason) by following the welfare policies favoured by the Conference of Catholic Bishops, than by trying to figure things out for itself. Waldron suggests that under the NJT, this would anoint the Conference of Bishops as an authority over Congress, and that this is problematic because even if it is true that Congress would do better following the Bishops, it seems wrong to say that

---

[9] Waldron thinks such a principle of 'institutional settlement' follows if we adopt a special conception of public authority, where A as a public authority is 'established to deal with questions of common concern arising among C1 and all the other Cs': Waldron, 'Authority for Officials', 68.

[10] Waldron, 'Authority for Officials', 69.

[11] Waldron, 'Authority for Officials', 69.

[12] Waldron can then build this principle of institutional settlement into his own justificatory theory, which rests upon the non-instrumental value of public acceptance in circumstances of disagreement. For the full theory, see Jeremy Waldron, *Law and Disagreement* (Clarendon Press, 1998).

the Bishops have authority over Congress, or even (probably) that they ought to have such authority. The Conference, according to Waldron, is not the right sort of authority; it does not occupy the sort of public position that would make it an appropriate decider of issues of common concern.[13]

According to Waldron, therefore, the NJT fails to capture a particular 'public or official' dimension of authority, which requires that a person or institution occupy a certain position in public life before it should or can be regarded as an authority.[14] Specifically, Waldron suggests that Raz's normal justification must be supplemented by a second and separate level, which requires that people who would be governed by the putative authority 'actually accept' that it satisfies the first level test (the normal justification test).[15] This is different from a purely procedural consent-based account; rather, it joins a test for an authority's substantive legitimacy with its subjects' acceptance that it meets the substantive test.

In response, Raz argues that not only is the interaction of authorities explicable within the terms of the NJT, but that phenomena of authority relations among officials actually serve to illustrate the operation and flexibility of that theory.[16] Raz argues that, according to the NJT, one institution is under the authority of another when the tasks of the lower authority 'would be better discharged if it were subjected to higher authority than if it were acting independently of such authority'.[17] He suggests that the NJT is put to use in this way within the principle of subsidiarity governing EU interactions with Member States, and that such a principle (where an institution is subject to the authority of another and must therefore defer only if deference would promote the performance of the lower authority's tasks) is the way we should think of 'the legitimate relations between higher and lower authorities'.[18] Furthermore, Raz argues, the NJT applies to the very question of when an authority is justified in determining that a situation requires an authoritative directive in order to coordinate behaviour.[19]

---

[13] Waldron, 'Authority for Officials', 63–65.

[14] Waldron therefore ends his argument at the point where he and others have previously challenged Raz—they say that the NJT cannot explain public or political authority, or at least that it cannot explain it well. The arguments are familiar and are not the focus of this study, but I raise Waldron's argument here because in the process of getting to his point about the special case of political authority, Waldron has made some important suggestions for my questions about relationships between authorities.

[15] Waldron, 'Authority for Officials', 66.

[16] Joseph Raz, 'Comments and Responses', 261–262.

[17] Raz, 'Comments and Responses', 262.

[18] Raz, 'Comments and Responses', 262.

[19] Raz, 'Comments and Responses', 259.

Raz's second response argues that the direction of authority relationships between institutions is determined by an institution's constitutional rules regarding other authorities—a factor that distinguishes inter-institutional relationships from inter-personal authority relationships.[20] Raz suggests that the answer to the question of when one authority should defer to another, in the case of institutional authorities, is largely settled by an institution's 'de facto constitution'.[21] He argues that the de facto constitution of an institution, whether or not it is justified or defensible, determines what the institution is in fact. His explanation of the phenomena of relationships between compatible or coordinated authorities is therefore to look at what social facts have established, by way of constitutional rules and their allocations of power.

3. Initial Clarifications

Before evaluating the success of either explanation, some useful clarifications can be made. First, the arguments can be organized by applying my earlier distinction between integrated and disjunctive authorities and the typology of inter-authority relationships. This reveals that Waldron's account shifts between examples of relationships between authorities that are integrated (eg courts and legislatures) and disjunctive (Congress and the Conference of Catholic Bishops), and that Raz's response does not clarify to which type of relationship his responses apply or consider different puzzles posed by compatible and complementary authorities. Although I will argue here that neither Raz's nor Waldron's solutions adequately capture justificatory distinctions between integrated/disjunctive and complementary/coordinated authorities, the failures occur for different reasons.

A second clarification makes a distinction between inter-authority relationships *of authority*, and other kinds of relationships between authorities. Waldron's target is sometimes unclear due to the use of mixed terminology about 'authority relations' and 'compliance' between officials, on the one hand, and 'relations of deference' and 'respect', on the other. Waldron suggests that requirements of respect can be 'rephrased' as ones of authority, seeing deference as 'an appropriate response to an authoritative directive' and one that goes beyond mere compliance.[22] Waldron at times seems to elide the difference between

---

[20] He therefore distinguishes the case of institutions from that of individuals, because 'what [institutions] can or cannot do is determined, to a large degree, by their constitution, formal or informal': Raz, 'Comments and Responses', 262.
[21] Raz, 'Comments and Responses', 262, n 7.
[22] Waldron, 'Authority for Officials', 52–55.

inter-authority relations of obedience (and duties to obey) or deference (and reasons to defer). Yet as a challenge to Razian authority theory, it seems important to preserve a distinction between obedience and deference, and to maintain clarity about which type of relation is under examination. Authority relationships exist where one institution or person is subject to the authority of another, while relations of deference can arise between institutions and persons who are not in authority relations, nor indeed in any sort of hierarchical relationship. Deference entails that an agent who defers has the capacity and the normative power to decide for herself; she simply chooses not to. This seems to be a necessary characteristic of deference to distinguish it from obedience: if you have legitimate authority over me, my obligation is to obey, not to defer. But if there is a reason to treat you as authoritative although you are not, this might be a sufficient reason to defer to you.

Raz's response clarifies that not all inter-authority relationships are themselves relationships of authority, but leaves open whether he accepts Waldron's assumption that deference between authorities is part of the practice of authority, even when the one deferring would make a better decision than the one deferred to.[23] The NJT cannot explain this sort of relationship, so Raz either needs to show that it is indeed something separate from authority or introduce a supplement/exception to account for the deviation from the normal test. From Raz's response, we might conclude that the NJT can explain authority relationships, but is neither aimed at nor applicable to other kinds of relationships. Along these lines, although Raz does not offer it here, one possible conclusion could be that the answer to Waldron's concern is that whatever explains deference between institutions, it is not a matter for authority theory because it is not a matter about authority.

However, even if Waldron's examples are discounted as instances of non-authority relationships and therefore outside the ambit of the NJT, the question remains whether such non-authority relationships between authorities might constrain the existence and/or legitimacy of the authorities engaged within them. An analysis should not solely be interested in whether the inter-authority relationships are themselves instances of authority and therefore explicable by application of the NJT, but in how they are part of the practice of authority that a theory of authority purports to explain.

---

[23] Raz, 'Comments and Responses', 262.

4. Compatible/Complementary Authorities and the Normal Justification Thesis

There are two key points to consider: first, the preliminary question of whether Raz's full account of authority (the pre-emption thesis, the dependence thesis, and the normal justification thesis) can generate the kind of relationships between authorities that interest Waldron; second, whether Raz's response (linking relationships among political authorities to the de facto constitutions that establish them) is sufficient to address Waldron's worry.

Raz's early works accepted that 'sometimes there are two compatible authorities whose powers overlap, as is the case with the authority of both parents over their children'.[24] Raz later confirmed that 'we can be subject to the authority of our parents, of our schools, and of the law, for example, at the same time, and regarding the same issue'.[25] When there is such overlap, Raz notes that sometimes only one authority will issue a directive, in which case that authority is the one to be followed. In my terminology, the authorities are compatible, and no worries about cooperation or conflict arise. Alternatively, and equally conveniently, there might be 'cooperative relationships among authorities' as occurs when legal authorities recognize the authority of schools or parents by 'lend[ing] them legal authority, by directing the relevant people to obey them or by enforcing their directives through legal procedures'.[26] In my terminology, this amounts to coordination between authorities. Raz sees no difficulties in such coordination, or at least no puzzles requiring further attention.

I think that Raz moves too quickly. To have multiple legitimate authorities on the same issue we need to show the possibility of facts that establish A *and* B as legitimate authorities over the same subjects. We can easily imagine facts giving legitimate authoritative force to A's commands only if A works *with* B. Some multi-level governments provide familiar, although sometimes controversial, examples, ie where a local or regional government has legitimate authority over subjects only if it cooperates with a national or federal government to achieve (for example) road maintenance or quality of education or another common objective. Yet even this seemingly straightforward application of the NJT shows that the legitimacy of A is dependent upon its relationship with B. This structure can apply not only to integrated authorities (as in the local-national government example) but also to disjunctive authorities that need to work

---

[24] Joseph Raz, *The Morality of Freedom* (Clarendon Press, 1986), 57.
[25] Raz, 'The Problem of Authority', 1021.
[26] Raz, 'The Problem of Authority', 1021.

together to be legitimate, but lack any normative arrangements to determine how they should do so. The application of the normal justification thesis to combinations of authorities illustrates one way in which the legitimate authority of one institution might be constrained by that of another, but it requires a more pluralistic and interactive view of authority-subjects and authorities. I will argue, in Chapter 7, that it also shows how the authority of agents should be understood as relative—that is, constrained by or dependent upon one another.

Equally interesting are facts rendering A and B as interchangeably legitimate authorities, that is, facts where right reason requires one course of action which could be achieved by following any of several authorities. Such plural authorities are indistinguishable under the NJT because reason requires obedience to either one. Imagine, for instance, that Sue negligently knocks over Tom, her neighbour, while driving into her driveway. Imagine that Sue now has reason to make amends, and that both A (a court) and B (a private arbitrator agreed to by Sue and Tom) would decide that Sue must pay Tom $1,000 in reparation. We might say that both the court's and the arbitrator's directives would enable Sue and Tom to better conform to reason than if they were left to their own devices (perhaps Sue is utterly unremorseful and would not offer anything to Tom privately, while Tom's idea of corrective justice is to run Sue over in return). If this pattern repeats on a regular basis, so that, more often than not, both the court and the arbitrator would generate greater conformity with the reasons that apply to Sue and Tom, then both would be legitimate. However, the court and the arbitrator would generate exactly the same outcome, so any difference in legitimacy between the authorities cannot be explained by the extent to which following their commands would entail conformity with right reason. So far so good, but there still seems to be an important difference between the authorities which might affect their legitimacy, and which depends upon moral or political theories attaching different values to different institutions or decision-making processes. Perhaps we are committed to public settlement of disputes and the visibility of corrective justice, and so would think a court's decision here more legitimate; or we might be committed to party autonomy in disputes and think it more valuable to let parties themselves decide how their disputes should be resolved. Under the NJT, the authorities are indistinguishable and their directives are compatible, but in political/legal practice there are different (and importantly different) implications of following one or the other.

This structure can repeat in larger-scale situations of compatibility. In the case of political authority, it may be necessary to disambiguate between authorities, and a theory of authority that cannot do so seems to miss something important in the way we normally think of plurality among political authorities. When there are multiple authorities, sometimes it is going to matter which one is obeyed, and which are not. Even where authoritative directives are compatible, it might still matter from whence they came.[27] For instance, imagine an 'official' national government which is challenged by a contending regime, in circumstances in which both are capable of securing compliance among members of the relevant community. Both might require the citizens of the state to do activity X (for example, that residents in a conflict zone obey a curfew, which would better enable them to conform to reason). We would normally think that in this scenario there is quite a difference, as a matter of legitimacy, between obeying each authority, even though the practical outcome and the extent of conformity with the reasons for doing the act would be the same whether either or both are obeyed. Those who obey the official government are making a certain commitment or allegiance to that authority, while the opposite commitment is made by those supporting the contender.

This is not to argue that affiliation must always be an element of a theory of political authority; rather that the idea of political authority might need something like an account of affiliation or other political values in order to distinguish between multiple legitimate authorities. This is particularly true in situations where the authorities command the same thing, and are therefore indistinguishable as a matter of Raz's 'conformity with reason' test. Importantly, these other political values are not incompatible with the NJT, but nor are they subsumed within it. Instead, I will flag here the argument that I develop in Chapter 6—that they are necessary supplements to the NJT in situations of plurality of authority.

The second puzzle concerns Raz's reliance upon the 'de facto constitutions' of institutions to determine inter-authority relationships. Raz's and Waldron's differences over the role of constitutional constraints reveal the key disjuncture between them. Waldron considered and rejected a fall-back onto constitutional rules to explain inter-authority relationships, because, in his view, a constitution contains a normative question about authority; it does not solve the question.[28] That is, the enquiry into legitimacy cannot end at 'the Constitution', because it begins there. For Raz, in contrast, the enquiry asks what is settled in fact, because the authorities at issue are institutions which can only act as their de facto constitutions direct. Raz says that we can find a positive conventional

---

[27] As Shapiro explains (although in pursuit of a different point), there is no reason to think that the choice of a particular system of authority is arbitrary. The choice of a particular authority, for many subjects or participants, will be an expression of a perceived obligation (eg to a system that has a popular mandate) or affiliation (eg to a system of religious law): J Shapiro, 'Law, Plans, and Practical Reason' (2002) 8 *Legal Theory* 387, 392.

[28] Waldron, 'Authority for Officials', 68.

source for a particular relationship, and use this to explain its character, and that the questions of what an institution *can* do and *should* do both depend upon the institution's de facto constitutional arrangements. The position is a clear instantiation of Raz's more general approach to institutional theory, which treats institutional arrangements (including legal arrangements) as matters of social fact, just as Waldron's is an instantiation of his generally normative approach to jurisprudence.[29]

Raz's social facts approach requires an account of what a de facto constitution is and how it can determine the hierarchies, deferences, and exclusions that operate between authorities. This raises some difficulties: (i) What is a de facto constitution? (ii) How does a de facto constitution constrain an institutional authority, if it does? (iii) How should we analyse multiple de facto constitutions? (iv) Why stop evaluating at the point of de facto constitutional constraints?

Raz does not clarify what he means by a de facto constitution. Typically, a constitution entails rules, hierarchies, principles, and conditions, which empower institutional actors and set limits on their activities, through express direction to constitutional actors and/or through protection of the rights of their subjects. Yet constitutions can be more or less formal; and constitutional content can be modified, expanded, or restricted by practice in a way that makes it misleading simply to read formal constitutional provisions and think one has understood constitutional content. Presumably, then, a de facto constitution refers to whatever the rules, hierarchies, principles, and conditions actually are, as a matter of constitutional practice, regardless of their formal or informal character. A de facto constitution can therefore be conceived as being responsive to practice in a way that a purely formal constitution is not. In this conception, however, an authoritative institution is not entirely constrained by its de facto constitution; it is instead partly an author of it—as it changes direction, or interacts with new authorities, or employs new tools in its dealings with subjects; it is in one sense remaking the de facto constitution. This seems to be at the heart of any distinction between a de facto constitution and a formal or de jure constitution.

This conception would suggest that an interaction between authorities is not limited by formal constitutional content; rather that the rules of interaction

---

[29] See also Joseph Raz, 'On the Authority and Interpretation of Constitutions', in Larry Alexander (ed), *Constitutionalism: Philosophical Foundations* (Cambridge University Press, 2001). If we apply this to specifically legal analyses, the difference invokes the key distinction between legal positivist and non-positivist approaches—the legal positivist's insistence that legal authority derives from social facts (conventional or otherwise) and the non-positivist's search for moral principles as the source of ultimate legal authority. This oversimplifies somewhat (for instance it elides the relationship between moral and social facts) and is not intended to characterize Waldron's approach as a natural law or other particular non-positivist argument.

are those actually operating in practice. Through that practice, the content of de facto empowerments and constraints upon an institution may be modified or even disregarded in ways that may entail the institution acting in previously unauthorized directions.[30] Practical examples in the legal context include those municipal courts or administrative tribunals which, as the international legal system has expanded in scope and authoritative content, have applied international law even when it is not incorporated. Earlier constitutions of those states, or more specifically those provisions empowering their rule-applying bodies, may not have permitted such reliance upon laws external to the national legal system, but along the way, as a matter of customary constitutional practice, those institutions have changed beyond the supposed constraints of their de jure constitution.

Both informal and formal de facto constitutions can change or be interpreted in ways that involve new relationships with other authorities. However, if de facto constitutions are constituted by flexible, responsive constraints, it is difficult to see how a de facto constitution constrains at all. If a de facto constitution is whatever rules are in effect at a given time, then those rules cannot reliably determine inter-authority relationships. Indeed, the opposite seems true: an institution's de facto constitution reflects what that institution is, given all the different developments it has undergone—developments that can be motivated by normative considerations. At this point, the normative enquiry that Waldron suggests we raise about how to understand inter-authority relationships is not just still in the picture of authority; it *is* the picture. For instance, take a formal national constitution that requires courts to defer to legislatures. The formal constitution governs both sets of institutions and tells them the terms of their interaction. But in the de facto constitution, courts might devise doctrines and mechanisms that show little deference to legislatures, for instance by practising extreme measures of judicial review which may even include precise instructions to the legislature about how it should be exercising its authority. In this circumstance, we can say that the formal constitution is not being upheld, and that a de facto constitution is trumping the formal constitution, but it seems that on Raz's view we would have to stop there; we could not go further into a normative evaluation of the substantive legitimacy of the relationship, to test its impact on legitimate authority.

The obvious response is that we might want to say a lot more about an inter-authority relationship (and specifically its legitimacy and its effect on

---

[30] Indeed, for matters on which a formal constitution is unclear or silent, such as final interpretive authority in the US Constitution or substantive restrictions on parliamentary sovereignty in Westminster systems, such unauthorized moves by institutions are the only means of (eventually) arriving at constitutional settlements.

the legitimacy of those engaged within it) than simply assessing its consistency with constitutional rules.[31] If a legislature in the above context starts leaving policy decisions to the judiciary, we might say there is an improper relationship because the legislature is not acting as it is supposed to according to the constitution, but we might also want to go into substantive normative detail about why this relationship is a problem. The dispute over who should decide matters of constitutional importance, including rights and duties of subjects and powers and limits of institutions, is a normative dispute which social convention might settle (and constitutionalize) incorrectly or unjustly. What is settled as a matter of fact is one thing, but legitimate authority is another. To side with Waldron on this question; matters of public authority are of such significance in social life that it would be odd simply to stop the analysis of inter-authority relationships with the acceptance of whatever social facts have produced, and solidified into a de facto constitution.[32]

Even if we subscribe to Raz's argument that the constitution does and should settle the matter, this aspect of Raz's response seems to be inconsistent with his prior argument that the NJT can be applied in order to justify relationships between authorities, unless we take the content of right reason to be determined, for institutional authorities, solely by the constitutional rules that apply to them. Even if we accept (with Raz) that institutional actors are not subject to the demands of practical reason directly, and are only artificial subjects of conventional rules, we can still test the legitimacy of the rules constituting the institutions and their relationship to see how they serve their subjects' conformity to reason. Furthermore, I will argue, we should ask whether these relationships are also part of the picture about the legitimacy of authority itself.

A third problem also emerges from Raz's strategy of explaining inter-authority relationships by reference to a constitution—de facto or otherwise. Raz's response to inter-authority relationships is a monist response, which does not account for pluralist practice. That is, when talking about disjunctive authorities—two or more authorities with separate constitutions—we cannot simply look to one constitution to constrain the relationship.[33] Even if we could use Raz's response

---

[31] For a comprehensive examination of arguments for and against constitutionalism, including Raz's conventional account, see Andrei Marmor, *Law in the Age of Pluralism* (Oxford University Press, 2007), 99 *ff*.

[32] The desire to analyse inter-authority relationships using normative theory is also a feature of much constitutional pluralist writing: see, eg Mattias Kumm, 'Conflicts of Authority' (unpublished 2012); Miguel Poiares Maduro, 'The Importance of Being Called a Constitution: Constitutional Authority and the Authority of Constitutionalism' (2005) 3 *International Journal of Constitutional Law* 332.

[33] Walker suggests that where there are different constitutional and meta constitutional sites and discourses, none of them answer and settle the legitimacy of power because they are all interacting: Neil Walker, 'Flexibility within a Metaconstitutional Frame: Reflections on the Future of Legal Authority

to explain the scenario of integrated authorities such as courts and legislatures within a constitutional structure, this does not help us examine relationships between disjunctive but overlapping or interactive authorities (such as Congress and an international institution, or the government of a foreign state, or the government of a tribal territory). When there are disjunctive authorities, without normative arrangements to integrate them, both might insist on the exclusivity or supremacy of their own institution (and constitution) relative to the other. Social facts themselves may not clarify that just one constitution is authoritative, as constitutional actors do not always give supremacy to their own constitution when it overlaps or interacts with others. Nor is it always possible to accommodate or integrate disjunctive constitutions in order to identify one as superior. The fascination with pluralism in European constitutional theory, for instance, is not simply an intellectual fashion; rather it seeks to make sense of actual practices that are more complicated than simply giving effect to either national or European constitutional supremacy.[34] Even if European/Member States' constitutions could be explained as a kind of ordered hierarchy, ie as integrated rather than disjunctive, this cannot be true of clearly separate authorities. For instance, compare the texts, principles, and purposes of a national constitution with that of the World Trade Organization (WTO), or compare the WTO constitution with that of the World Health Organization (WHO). Conventional hierarchies or integrations cannot be found in those cases where constitutions do not speak to other constitutions.

If social facts cannot settle the requirements of inter-authority relationships, our explanation of them is either limited to describing relationships of mere power, which can explain why those relationships operate the way they do, or we can look elsewhere to engage in normative enquiry about the justifiability of the authorities and their relationships by appealing to political and moral principles. Then it is the principles that are justifying the inter-authority relationship, not either or both of the authorities' constitutions.

5. Compatible/Complementary Authorities and Procedural Justifications

Turning to Waldron's account, some of the same criticisms arise. Waldron offers the principle of institutional settlement as a contender for the role of

---

in Europe', in Grainne De Búrca and Joanne Scott (eds), *Constitutional Change in the EU: From Uniformity to Flexibility?* (Hart Publishing, 2000).

[34] Kumm, 'Conflicts of Authority'.

justifying one kind of inter-authority relationship, so that once a settlement has been achieved, deference is required because it protects order against disorder. In my terminology, the idea is that relationships of deference transform situations of potential conflict into situations where the authorities are compatible, not conflicting, because only one actually exercises its authority. However, Waldron's solution is vulnerable to the same pluralist critique made of Raz's constitutional solution. Questions of common concern can arise between different normative systems, and even a principle of institutional settlement that could establish the primacy of authorities within each system could not resolve which systemic settlement should prevail. In other words, where there are two or more disjunctive authorities that could adequately secure coordination around matters of common concern arising within their shared/overlapping/ interactive subject-communities, then even if we prioritize public institutional settlement we could not know which settlement attracted that priority. Recall the example offered in Chapter 3 of a tribal authority in a relationship with a state with which it shares subjects. If the tribal authority determines that its subjects should disregard or act contrary to a directive issued by the state government relating to tribal property, this unsettles the primary relationship that exists between the state and members of the tribe who are subjects of both authorities, but so too would the state's directive unsettle the relationship between the members of the tribe and the tribal authorities. The question of priority or deference between them cannot be settled by an account of institutional settlement if both are salient and capable of securing compliance and order in their community or communities.

The other core argument against reliance upon a principle of institutional settlement to justify inter-authority deference is that some non-deferential relationships may be justified despite the confusion they cause. There may be value in unsettling or challenging the relationship that exists between authorities and subjects, and a competition for authority might be one way of doing so. Depending on the issues at stake and the context of the authority relationship, we might not want the clarity that comes from having just one authority making decisions. This inadequacy of the institutional settlement explanation is consequent upon Waldron's narrow interpretation of the value of deference. In his account, deference is valuable when (and because) it helps to secure public coordination over questions of common concern. But deference can serve wider values than simply avoiding confusion or promoting the clarity of authority. Deference can be invoked and practised to serve values associated with pluralism, with toleration, and with self-determination. However, some of these principles are in direct opposition to the idea that settled solutions to questions of common concern should be protected against competition, so that to explain deference between authorities we must consider the distinct values and limits of deference on their merits, rather than prioritizing one value without further argument.

This reveals a final and larger problem: is it necessary or even preferable to individuate a single authority to which other authorities should defer? Even if those matters of common concern or coordination to which Waldron would apply the principle of institutional settlement do require the presentation of salient solutions, this need not entail that only one authority (or one set of integrated authorities) must be anointed over others. As my account of relative authority in the following chapters argues, inter-authority relationships of cooperation, and even relationships of contest, can establish salient solutions along which subjects can coordinate; and in at least some matters of common concern, such relationships might even be more desirable than simply empowering one authority to decide. As Waldron himself notes, questions of common concern are likely to attract different and competing solutions.[35] It might be that the way to reach common answers *and* to secure genuine conformity with them is to allow competition between public authorities, or to require them to work together cooperatively, rather than prioritizing one or other by insisting upon a practice of deference.

Thus, although both Waldron and Raz have raised the prospect that relationships between authorities might be a matter for a theory of authority, neither account has adequately explained the impact of either integrated or disjunctive relationships upon the legitimacy of authority. Inter-authority relationships cannot be justified simply by referring to monist de facto constitutional arrangements (Raz's answer) or a monist de facto public settlement (Waldron's answer). Even relationships between compatible and complementary authorities, which are the easiest types of plurality to conceptualize and justify, are under-explained by those theories because they do not attend to the plurality of settlements and constitutions, or the plurality of authority itself. Yet the core assumption of both accounts—that inter-authority relationships must be understood by reference to the primary authority relationship, and that the relation between A and B within the official realm is somehow '*about* the relation between officialdom in general to C1, and his fellow citizens'—seems promising.[36] We just need to explore the character and implications of the connection between the primary and secondary authority relationships more carefully. Waldron places the primary relationship as a sort of trump whereby once a primary relationship exists, secondary relationships between authorities must be managed so they do not unsettle it. There are other possibilities, including my own argument that a secondary relationship between authorities, although

---

[35] Waldron, 'Authority for Officials'; see also Waldron, *Law and Disagreement*.
[36] Waldron, 'Authority for Officials', 67 (emphasis in original).

not conceptually prior to the primary relationship between authority and subject, nevertheless can condition the legitimacy of the primary relationship so that we cannot simply say that one gives way to the other.

6
Actual and Apparent Conflict

Compatibility and complementarity between authorities are the most convenient types of plurality of authority, but they do not exhaust the field. The bigger challenge for a pluralist analysis of authority is to ask whether it is possible to have conflicting legitimate authorities in the same domain, and, if so, how (if at all) this affects the legitimacy of those authorities. The possibility question is no preliminary or introductory matter; it requires asking whether all apparent instances of conflict can be explained away, either by locating legitimate authority in networks of integrated authorities, or through determining that only one among competing claimants is a truly legitimate authority. Understanding the possibility of plurality thus requires close attention to the distinction between multiple claims to authority, and multiple claims to authority that are actually true.

This chapter asks, first, whether, under either substantive or procedural justifications, it is ever possible to have conflicting legitimate authorities in a single domain. The analysis in section 2 then isolates the most complex problems within Raz's service conception, under which conflicts of legitimate authority are especially problematic. Having argued that conflicting legitimate authorities are possible even within Raz's conception, section 3 argues that conflicts of authority reveal two intractable problems: one of ranking authorities, and the other of identifying authorities. Section 4 then concludes with an argument that in circumstances of conflicting plausible claims to authority, a substantive conception alone cannot explain conflicts of legitimate authority; rather it is dependent upon procedural theories to do the work of identifying and legitimizing authority. This reveals the need for a hybrid or conjunctive justification, which is the focus of Chapter 7.

1. The Possibility of Conflicting Authorities

Any of the procedural justifications of authority—whether justifying authority by consent, affiliation, democracy, or other procedures—straightforwardly leave open the possibility that any one of these forms of participatory affirmation could generate more than one legitimate but conflicting authority, or they could operate in parallel to generate multiple conflicting authorities with concurrent or overlapping powers not integrated by a common normative framework. Where that occurs, there may be additional questions to ask about situations of practical conflict between authoritative obligations, but the mere possibility of such plurality is theoretically coherent and unproblematic.

Conflicts of authority pose more difficulty under the substantive justifications, and indeed pose difficulties for those accounts. Substantive accounts import a success condition which requires that authority is only justified if it is successful in providing the service or value that authority is supposed to provide. On these accounts, if success is undermined by the presence of multiple conflicting authorities, even de facto ones, then authority cannot be justified. Raz's service conception is more difficult still, because the success condition within Raz's account is not simply tied to the justification of authority, but to its very existence. As authority is justified by its service of subjects' conformity to reasons, not by the actions or relationships of standing between persons, there can only be conflicts of legitimate authority on Raz's theory if it is possible for more than one authority in the same domain to be able to serve subjects in this way.

Chapter 5 demonstrated Raz's view that plurality of authority will often manifest in unproblematic complementary or compatible relationships, but he also anticipates that plurality may generate conflicting claims to authority. Such claims are also thought to be unproblematic for the service conception. In *The Morality of Freedom*, Raz explained:[1]

> a complete justification of authority...has to establish that there are no reasons against its acceptance which defeat the reasons for the authority...One recurring kind of reason against accepting the authority of one person or institution is that there is another person or institution with a better claim to be recognized as an authority. The claim of the second is a reason against accepting the claim of the first only when the two authorities are incompatible, as are the claims of two governments to be legitimate governments of one country.

Raz does not elaborate on the possibility that multiple claims to authority might actually be made by multiple authorities (not just multiple claimants of authority), but he does tell us that when there are contending authorities, the normal justification thesis (NJT) offers a device for resolving conflicts, by revealing when one authority is justified in excluding another. According to Raz:[2]

---

[1] Joseph Raz, *The Morality of Freedom* (Clarendon Press, 1986), 56–57.
[2] Joseph Raz, 'The Problem of Authority: Revisiting the Service Conception' (2006) 90 *Minn Law Review* 1003, 1021.

The question whether a given authority's power extends to exclude the authority of another is to be judged in the way we judge the legitimacy of its power on any matter, namely, whether we would conform better to reason by trying to follow its directives than if we do not.

Thus, Raz treats conflicts of authority as situations of merely apparent conflict: when there are multiple claims to authority, we can treat the better claim as a reason against the weaker claim; we can apply the normal justification in order to exclude one of them. Raz then makes light of both apparent and actual conflict between authorities, indicating that the service conception offers tools for individuating or prioritizing one authority (or one claimant) over others. I think that Raz has moved too quickly over both the impact of conflicting claims and the possibility and impact of actual conflict. More work is needed to explain both phenomena, and to consider their impact upon the plausibility of the service conception.

2. Conflict and the Service Conception

Raz imposes two general conditions upon the existence of legitimate authority, which are also constraints on the possibility of conflicting legitimate authorities. To see whether or not there is genuine multiplicity and actual conflict of legitimate authority, not merely pretenders or purported authorities generating apparent conflict, we must apply the 'de facto condition' and the 'moral condition'.

a. The de facto condition

According to this condition, a person or institution must have de facto authority if they are to have legitimate authority. De facto authority requires that a person or institution both claims to exercise and is treated as having legitimate authority by some set of subjects.[3] In Raz's words:[4]

> …only bodies that enjoy de facto authority (i.e., that are in fact followed or at least conformed with by considerable segments of the population) can have legitimate authority over all these matters. Hence there cannot be an unknown political authority. Similarly, there cannot be a political authority that does not exercise its authority, i.e., does not issue directives that impose duties, confer rights, etc.

---

[3] The claim to legitimate authority is necessary to distinguish de facto authority from de facto (mere) power.
[4] Raz, 'The Problem of Authority', 1036.

This 'de facto' condition constrains the types of cases in which multiplicity of legitimate political authority can arise, by limiting it to cases in which more than one body can succeed in achieving coordination around its directives. Plurality of authority can therefore only occur when there are two or more authorities that are able to communicate their claims to their subjects and whose claims either are or are likely to be accepted.[5] If there are social facts, such that authority A is able to communicate its commands and be taken seriously (or force compliance), but all other purported authorities would be ignored in that particular domain, then only authority A is a candidate for legitimate authority, and there can be no plurality. In many domains this is the way our social practices work. For instance, we have social and constitutional principles, laws, and customs which dictate that a panel of media experts does not share the domain of a court; that a university council's domain is more restricted than that of a legislature, and so on. Raz deploys this condition to dispose of obvious non-starters and to reduce the likelihood of plurality of authority.[6] Although these facts are contingent and at times their identification is controversial, they play a significant role in limiting the likelihood of finding more than one legitimate authority in a single domain.

Yet the possibility of conflict remains. Consider two potential readings of the de facto condition. A strict reading would limit legitimate authority to those bodies that already have effective authority; a looser reading would require that legitimate authority could attach to bodies that could have effective authority. Raz himself has explained that the de facto condition allows for authorities that are 'soon likely to enjoy effective power'.[7] This reading has the advantage of not precluding new competitors from being candidates for legitimate authority, as well as helping to deal with the problem that it will sometimes be difficult to work out whether a particular power is or has the capacity to be effective. Even in the strict sense, however, the de facto condition would not rule out multiplicity, as competition and conflict could still occur between authorities who already exercise de facto authority over different but integrated or proximate segments of a population, ie where the domains of authority overlap one another, or are unclear or contested.

[5] Raz calls these the non-moral or non-normative conditions for authority. They include a condition that an authority fails to be legitimate if it 'cannot communicate with others': Joseph Raz, *Ethics in the Public Domain* (Oxford University Press, 1994) 202.

[6] For instance, responding to the example suggested by Waldron: although the United States Congress and the Conference of Catholic Bishops might both enact welfare policies, the Conference of Bishops could not have de facto authority over the polity and could not secure conformity to its commands. In practice, only Congress has de facto authority over the society as a whole; only Congress is therefore a contender for legitimate authority in that broad domain: Joseph Raz, 'Comments and Responses', in Lukas H Meyer (ed), *Rights, Culture and the Law* (Oxford University Press, 2003).

[7] Raz, *The Morality of Freedom*, 75–76.

b. The moral condition

The de facto condition might be thought to be a preliminary constraint upon who can have legitimate authority, which, if met, triggers the application of the moral condition. In Raz's terms, one cannot have legitimate authority if 'the moral or normative conditions for one's directives being authoritative are absent'.[8] The moral condition is, in part, met by satisfying the normal justification condition wherein an authority's directives enable its subjects to better conform to reason than they would by acting alone. Yet the normal justification thesis does not by itself provide transit through the moral condition, which also requires that there are no undefeated reasons against having the authority. As Raz notes, the normal justification thesis is silent on the matter of reasons against having authority, but if these reasons outweigh the reasons for having authority, then even an authority that would meet the normal justification condition will fail to have legitimate authority.[9]

The question is whether both parts of the moral condition leave open the possibility of plurality.

Part one: the normal justification thesis (NJT)

Starting with the normal justification thesis itself, we need to ask whether the facts creating first-order reasons to obey, and second-order exclusionary reasons to not act on one's own judgment, can only anoint one authority at a time. Put another way, we need to ask whether it is possible for facts to establish the legitimacy of more than one authority in a single domain. Chapter 5 indicated the possibility of facts rendering A and B legitimate authorities when they are working together. The question here is about the possibility of facts that would render A *or* B as *alternative* legitimate authorities. This could occur (i) if right reason recommends more than one course of action equally, and those courses of action could each be achieved by following different authorities; or (ii) if right reason renders eligible more than one course of action whose values are incommensurable, and those courses of action could each be achieved by following different authorities.

Plurality of authority in each of these circumstances is made possible by Raz's notion of legitimacy. Consider two purported authorities (A and B) and a purported subject (C). If A commands C to do X and B commands C to do Y, and by following either authority C would better conform to reason than if

---

[8] Raz, *Ethics in the Public Domain*, 218. On the authority of legal systems, Raz argues that to genuinely claim authority a system must be 'of a kind which is capable in principle of possessing the requisite moral properties of authority' (p 202).

[9] Raz, *Ethics in the Public Domain*, 218.

she acted on her own judgment, then both A and B are legitimate authorities for C. This structure then splits into three—depending upon the content of the directive and the reasons involved:

(i) If reason equally recommends doing either X or Y, then C's better conformity with reason will be achieved equally, whichever authority is obeyed.[10]

(ii) If reason were neutral between doing X and Y because they are incommensurable, then each option would secure C's conformity with reason differently, but to the same extent.

In both (i) and (ii) there are multiple legitimate authorities. Possibility (iii) is more complicated, throwing up two possibilities:

(iii) If reason recommends X over Y, then

(a) is there no plurality because A is *more* legitimate than B and B drops out of the picture?; or
(b) is A *more* legitimate than B but both are legitimate for C because she would still do better by following B's command than she would acting alone?

In short, do we read the normal justification as an absolute or sliding-scale test of legitimacy?

The canonical formulation of the NJT is concerned with the subject doing better by following authority, not with the quest to find one 'best' authority. On this approach, the NJT is most naturally read as a sliding scale test, where more or less legitimacy can attach to different authorities. On this reading there can be more than one legitimate authority even where one is more legitimate than others. This presents an easy explanation of plurality of authority, one which entails a lexical ordering of authorities according to their legitimacy under the NJT. The question immediately follows, however, whether we should read the NJT as an absolute test by substituting 'better' for 'best', so that the only truly legitimate authority is the one which does 'best', ie which gets the subject *closest* to conformity with reason. Any conflict between authorities would then be merely apparent conflict, awaiting a determination of which is the truly legitimate authority. If conformity to reason is the basic standard by which the legitimacy of authority is measured, it might make

---

[10] If the problem is a coordination problem, then this would hold only if everyone obeys the same authority, even though it does not matter which they obey. The coordination condition generates the strongest reasons to want one clear authority or hierarchy of authority, rather than plurality. It provides an independent (although not necessarily conclusive) reason against plurality of authority. See discussion in Ch 5.5.

sense to favour the absolute reading, although an argument could be made that what matters is simply for the subject to do better, not best.

This debate does not matter for the purposes of showing the possibility of plurality, for even the absolute reading would leave open the possibility of plurality whenever right reason renders eligible two or more equal or incommensurable alternatives, corresponding to the directives of two or more different authorities. This may take some explaining, for although it is widely accepted (including by Raz) that reason can recommend actions equally or neutrally,[11] we would still need to show that different authorities could recommend such distinct actions when they have based their decisions on the same reasons applying to the subject. This outcome is easily conceivable in coordination-convention situations: for instance, authority A might examine all the relevant reasons then issue a directive that subjects must drive on the left, while authority B might weigh up the same reasons then command that subjects drive on the right. However, the problem of incommensurability is more difficult. To be incommensurable, there must be no common measure between two bearers of value. This is clear enough in the examples Raz himself offers, where an individual faces choices between equally successful careers, neither of which is intrinsically more valuable than the other. Can the same be true of authoritative decision-makers? The easiest example would be one parallel to the individual choice, where reason might be neutral between (for instance) equally successful public spending on the arts or the sciences, or between equally successful public health policies promoting physical exercise or healthy eating. Although the decisions faced by a public authority making choices for a community of subjects look different from those facing an individual, the structure of support or neutrality from reason does not change. That is, as long as we follow Raz in saying that an authority should base its decisions upon the reasons that apply to the subject, then any incommensurable options that reason would throw up for the subject will be thrown up again for the deciding authority. At that point it is conceivable that one authority might decide on one option, while another would favour the alternative. As in the individual scenario, both choices would be justified, and there would be an actual conflict of authority.

Part two: reasons for decision

Raz's moral condition requires that authority is legitimate when it meets the NJT *and* there are no undefeated reasons against having the authority. Here

---

[11] Raz seems to be committed to the possibility of this sort of pluralism, both where reason is neutral between equally good contenders and where reason generates incommensurable contenders. For Raz's discussion of incommensurability, see Raz, *The Morality of Freedom*, 321–345.

we need to clarify a distinction made in Raz's account, which is easily overlooked or confused. There is an important difference between reasons for action and reasons about the value of an authoritative decision-making process, which I will call 'reasons for decision'. Reasons for decision do not bear directly upon doing a particular action and are not subsumed within the normal justification for authority; they are independent of the reasons that apply directly to the subject(s) of authority. In Raz's terminology, directly applicable primary reasons for action are called 'dependent reasons'—because they are the reasons upon which an authoritative directive should depend. Raz then distinguishes these reasons from his 'independence condition', which is an example of a reason about the most important decision-making process. Specifically, the independence condition acknowledges that sometimes it is more important for individuals to decide independently than to conform to reason by following authority. My terminology clarifies the difference between dependent and independent reasons by simply distinguishing reasons for/against a particular course of action ('reasons for action'), from reasons for/against wanting the authority to decide ('reasons for decision'). The question is then whether any of these rule out plurality of conflicting authority.

With his focus upon reasons for action, Raz does not tell us much about reasons for decision, just that the category includes reasons affecting 'the desirability of issuing the directive', side-effects, and reasons about how we should decide what to do.[12] We do not get any more specific guidance about the content or forcefulness of such reasons within the service conception, but if the independence condition is taken as illustrative, we can see it as an expression of procedural values about types of decision-making and the value of authority.

To explore these reasons for decision, it is useful to distinguish two types of reasons: procedural reasons and reasons about side effects. Procedural reasons are reasons about the value of different forms of decision-making (for example authoritative or autonomous), and are the subject of dispute between political theorists who defend the values of different decision-making procedures. Raz's independence condition is his most detailed example of a procedural reason, requiring that authority would not be legitimate over matters on which it was more important for the subject to decide autonomously. Reasons favouring autonomy over certain types of practical action (such as choosing one's friends or career) can therefore be seen as undefeated reasons that would tell against having authoritative determination on matters.

Far from ruling out plurality, procedural reasons seem to generate it, because different authorities will be valuable for different reasons. One authority might

---

[12] Joseph Raz, 'Government by Consent', in J Rowland Pennock and John W Chapman (eds), *Authority Revisited* (New York University Press, 1987), 349.

be valuable because it is representative of a community with actual associative obligations; another because it has been consented to; another because it will deliver just outcomes or meet other criteria of value. If procedural reasons conferring value on two different authorities are unequal, we are left with a lexical ordering of legitimate authorities just as we can have under the NJT. Yet if they are equal or incommensurable, then even if there is a reason to want just one authority, procedural reasons themselves will not single out one particular authority over another that is equally or incommensurably valuable.

In contrast, side-effect reasons are about the effects of authority other than effects upon individual subjects, (for example effects on non-subjects or effects upon the community as a whole). This second category of 'considerations of side effects' is not explained by Raz as part of his explanation of authority— but if we are to distinguish these considerations from the reasons for action applying to the subject, side-effect reasons must be reasons about the exercise of authority that are not directly or indirectly reasons for action for the individual subjects. It is not clear whether Raz thinks that these side effects can amount to side constraints or even duties upon the authorities; but at the very least, the consideration of side effects suggests that an exercise of authority could be outweighed if it causes unjustified harms (and perhaps, although not necessarily, rights-violating wrongs) to non-subjects or to communities.[13] This category is not subsumed within the normal justification. Although the NJT does require that an authority help subjects achieve their inter-personal obligations—including any obligations owed to non-subjects[14]—there may be side effects of authority that are independent of the obligations owed by subjects to non-subjects. Side effects thus present a potentially broad restriction on the plurality of authority, for side effects are contingent upon actual circumstances which are infinitely variable, and any number of possible side effects might rule out having a particular authority. Yet there is no conceptual difficulty for the possibility of plurality. Indeed, as with procedural reasons, there are conceivable circumstances in which side-effect reasons would favour having plural authorities as a way of mitigating the negative side effects that just one authority might generate.

---

[13] I do not think that we should read Raz here as invoking the Nozickian position in which someone's rights are side constraints on others' actions. Nozick argues that rights function as side constraints on the actions of others towards the rights-holder. Raz, however, sees rights as interests that are sufficient to hold others to duties. Duties seem to be more onerous than side constraints, which could simply be limits upon how an action is performed, rather than constraints upon whether an action is performed; hence, side constraints, rather than constraints. For Raz's discussion of rights, see Raz, *The Morality of Freedom*, 171–192.

[14] The reasons applying to subjects, to which authority is supposed to assist subjects in conforming, include reasons applying between persons.

The moral condition, consisting in the normal justification thesis and reasons for decision (including procedural reasons and side effects), therefore leaves open the possibility that individuals could be subject to multiple legitimate authorities in the same domain, at the same time. However, the moral and de facto conditions are not the only barriers to the possibility of plural authority. Together, they reveal a set of intractable problems, and the critical role played by the question of what amounts to a 'reasonable enquiry'.

3. The Identification Problem, the Rankings Problem, and Reasonable Enquiry

If conflicts of legitimate authority are not ruled out by the service conception, and/or cannot be subsumed within Raz's normal justification for authority, then we need to consider any implications those conflicts have for the service conception as a whole. The combination of the moral and de facto conditions, which permit circumstances of plurality, together generate two significant problems arising out of that plurality. I call these respectively the 'rankings problem' and the 'identification problem'.

a. The rankings problem

The rankings problem is straightforward to explain. As the name suggests, the service conception leaves open the possibility that there can be multiple legitimate authorities that cannot be ranked according to their legitimacy. This possibility follows directly from the analysis in section 2. A rankings problem arises whenever there are equally or incommensurably legitimate authorities (ie authorities that would help their subjects conform to reason in equally or incommensurably better ways than if they were left to their own devices). In this situation it is impossible to rank authorities by reference to their legitimacy. Although there might be all sorts of other ways in which to rank them (ie by reference to other reasons about the value of the authority, its importance, or its effectiveness), that ranking would have to be based on factors outside of the core account of legitimate authority that Raz offers.

The rankings problem is, however, not as critical for the service conception as it is for purely procedural justifications of authority, which justify authorities by reference to how they are selected rather than what outcomes they produce. Those justifications include no standard against which multiple procedurally legitimate authorities can be ranked, and it is no answer to suggest that the procedures themselves can be ranked according to their value, or fairness, inclusiveness, or other such principles. As with the substantive justifications, there might be equal or incommensurable justifications—this time not for outcomes, but for procedures. In situations of conflict, particularly conflict between overlapping authorities, the presence of the same (or very similar) procedures would make such a ranking impossible, or at least very difficult.

b. The identification problem

By far the bigger problem, for the Razian account at least, is the identification problem. Under the service conception of authority, the subject needs to be able to identify a legitimate authority in a particular domain in order to try to follow its commands (and so better conform to right reason). Raz himself tells us that the identification of an authority is not simply an epistemic problem; legitimate authority can exist only if a reasonable level of enquiry reveals it to exist.[15] ... In Raz's own words:[16]

> To fulfil its function, the legitimacy of an authority must be knowable to its subjects.... How much it can be expected to improve our conformity to reason, and how important the matter is, establish what inquiry is reasonable to undertake. When reasonable inquiry will not reveal the case for authority, that case, if it exists at all, is unknowable. It follows that people are not subject to any authority regarding those matters. This argument is used here to establish not merely that it is not rational or not worthwhile, to carry on with the inquiry about the existence of certain reasons, but that those reasons, authoritative directives, do not exist. There is no authority over the matter, because to exist, authorities must be knowable.

Conflicts of authority bring to light the fragility of authority on Raz's account. Under the service conception, when two or more purported authorities issue conflicting directives, the difficulty of working out which (if any) ought to be obeyed can lead to the collapse of any authority whatsoever. The identification problem is, put simply, that it is necessary to know who actually has authority before one can determine its legitimacy.

More precisely, there are two types of identification problem. The first occurs where the subject has no way of determining the legitimacy of contending authorities other than by revisiting the primary reasons for action—the very reasons the authority is supposed to pre-empt according to Raz's pre-emption thesis. If a subject must determine which of two (or more) authorities is truly

---

[15] Raz addresses this issue of identifying authoritative content while arguing for his much-discussed exclusivist legal positivism—that the content of authoritative legal directives cannot include moral principles. There, he suggests that subjects can be served by authoritative directives 'only if they can establish their existence and content in ways which do not depend on raising the very same issues which the authority is there to settle': Joseph Raz, 'Authority, Law and Morality' (1985) 68 *The Monist* 295; Raz, *Ethics in the Public Domain*, 219.

[16] Raz, 'The Problem of Authority', 1025–1026; Joseph Raz, 'Comments and Responses', 254.

legitimate by examining the very reasons each authority's command is supposed to exclude, the authority of each is vitiated. The second type of identification problem arises where, although a subject could determine legitimacy by reference to non-pre-empted reasons, he cannot do so without going to unreasonable lengths. To explore the first problem we need to know what content the subject's enquiry can involve; for the second, we need to know what amounts to reasonable enquiry.

To avoid vitiating authority altogether, a subject's enquiry must be limited to non-pre-empted reasons—that is, reasons on which it is better for the subject to decide. The content of a subject's enquiry therefore depends on what kinds of reasons are pre-empted. If an authority pre-empts reasons for action only, then a subject can enquire into reasons for decision in order to determine the legitimacy of authority. Yet if an authority pre-empts both reasons for action *and* reasons for decision, the subject has a much more difficult task. One might think from Raz's insistence upon the independence condition that only reasons for action would be subject to pre-emption.[17] This also seems a logical implication from Raz's 'dependence thesis'—that a legitimate authority is supposed to base its decisions on the reasons applying to the subject directly, namely the reasons for and against doing a particular action. Legitimacy would then depend on the outcome of that decision, not the value of having an authority make it rather than following a different decision process. But Raz expressly takes the opposite approach, telling us that:[18]

> there are two kinds of reasons the preemption thesis affects. First, it preempts reasons against the conduct required by the authoritative directive. Second, it preempts reasons that do not necessarily bear on the pros and cons of behaving as the directive requires, but that do militate against the desirability of issuing the directive. These may be that the matter should be left to individual discretion, or that the directive will have undesirable side effects that make it undesirable, and so on.

Thus on Raz's view, at least some of the reasons telling against the value of the authority and/or the importance of having an authoritative determination of that matter are pre-empted. This does not seem problematic when the reasons for decision are obvious, for instance when comparing questions about the organization of national defence with questions about choosing a friend or partner. It is clear that the second enquiry is one best made individually, and the first is best made by authority, because there simply is no value in having

---

[17] Hershovitz interprets Raz in this way: Scott Hershovitz, 'Legitimacy, Democracy, and Razian Authority' (2003) 9 *Legal Theory* 201, 219–220.

[18] Raz, 'The Problem of Authority', 1019, fn 19.

authority on the second question, while there is significant value on the first.[19] Often, however, it will be more difficult, and it will be particularly difficult in situations of plurality, where the reasons against the value of following the directive include reasons about the value of different authorities—ie a reason against having one authority decide might be that the matter could be (or perhaps has been or will be) decided, equally well, by a *different* authority, carrying a different value.

If we accept Raz's argument that both reasons for action and reasons for decision can be pre-empted, it becomes critical to know the extent of pre-empted reasons. If the zone of pre-emption is determined by right reason, and right reason requires that it is better for the subject to decide when one particular authority should prevail over others, then those reasons for decision, including reasons about the values of different authorities, are not pre-empted and a subject can enquire into them without vitiating authority. Alternatively, if an authority could pre-empt all reasons, there would be nothing left for the subject to rely upon in his quest to identify which of competing authorities is legitimate.

Raz himself tells us that authorities only have the power to determine when authority is needed if the normal justification thesis 'vindicates their possession of the power'.[20] This suggests that the zone of exclusion is indeed determined by what would best promote conformity to reason. Yet this does not help address problems where the very selection of which authority to follow, among competing options, is itself a coordination problem on which it is better to have an authoritative determination. As Besson has argued, 'it would undermine the whole point of authority to have to identify it as a co-ordinative authority before it can effectively be such'.[21] If right reason dictates that it is better for *the authority* to determine when it should prevail over other authorities, then reasons about the value of other authorities would be pre-empted and the subject would not be able to act upon a private evaluation of their respective values. Yet this would amplify the identification problem, because in circumstances of a genuine conflict between incommensurable or

---

[19] Even the example of choosing one's career might be contested—building up and maintaining an army during war time might be thought more important than allowing young men and women to choose their own career path.

[20] Raz, 'Comments and Responses', 259: 'they have the power to determine that a given situation justifies or requires coordination when the general doctrines of authority determine that they do. For example, when the normal justification thesis vindicates their possession of the power, namely, when people or institutions would better conform to reason if that power were exercised by an authority than otherwise'.

[21] See Samantha Besson, 'The Authority of International Law—Lifting the State Veil' (2009) 31 *Sydney Law Review* 343, 355. Besson goes on to argue that this problem shows that consent plays an important role in allowing subjects to recognize legitimate authority.

equally valuable authorities, if it is better for an authority to decide which authority should prevail then, necessarily, it would be better for *each* authority to decide whether it (and not the subject or the other authority) should work out which of the competing authorities is to be obeyed. This results in a cycle of identification problems, in which the normal justification thesis offers no way of distinguishing which authority ought to be obeyed, because there is no way to separate the extent to which each can bring about their subjects' conformity to reason, and no way to remove decisions about their desirability for determination by the subject.

A case could be made that, to promote conformity to reason, decisions on which of multiple authorities should be obeyed should normally be made by the subject, in order to avoid simply accepting the self-image of an authority and to preserve the subject's autonomy. The first type of identification problem would be avoided if a subject could work out which authority to obey by reference to non-pre-empted reasons (reasons upon which it is better for the subject to decide). However, this is where the second identification problem becomes crucial—what lengths of enquiry are reasonable in order for a subject to determine the existence of legitimate authority?

Reasonable enquiry must be sensitive to subject matter and the importance of an authoritative resolution. When there are important issues of public order or justice to be decided, a great deal more deliberation will be reasonable than for trivial matters or matters which could be decided privately. We might therefore argue that a circumstance of plurality of purported authorities simply extends the enquiry that it is reasonable to undertake in order to work out which authority is to be followed. As the urgent questions of coordination and interaction between subjects of competing authorities become more complex, so too does the level of enquiry that subjects can be expected to undertake. So long as the options are visible and salient for the purported subjects, it is no less reasonable to enquire into the respective value of purported authorities than it is to enquire into the value of authority itself. On the other hand, perhaps it is unreasonable for a subject to have to enquire not simply about the legitimacy of one authority relative to individual decision, but about the contending legitimacy of multiple authorities, where this means weighing up and navigating through competing values and conflicting directives, while also anticipating how relationships between multiple authorities themselves might affect their effectiveness and therefore their legitimacy. In situations of plurality of purported authorities, an enquiry into the existence of legitimate authority is likely to be difficult at best, and if that difficulty is unreasonable, the service conception tells us there will be no legitimate authority whatsoever.

For now, it is enough to consider the implications of both arguments. I do not need to settle this dispute here because, in either case, the implications are that the service conception either leads to the collapse of authority, or authority becomes dependent upon procedural justifications. If it is not reasonable for a subject to have to determine where legitimacy falls between two or more authorities which would both be legitimate under the normal justification, or even between authorities which only appear to be legitimate, then there can be no authority whenever there is reasonable doubt about who has it. Alternatively, if it is reasonable for subjects to make that enquiry, they can do so only by relying on non-pre-empted reasons for decision, ie reasons determining the most important decision procedures for deciding a particular substantive question. Just as Raz acknowledges that sometimes autonomy is more important than acting in conformity with right reason, it may at times be more important to give effect to procedural values such as democracy.[22] None of these procedural values is provided within the service conception of authority; we would need to look to non-instrumental theories about what kinds of decision procedures are valuable, and in what circumstances one is more valuable than another. When we are inquiring about the value of authoritative decision-making in different locations, we have to look to moral and political theories about higher-order values of autonomy or equality, and/or political theories about justice, representation, affiliation, or efficiency. But when we do so, the values that are used to justify having one authority rather than another then end up doing all the work of sustaining the very existence of legitimate authority.

4. The Limitations of the Service Conception

All of this reveals a key feature of Raz's theory, which, despite its claim to explain authority without making any assumptions about who actually has authority, can only explain legitimate authority where there are clearly identified and uncontested singular authorities or where authority is at least organized through clear hierarchies which make it obvious to potential subjects. Yet the practice of authority is no longer like this, if it ever was. Different purported authorities compete for legitimacy over the same or overlapping domains, and they compete for control of situations in which their separate domains must interact.[23] Wherever there is plurality of prima facie authorities issuing

---

[22] Examples of such arguments appear in Scott J Shapiro, 'Authority', in Scott J Shapiro and Jules L Coleman (eds), *Oxford Handbook of Jurisprudence and Philosophy of Law* (Oxford University Press, 2002), 431–438; Hershovitz, 'Legitimacy, Democracy and Razian Authority', 216–219.

[23] For example, on the overlap and contest over domains between international and state authorities, see Besson, 'The Authority of International Law', 358–366.

incompatible directives to subjects, then even if there is one authority that would (in the end) be more legitimate under the NJT than its contenders, the subject will struggle to work out which one it is. Even situations of apparent conflict, therefore, will vitiate authority unless there are non-pre-empted reasons which the subject can, upon reasonable enquiry, use to work out where legitimacy lies.

The point is not that there must always be a way to resolve conflict between legitimate authorities or find a way to individuate one over others. Sometimes it will be necessary to resolve conflict, but at other times conflict can be a useful way of keeping alive competing values, and the contest of reasons that they embody. Similarly, it will not always be necessary to have just one authority, when two or more can coordinate in service of their subjects.[24] Rather, the point is that the normal justification is parasitic upon the identification of authority.

The conflicts phenomenon, and the identification problem generated by both actual and apparent conflicts, thus reveals that procedural justifications become *necessary supplements* to Raz's normal justification, and are not merely subordinate or secondary, as Raz has allowed.[25] When the NJT cannot separate between equally or incommensurably legitimate authorities, we must turn to some other theory whenever we need to disambiguate in order to sustain the very existence of authority. As was suggested in Chapter 2, the normal justification of conformity to reason cannot encompass and incorporate these other moral or political theories without becoming redundant.[26] If, for instance, we said that people have duties to comply with democratic decisions, either because they have consented to the process or as part of a duty of fairness, and that obeying democratic authorities helps us to conform to this duty so those authorities are justified indirectly under the NJT, we would render the NJT empty and all the normative work would be done by whichever theory is telling us that reason favours democracy. As Hershovitz argues, 'we would need on all occasions a further (and different) criterion of

---

[24] I return to each of these possibilities in Ch 8.
[25] Raz has argued that consent to authority plays a 'subordinate but nonetheless valuable role' by reinforcing other reasons that may not be obvious to those subject to authority, though it cannot replace them: Raz, *The Morality of Freedom*, 89–90.
[26] The whole point of the separateness of the Raz independence condition is that it carves out of the normal justification a sphere of activity in which conformity to reason is not the primary value. See also Hershovitz, 'Legitimacy, Democracy and Razian Authority', 219: 'In order for the normal justification thesis to be a competitor with other theories of legitimacy, it cannot be the case that it subsumes or gives way to any theory that on its face conflicts with it but turns out to be true'.

legitimacy to assess whether the normal justification thesis was fulfilled'.[27] This is why the answer to Raz's exchanges with advocates of various procedural justifications does not simply start and finish with Raz saying that the NJT absorbs these procedural justifications insofar as they are true. In my terms, and most significant for this project, is the worry that the NJT must either be read so narrowly that it becomes unable to differentiate between authorities whose directives reason recommends equally or neutrally, and thus ends up denying authority altogether because of the identification problem, or be read so broadly that it subsumes all correct theories about what makes these authorities valuable.

The problem therefore remains that when there are genuine or even apparent conflicts of authority, the service conception offers no account that can preserve the authority of either or both contenders. The service conception tells us that in situations of genuine conflict there is no authority, and in situations of apparent conflict there is at least an existential threat to authority. Yet the service conception's 'one authority' or 'no authority' implications do not seem to fit the existing practice of authority, where authority is contested by plausible claimants and shared between different levels of governance or constitutional orders, and not always aligned in tidy hierarchies. It would be odd to treat the justification of authority over subjects as if that power were always exercised by singular or at least integrated authorities within an isolated subject community, because this is not the contemporary reality. The practice of authority no longer singles out salient, clear authorities or hierarchies with clearly bounded domains. Different purported authorities, including international and state authorities, compete for legitimacy over the same or overlapping domains, and they compete for control of situations in which their separate domains must interact.[28] This is particularly evident in the dialogical practices of international, regional, and national courts where concurrent or overlapping jurisdictions are commonplace and yet still seem to have authority. Their subjects or officials do not treat overlapping or conflicting outcomes as vitiating those courts' authority, and the courts themselves engage in practices of deference or referral designed to recognize and respond to one another's authority.

I suggest in the following chapters that 'one or none' is not the right way to think about the practice of authority, and that in situations of plurality, neither conflict nor incompatibility negates authority. I do not think that we

---

[27] Hershovitz, 'Legitimacy, Democracy and Razian Authority', 220. My analysis in Ch 7 suggests that Raz himself has imported the second kind of criterion into his account, and so requires the kind of additional criterion of legitimacy that Hershovitz says was not intended to be required.

[28] Besson, 'The Authority of International Law, 358–366.

should accept the service conception of authority unless there is no way to explain legitimate authority in circumstances of actual or apparent conflict, and build inter-authority relationships into that account.

I have argued here that Raz's service conception cannot adequately explain plurality of authority. Yet the problems plaguing Raz's account must be seen as general problems plaguing any purported justification of authority that seeks to justify authorities independently. The identification and rankings problems also plague other, non-Razian, substantive theories of legitimate authority, and both problems generate parallel difficulties for procedural theories. For instance, because a consent-based theory leaves open the possibility of consent to multiple conflicting authorities, it generates the same risk that subjects will be unable to identify which of the contenders to follow, because both are legitimate; and the same risk of a rankings problem because there is no way to reasonably rank contending, consent-based authorities. The rankings problem is even more troubling. If consent is considered both necessary and sufficient for the legitimation of authority, then there would be no standards to appeal to in order to rank authorities. Or, if consent were considered necessary but not sufficient to justify authority, and so there could be other standards used to rank an authority, then any resulting ranking which placed one consented-to authority higher than another would seem to disrespect the worth of the consent of those subjects of the lower-ranked authority.

Both the identification and rankings problems seem intractable for existing substantive and procedural theories of authority. In the following chapters I argue that the justification of authority must first marry the procedural and substantive justifications, and then move away from trying to justify authority independently. Authorities and their subjects are interactive and engaged beyond their immediate communities, and authority can continue in circumstances of plurality through arrangements of cooperation, deference, and toleration, which all preserve authority while loosening the grip of any one particular authority. In order to explain such practices, we need a pluralist conception of authority.

PART III

A PLURALIST CONCEPTION OF AUTHORITY

7
A Conjunctive Justification

A pluralist account of legitimate authority must address the rankings and identification problems generated by circumstances of plurality. This chapter proposes that to do so, a pluralist account must first marry the procedural and substantive justifications of authority into a conjunctive justification, which integrates and gives equal importance to procedural and substantive values, and to reasons for decision and action. Both are needed because they do different normative work; and, importantly, they generate different normative outcomes together than each can on its own.

An attempt to combine procedural and substantive justifications is not particularly novel, but their priority and respective roles in a justification for authority remain controversial. As examined in Chapter 2, Raz's account acknowledges that both reasons for action and reasons for decision play some role in the justification of authority, but makes reasons for decision secondary to the test of helping subjects conform to the reasons for action that apply to them. Furthermore, the question of who can have authority (or, in other words, by what process a particular entity becomes authoritative) is irrelevant to the normal justification of authority. In contrast, an account such as Waldron's gives precedence to the procedural question of who or what can have legitimate authority, while the substantive question of what an authority can do is not a necessary part of the justification of authority itself. This means that the 'authoritative' answer and the 'right' answer need not and often will not be the same. A third option suggested by Christiano and given some support by Hershovitz, may combine procedural and substantive justifications, arguing either that good procedures generate good outcomes, or that procedures can carry substantive values.[1] Any such hybrid option, however, runs the risk of eliding the significant differences between procedural and substantive justifications or the complexity of their interaction.

In a situation of singular or clearly ordered authorities these explanations might be defensible on their own, but they are far less attractive in circumstances

---

[1] See Tom Christiano, *The Authority of Democracy* (2004) 12 *Journal of Political Philosophy* 266; Scott Hershovitz, 'The Role of Authority' (2011) 7 *Philosophers' Imprint* 4.

of plurality with its attendant identification and ranking problems. On its own, a procedural justification establishes when a particular candidate can have legitimate authority, but it does not tell us what (if anything) that authority can do or the limits (if any) upon the exercise of authority. The substantive justification, in contrast, tells us what an authority can and cannot legitimately do, but not who or what can be a legitimate authority. Yet if we group procedural and substantive justifications together without working out how they might interact or their potential priority, we might face both of these defects simultaneously.

The parallel puzzles accompanying plurality reveal the need for a justification that can answer both the question of who can have authority, or what I call the question of 'standing', and the question of what those authorities can do, or the question of 'standards'. This chapter takes each of those questions in turn. Section 1 addresses first 'standing', then 'standards'. Section 2 examines the nature of reasons within a conjunctive justification, and introduces a new and important category of 'governance reasons' to capture reasons that concern how authority is structured and organized. Finally, section 3 illustrates that, although a conjunctive justification goes some way towards explaining plurality of authority, it does not go far enough.

1. Standing and Standards of Authority

a. Standing

Reasons for decision, including the procedures by which a person or body attains a position of authority, do two important things. First, they have an epistemic significance: if the procedures are sufficiently salient and supported by potential subjects, they identify particular bodies or institutions as prima facie authorities around whom subjects can coordinate. As we saw in Chapter 6, in some circumstances these procedures will provide a complete solution to the identification problem, by singling out just one person or body who is both procedurally justified and able to achieve a better substantive outcome for subjects.

Second, and more importantly, reasons for decision can do the normative work of conferring standing upon particular authorities. I agree with Raz that the first step in any justification for authority must be the existence of an outweighing reason to have authority at all (this is the point of Raz's independence condition which precludes authority when reasons for having authority are outweighed by reasons for autonomous decision-making). My argument then departs from Raz's approach by insisting that any outweighing reason to have a public authority over rational and autonomous persons must simultaneously be a reason to have an authority which satisfies a justified selection procedure, and not simply a reason to have anybody who happens to be able to be effective at getting persons to better conform to right reason.[2] On this view, the values protected by reasons for decision determine not only whether authority is worth having, but, if so, who should have it.

This alteration makes the justification of a particular authority sensitive to autonomy and rationality, not just rationality, on the basis that although a reason to have authority can outweigh a reason to have autonomous decision-making, it cannot exclude the value of autonomy altogether.[3] Autonomy never drops out of the justification. Even when there is a reason to surrender a decision to an authority, the value of autonomy continues to act as a constraint upon the justification, by requiring that subjects have some say in the process of working out who 'their' authority is.[4] Thus, only when that process includes some kind of participatory role for subjects can it confer the standing or role of authority upon the persons or institutions that pass through it.[5]

Standing is not normatively neutral or empty, rather the office of authority is a role constituted by moral standing. Unlike some morally significant roles that one can assume simply by choosing to do so or at least acting in a way that brings about that role (eg parent, friend), it is crucial that for public authorities such standing can only be conferred on a person or body by other persons or bodies. Standing can be claimed for oneself but that claim has no normative impact. Nor is the standing of authority simply an outcome of social practice.[6] In the case of political authorities, only morally justified selection procedures

---

[2] This also follows the lines of Darwall's objection to Raz, namely that Raz shows when it would be rational for someone to have authority but not that they actually have it: Stephen Darwall, 'Authority and Second-Personal Reasons for Acting', in David Wall and Steven Sobel (eds), *Reasons for Action* (Cambridge University Press, 2009), 134–154. For related criticisms, see Allen Buchanan, *Justice, Legitimacy, and Self-Determination: Moral Foundations for International Law* (Oxford University Press, 2007), Ch 5; and Allen Buchanan, 'The Legitimacy of International Law', in Samantha Besson and John Tasioulas (eds), *The Philosophy of International Law* (Oxford University Press, 2010), 83–84, arguing that Razian authority does not justify one in attempting to rule over others.

[3] Indeed, on Raz's account the value of autonomy is at the heart of the substantive justification, which applies once there is sufficient reason to have authority. Even if we treat a reason to have authority as an exclusionary reason in the Razian sense, it only excludes autonomous decision-making on that point. It has nothing to say about how an authority should be chosen or who should have authority.

[4] This is, of course, the core idea of liberal political thought from Kant, through Rawls and Korsgaard, to the discourse theory of Habermas.

[5] I have in mind here a version of Darwall's basic point that authority requires a background relationship of moral standing. Darwall, 'Authority and Second-Personal Reasons for Acting'.

[6] Hershovitz suggests that the justification of authority is dependent upon the justification of the practice which assigns the roles of authority and subject. He argues that 'to justify political authority, we need to show that people are obligated to occupy roles they are born into, rather than ones they choose' and that 'the question whether there are legitimate political authorities depends both on the roles involved in political practice and on the justifications we might give for those roles': Hershovitz, 'The Role of Authority,' 16.

confer a moral standing upon those they select, as opposed to the default or de facto roles that some authorities may acquire over time. Thus, a person or body (eg a private citizen or occupying force) who has not been selected or elected or appointed or confirmed according to a justified process can have no subjects; they may have only followers or people over whom they are influential or coercive. The often-cited example of the random person who takes charge of a panicking crowd of strangers in a burning theatre is, on this approach, not an instance of a public authority because although there is a reason to want authority and it would be rational for the crowd members to follow an authority, there is no procedure which entitles some person to have authority. The person who takes control has no standing to have authority—and, indeed, she is not a standing authority, but simply a natural leader whom other people have an interest in following.

Of course, this all skips over the big question of which selection procedures are morally justified, and all the details of what autonomy is and how it is linked to political legitimacy. Working that out would require a full-blown moral theory about value, a theory of the person and their practical reasoning that explains the value of autonomy, a theory of the determinants and value of the political community, a political theory that explains how autonomy can be applied to generate political legitimacy, and sensitivity to any other restrictions imposed upon autonomy and legitimacy that are required by theories of justice. These are the core questions of liberal political philosophy, and I cannot recount the work that has been done on them or offer any original alternative to the contending approaches.[7] Here, I merely want to explore a type of justification for authority without defending any particular content in either its procedural or substantive parts.[8]

b. Standards

However it is achieved, conferral of standing does not complete the normative work necessary to justify legitimate authority. We still need to show that

---

[7] For recent contributions to understanding autonomy, see Stephen Darwall, 'The Value of Autonomy and Autonomy of the Will' (2006) 116 *Ethics* 263, 263–284.

[8] In the interests of signaling future paths for my analysis, I see most promise in deliberative-discursive accounts of democratic legitimacy, which seek to capture the interaction of private and public values, liberal and republican concerns, and freedom and fairness in communities. The preference is broadly but not exactly Habermasian because it does not necessarily follow the entire discourse-theoretical account of democracy, or Habermas' thoughts on its implications for transnational communities. See, eg Jurgen Habermas, *Between Facts and Norms: Contributions to a Discourse Theory of Law and Democracy* (MIT Press, 1996). Compare Seyla Benhabib, *Democracy and Difference: Contesting the Boundaries of the Political* (Princeton University Press, 1996); Seyla Benhabib, *The Rights of Others: Aliens, Residents, and Citizens* (Cambridge University Press, 2004).

the procedure has normative force, which it can have only if it is consistent with the autonomy of those who participate in it. Once again, autonomy does not drop out of the justification. Participation in the selection of an authority by itself is not enough if the authorities that are selected as a result would act inconsistently with their subjects' autonomy. We therefore need to add Raz's substantive condition (or something close to it) to the procedural justification, so that once a particular body or institution carries the standing of authority, so is entitled (or has a duty) to govern subjects or a community of subjects, we then ask about its legitimacy in helping subjects conform to the reasons that apply to them. Legitimacy of authority therefore depends upon how those who have the standing of authority actually use their authority. They can only change the reasons that apply to the subject if the exercise of their authority would help those subjects to conform to the reasons that apply to them.[9]

So far, there is nothing particularly pluralist about this conjunctive justification, but it does allow us to see how choices between different authorities slot into the different parts of the justification of authority. Once there is a reason to have authority, we can weigh the different values and different decision procedures that confer standing upon different authorities. Sometimes this might remove the possibility of having more than one legitimate authority, other times it will keep that possibility alive, still other times it may amplify its likelihood. We are therefore left with a conjunctive justification that is more persuasive than either a substantive or procedural justification alone can be, because either of those paths cannot accommodate the merits or remedy the drawbacks of the other.

However, the conjunctive justification's sensitivity to both the standing and the standards requirements still leaves us with just as much plurality and just as many (if not more) potential inter-authority relationships to be explained. How does such a justification help at all in a quest for a pluralist theory of authority?

The key contribution is that a conjunctive justification allows us to let go of the messy contest between procedural and substantive theories in order to more closely examine both the reasons for decision and the reasons for action that go into the overall test for legitimacy. Both kinds of reasons look somewhat different in pluralist circumstances than they do in their typical monist contexts.

---

[9] Whether this happens through pre-emption in the way Raz describes, or simply through creating outweighing authoritative reasons, is not critical here.

2. Reasons in a Conjunctive Justification

a. Plural reasons for decision

The circumstances of plurality bring reasons for decision into sharper focus and reveal their crucial role in justifying pluralist authority, while also altering their content. In circumstances of plurality the ordinary procedural reasons that can confer the standing of authority can be multiplied and variable between different authorities, while side-effect reasons come to include concern for the impact of authority upon subjects shared between overlapping authorities and subjects of interactive authorities. Most importantly, the circumstances of plurality reveal a special category of reasons for decision which, I argue, arise only in circumstances of plurality, and which I will call 'governance reasons'.

Governance reasons are reasons about how to govern—they refer to the values attached to different kinds of governmental organization or the advantages and disadvantages of different modes of governance—centralism and hierarchy, on the one hand, or plurality and heterarchy, on the other. Governance reasons thus include concern for the necessity of inter-authority coordination and the permissibility of conflict, determining whether conflicting authorities need to be coordinated through subjection to a harmonization or adjudication process, or whether the existence of conflicting directives is justifiable or at least morally permissible. Governance reasons can point in either direction. If there are undefeated reasons favouring strongly centralized or even singular authority in respect of a certain matter, then plurality of conflicting authorities would be unjustified and we would always need some way to resolve conflicts between authorities. On the other hand, governance reasons might permit or even favour conflict or incompatibility between overlapping or interacting authorities.

Although all governance reasons are specific to different circumstances and will often be contested, some easy examples might be illustrative. On some matters it is more important to have an apex of decision-making which gives one authority primacy over others, or establishes a hierarchically organized structure of complementary/compatible authorities. This might frequently apply to coordination problems, where a reason to have coordinated action can also be (but is not necessarily) a reason to have a singular/hierarchical location of authority. Or there might be circumstances in which risks to subjects' physical security generate overriding reasons for a hierarchy of authorities. For instance, whatever benefits might arise from decentralization or plurality of public authority, an army in wartime should probably not have conflicting chains of command. On the contrary, some questions of a political nature might be better served by having plurality of authority which keeps alive contests between values or reasonable beliefs about values.[10] For instance, plurality of authority might be desirable for its ability to give effect to self-determination and/or individual autonomy, and this might outweigh concerns created by conflict between authorities. Governance reasons may also recommend prioritizing different levels of governance: sometimes there is a reason to want decision-making at the most local level with a system of checks and reviews in place above it; while sometimes there is reason to want decisions made at the most removed or highest level. All of these are reasons about the way to reach a desired outcome—they are reasons about how decisions should be made and, specifically, about the best forms of governance.

Plurality of authority also modifies the other types of reasons for decision. Side effects become particularly complex in circumstances of plurality because there is no longer simply one category of subjects and one category of non-subjects; rather there are different persons who are subjects of overlapping or interactive authorities. The presence of overlapping and interactive authorities generates additional layers of obligations, reasons, and potential side effects between and among subjects, non-subjects, and (now) shared subjects. In addition to the ordinary side effects upon non-subjects of an authority, possible side effects of the exercise of pluralist authority include: (i) upsetting relationships that non-subjects have with other authorities to whom they *are* subject; and/or (ii) upsetting relationships that subjects of one authority have with another authority of which they are also subjects in a shared domain.

We can revive the state-tribe example to illustrate this complexity. Recall the example from Chapter 3, in which legitimate state (S) and tribal (T) authorities issue conflicting directives over property in marine resources. Even if we say that subjects of S owe obligations of non-interference with property to subjects of T, we have not fully captured that S's directive interferes with T's authority relationship with its subjects on two fronts: it interferes with the obligations owed to T by subjects of T, and it interferes with T's ability (and perhaps duty) to govern those subjects effectively. From the other perspective, even if we say that subjects of T owe obligations of respect for property to subjects of S, we have not fully captured that T's directive to its members interferes with the obligations owed by subjects of S to S, and with

---

[10] It would be a mistake to equate these positions of centralized order versus pluralism with values of coordination versus anarchy. An observation of the pluralist practice of authority reveals that there can be coordination through plurality just as there can be anarchy despite centralism or hierarchy. Any need for a single coordinated action from subjects of authorities does not equate to a need to have just one authority coordinating that solution.

S's effective governance of its subjects.[11] The nature of the interference differs depending on the character of the relationship between the authorities. If there is a relationship of separate domains so that subjects of T are non-subjects of S and vice versa, we might think that the interference is merely an inconvenience which could cause confusion or perhaps tension between the respective subjects due to the interaction between these domains, but that the separateness of the domains means that there is no real change to the authority-subject relationships for either S (and its subjects) or T (and its subjects). Yet as discussed in Chapter 6, the mere presence of confusion about the applicability of different authorities' directives, and the existence of conflict resulting from inconsistent directives, can upset the ability of an authority to achieve coordination and so better enable subjects to conform to reason when coordination is needed.

Now imagine that there is some overlap in the domains of the authorities, as members of the tribe are legitimately subjects of both S and T. (For this to occur we must imagine that both are procedurally justified and that reason equally or incommensurably recommends both the preservation of the shellfish resources under tribal control and free access to pursue recreational fishing.) In this scenario there are two legitimate authorities whose directives are not only in conflict, but are also purporting to exclude the effectiveness of the other, and the obligations owed by subjects to the other authority.

Finally, plurality necessitates a closer look at the procedural reasons working to confer the standing of authority, as these can now include different procedures conferring standing upon different authorities—perhaps the state is democratically elected by a majority and the tribal government is too, or has the consent of tribe members expressed through a different justified process. The multiplication of procedural reasons which justify particular authorities can augment the puzzles of plurality, and weighing up their respective values will not always produce a priority or lexical ordering of justified authorities, because the possibilities of equally or incommensurably justified procedures remain. Furthermore, procedural reasons may fail to do the epistemic work of identifying a salient authority. There may still be a coordination problem over who is to exercise authority, and a prospect of disagreement or confusion which could defeat the existence of authority altogether. Communities of subjects will not always see one salient authority among many, precisely because there is obvious incommensurability between the values they respectively protect.

---

[11] The example is written so that S and T are interchangeable; ie the example works in reverse and is not dependent upon any particular value of either state or tribal governments.

b. Plural reasons for action

Once we accept that incommensurability and/or equality of primary reasons for action can leave open the possibility of plurality of authority, it is an obvious step to say that these phenomena can also generate such plurality. Incommensurability and equality, however, are not the only generators of multiple primary reasons for action and multiple authorities helping subjects towards good outcomes. The second driver is the newly complex idea of the subject(s) of authorities. Under a monist substantive account of authority, the values or the reasons for action that authorities are supposed to help subjects achieve are simply the reasons applying to individual subjects. The subject is not an interesting part of that account; his identities and activities matter only insofar as they are relevant to working out what reasons for action he is actually subject to. In contrast, a pluralist substantive account of authority is suddenly aware of multiple subjects or groups of subjects, whose identities and activities engage them with other subjects and indeed other authorities. Peoples' activities and identities can tie them to distinct authorities. The reasons for action applying to those people will be correspondingly more complex and more likely to engage different authorities in their realization.

This is where the difference between primary and secondary reasons for action becomes important. Where there is overlap or interaction between subjects of different authorities, the content of applicable reasons for action is affected. In cases of interaction, where a subject of one authority must interact with a subject of another authority in order to conform to reason, then the relevant reasons for action come to involve the directives of the other authority and they may even include a reason for a subject to obey the other authority rather than her own. In cases of overlap between subjects of different authorities, primary reasons for action will be sensitive to the overlap itself and may end up looking different for it. In both cases, the existence of more than one legitimate authority can generate new reasons for action that would not exist in the monist situation.

In contrast, plurality of secondary reasons for action affects the structure or the pattern of applicable reasons. Recall that on the monist Razian account, the directives of a legitimate authority function as positive secondary reasons for action as well as exclusionary secondary reasons not to act on some primary reasons. In a pluralist context, there are multiple positive secondary reasons for action as well as multiple exclusionary secondary reasons for action. This results in a complex matrix of possible interactions between those reasons. A positive secondary reason to follow one authority might be paralleled by a positive secondary reason to follow another authority. Alternatively, exclusionary reasons to follow two different authorities (instead of acting on one's own judgment), might directly conflict with one another. Another possibility sees a positive secondary reason to follow one authority, alongside an exclusionary reason not to follow that authority. In any of these situations, there seems to be a stalemate or deadlock of secondary reasons for action. It is unclear whether this stalemate is the end of the story, but, if so, it provides an unsatisfactory explanation for plurality of authority.

3. Is a Conjunctive Justification Satisfactory to Explain Plurality of Authority?

If we take the newly complex primary and secondary reasons for action and add them to the account of reasons for decision offered in section 2.a, we end up with a conjunctive justification for pluralist authority.

We can state the test as follows. Authority is justified if:

(1) there is an undefeated reason to have authority rather than private decision-making;
(2) a particular person or body has the standing of authority conferred upon it through a justified procedure;
(3) that authority is supported by or is consistent with the balance of governance reasons;
(4) that authority is supported by or is consistent with the balance of side-effect reasons; and
(5) its exercise would better enable subjects to conform to the reasons for action that apply to them, including both primary and secondary reasons to follow or exclude the directives of other relevant authorities.

This test leads to three important observations. The first is that the conjunction of the substantive and procedural elements of the justification can be mutually constraining. A really good dictatorship, even one which generally produces substantively better results than private decision-making would produce, cannot be authoritative if it carries no procedural values; while a thoroughly democratic and participatory regime cannot be authoritative if it generally produces worse substantive results than could be reached through private action.

The second is that the conjunctive test still leaves open the possibility of plurality of legitimate authority. The conjunctive justification can indeed generate plurality due to the diversity of procedures and outcomes through which different agents can have legitimate authority. We can end up with many different authorities that are (for instance) democratically elected by different communities, and which all govern soundly and with legitimate substantive outcomes. We might also end up with different authorities within a single community that are justified by incommensurable, or equal, reasons. The conjunctive justification is thus not a cure-all for the identification and rankings problems, which remain intractable at this point.

The third observation is that the conjunctive justification puts forward a very stringent test, and there is a real possibility that no authority could actually satisfy this test in circumstances of plurality. For instance, if the pattern and content of reasons for action result in a stalemate or deadlock of reasons, then criterion (5) above becomes very difficult to satisfy. Or, if the balance of governance reasons and side-effect reasons together point towards having a singular or hierarchical authority, but there is no justified procedure providing suitable standing to a particular candidate, then no particular authority would have legitimacy. This opens up several responses. One would be to give up on thinking about legitimate authority and say that all that matters is de facto power and path-dependent outcomes. Another would be to say, as Raz does of his own theory, that the fact that a test may rule out many or even most purportedly legitimate authorities shows no defect in the test itself. Creating a stringent test can also be a way of expressing a kind of radical aversion to authority, without going so far as to say that it can never be justified.

That is not my aim here, and I think that there is a different way forward. We need the conjunctive justification test in order to minimize the ranking and identification problems, but these prove intractable. Even if we combine accounts of standards and standing, and are sensitive to the newly complex reasons for decision and action that plurality generates, we still do not have a way to determine whether candidates for legitimate authority actually have legitimate authority, given their plurality. The solution, I think, is to change the way in which the test for justification is applied, and revise our understanding of the legitimate authority it is testing for.

8

'Relative Authority'

The previous chapters have shown that if we treat the procedural and substantive values of multiple authorities as if both the values and the authorities are independent of one another, we face two problems. The first, and most urgent, is to explain whether the very existence of authority can be sustained when not only the substantive and procedural justifications, but also their conjunction, result in plurality. The second problem is that evaluating authorities' legitimacy independently leaves nothing with which to evaluate relationships between authorities that are separately justified by the same reasons, or are separately justified by different reasons. There may be many different authorities which are (for instance) democratically elected by different communities, and which all govern soundly and with legitimate substantive outcomes, but with nothing to indicate how their interactions, when they occur, should be conducted. Alternatively, there might be different authorities within a single community that are justified by incommensurable reasons; again, with no indication how their interaction should proceed or whether one can legitimately exclude, tolerate, or cooperate with another. In practice, the interactions of authorities form a large part of their activities. If they are involved in projects with another authority, or if their subjects interact or are shared, then authorities' interactions cannot simply be explained as something parallel to their authority. Instead, that explanation needs to feature within an account of authority itself.

The intractability of the identification and rankings problems, and the inevitability of plurality of purportedly legitimate authority and its resulting interrelationships, suggest the need to re-imagine what it means for authority to be legitimate. This chapter presents a pluralist account of what authority is, and a justification for authority in circumstances of plurality, which integrates inter-authority relationships into the conditions for those authorities' legitimacy. This is achieved by combining the conjunctive justification from the previous chapter with a 'relativity condition', which tests the *interdependent* legitimacy of authorities and requires *justified relationships* between overlapping or interactive authorities. The resulting pluralist theory of authority conceives of legitimate authority as relative, and holds appropriate inter-authority relationships to be included within the conditions of an authority's legitimacy. It not only conceptualizes the phenomenon of plural authority directly and explains how authority can continue in the face of plurality, but also establishes how interaction between plural authorities can be a factor in their legitimacy.

The argument proceeds as follows. First, section 1 explains the conception of relative authority as a shared or independently held normative power, and presents a relativized justificatory theory in which authorities can be interdependently rather than independently legitimate. Section 2 argues that this is a better way of explaining and justifying authority in the contemporary pluralist circumstances of political, legal, and constitutional practice. Section 3 then offers a complete justification for public authority, which combines the conjunctive justification with the relativity condition; while section 4 concludes by assessing the case for pluralism upon which the pluralist account of that authority (indirectly) depends.

1. Relative Authority and the Relativity Condition

There are two senses in which authority might be conceived as relative. The first, and perhaps the most natural sense, is the idea that one agent has more or less authority when compared with another agent. Thus, we might colloquially say that Parliament has relatively more authority than a court in respect of some particular question to be settled. This treats relativity as a measure of the quantity or the quality of authority held by different bodies, and suggests that there can be degrees of authority rather than treating authority as necessarily ultimate. For instance, much discussion of the 'relative' authority of EU and Member States' constitutional law is concerned with evaluating those laws' separately legitimate authority against some common standard of legitimacy which acknowledges the variable, non-ultimate intensity of authority.[1] This first sense of relativity is relevant to the work presented here, which accepts that authority may be measured proportionately between authorities, and that this is a useful measure for examining relationships that are arranged in some formal integrating structure which allocates and distributes authority. As the previous chapters' discussions have argued, however, a structured organization does not tell the whole story of the authority of those agents engaged within that organization, for it is still crucial that the relationships and the rules organizing those relationships be evaluated in order to determine the legitimacy of the authorities. Furthermore, a proportional, measuring sense of relativity still measures

---

[1] See, eg Mattias Kumm and Jan Komárek, 'Rethinking Constitutional Authority', in Matej Avbelj and Jan Komárek (eds), *Constitutional Pluralism in the European Union and Beyond* (Hart Publishing, 2012).

the authority of the relating agents as though it is independent, and indeed that separateness is crucial to maintaining the ability to measure one against the other(s). Any such work that does not tie the conditions of legitimacy together into an integrated test is, I think, better understood as an account of 'respective' rather than relative authority.

A second sense of 'relative' is the one I am going to use here. This uses 'relative' to mean 'dependent' or 'interconnected', or, in dictionary terms, 'existing or possessing a specified characteristic only in comparison to something else; not absolute or independent'.[2] Relative authority here means more than simply concurrent or co-existing or comparable authority; rather it is authority whose legitimacy is mutually constitutive and mutually constraining between two persons or bodies which prima facie have the standing of authority, but which cannot alone have independent legitimacy because of the existence of the other and the need for interaction. The generator of all this relativity is, of course, the characteristics of the authorities' subjects, who are either shared between the authorities or whose activities bring the authorities into interaction. The conception of relative authority explains that, whenever authority is shared or overlapping as a result of these subjects' characteristics, that authority is not independent and its legitimacy cannot be assessed as if it is. Instead, that authority is relative.[3]

The idea of relative authority switches the focus of a theory of authority on to the relationships that exist between interactive and/or overlapping authorities. In different ways, relationships between these relative authorities become a condition of those authorities' legitimacy. Thus, a 'relativity condition' can be stated simply as follows: *in circumstances of plurality of prima facie authorities, the justification of authority depends upon a justified inter-authority relationship.* This is shorthand, for it is still necessary to fill in all the details of what constitutes a justified relationship, and these will depend upon the reasons for action and decision applying in the particular circumstances. It is also necessary to modify the procedural and the substantive branches of the conjunctive

---

[2] *Oxford English Dictionary*, 'Relative, N., Adj., and Adv' (Oxford University Press, 3rd edn, 2009), entry B.2.a.

[3] I have not been able to find other accounts using the same sense of relativity of authority. The closest is the idea of 'relative legal authority', which is expressly employed in Cotterrell's work on transnational law. See Roger Cotterrell, 'Transnational Communities and the Concept of Law' (2008) 21 *Ratio Juris* 1. However, as Cotterrell makes clear, the notion of relative legal authority is 'linked to a notion of degrees of legality' and is determined by 'negotiation and mutual recognition from diverse perspectives and standpoints' (p 15). In that work, the concept which is made relative is not so much authority, as legality. A full discussion of this perspective appears in my Chapter 9 on law's relative authority.

justification of authority. Having already made these branches pluralist, now we must make them relative.

The first step is to consider the two different ways in which the conditions of legitimate authority can entwine multiple authorities:

(1) Different purported authorities that are procedurally justified need to cooperate or coordinate if they are to be substantively justified (ie if they are to succeed in serving their joint or respective subjects' conformity to reason/values). (I call this *substantive relativity*.)

(2) Multiple purported authorities do not need to work together to be substantively legitimate, but there are procedural reasons, governance reasons, or side-effect reasons that cause their relationship to be a constraint upon each other's procedural legitimacy. I call this *procedural relativity*.

Substantive relativity is the most straightforward to explain. In situations of overlapping domains, it occurs: (i) if shared subjects have an undefeated reason to avoid a practical conflict between different directives issuing from the overlapping authorities; or (ii) if subjects shared between different authorities in an overlapping domain could only do better in conforming to reason if the authorities cooperated or coordinated their activities.[4] Situations of interactive domains can generate the same need for cooperation or coordination in order to meet the substantive justification, but only where there are matters of common concern such that neither authority alone could be substantively justified. This situation is complicated somewhat by the possibility that a relationship between authorities in interactive domains might have lop-sided effects on their substantive legitimacy. That is, one authority might help its subjects do better by cooperating, while the other would help its subjects do better by excluding the other and acting unilaterally. A genuinely pluralist account of authority must therefore modify the substantive part of the conjunctive justification to require that a cooperative or coordinative relationship between authorities is justified when it improves *or does not diminish* the prospects of either subject's conformity to reason. The relativity condition

---

[4] Note, however, that practical conflicts are not always cause for concern and need not always be resolved. See Raz, 'Personal Practical Conflicts', in Peter Baumann and Monika Betzler (eds), *Practical Conflicts: New Philosophical Essays* (Cambridge University Press, 2004). Where a practical conflict can be left unresolved, without harm to the subjects, there is no requirement that the different authorities coordinate or cooperate. The obvious examples of reasons to avoid conflict appear in coordination problems such as road rules, but matters of fairness could also fit this category. For instance, in a federal system where both national and state authorities can collect taxes upon their shared subjects, the tax levels will need to be mutually responsive to ensure that the overall level of tax being paid is justifiable.

therefore provides a modification of the substantive part of the conjunctive justification while keeping intact its basic content.

Things get more complicated in explaining procedural relativity, in which authorities are entwined by their procedural justifications. Any of three types of reasons for decision (procedural reasons, governance reasons, or side-effect reasons) can render the legitimacy of authorities relative. First, the procedures that confer the moral standing of authority might, in order to confer that standing, be contingent upon other procedures which are designed to manage an overlap or interaction with the domains of other authorities. For example, and depending on context, a state's democratic procedures might need to include special representative, consultative, or review mechanisms which protect the participation of subjects who are shared between that state and other (internal or external) authorities. Still depending on context, it is conceivable that in order to be justified, those procedures would have to include the participation of subjects shared with other authorities, or even non-subjects who are in close proximity to the subjects and who are affected by the exercise of the authority.[5] Alternatively, legitimacy might require that the selection procedure for conferring standing upon a particular authority include a process of cooperation or coordination with another authority. The important value here is not the achievement of cooperation or coordination (which is built into the conditions of substantive relativity), but the process of cooperating or coordinating, because this respects the standing of authority that subjects (whether shared or overlapping) have conferred on both authorities.

Side-effect reasons can also condition legitimacy between both overlapping and interactive authorities. These conditions stem from a cosmopolitan view of subjects as interactive individuals, whose interactions have moral relevance not just within the communities of people with whom they share a single authority, but also across those boundaries. According to the relativity condition, the interaction of subjects with non-subjects creates conditions upon the legitimacy of the subjects' authorities. In part, these are encompassed within the substantive branch of the conjunctive justification—because whenever subjects have reasons to respect the autonomy of non-subjects and to give effect to any obligations owed to them, their authorities must help them conform

---

[5] Arguments to that effect are made by proponents of 'affectedness' theories of participation, where those who are affected, or more often 'significantly affected' or 'specially affected', are entitled to some form of participation in decisions. These are controversial positions but are often proposed as one principle of good governance for decision-making at supra-national and international levels. See, eg Nico Krisch and Benedict Kingsbury, 'Introduction: Global Governance and Global Administrative Law in the International Legal Order' (2006) 17 *European Journal of International Law* 1. For analysis, see Anne Peters, 'Dual Democracy', in Jan Klabbers *et al.* (eds), *The Constitutionalization of International Law* (Oxford University Press, 2009).

to these reasons. However, these conditions are also generated by reasons for decision. The moral standing conferred upon an authority cannot include a standing to interfere with those who do not participate in that process of conferral. Standing can only legitimize authority over those who confer it; it does not entitle the authority to interfere with others any more than the subjects themselves could do so privately.[6] Where there are overlaps or interactions between two or more authorities with standing, therefore, they must at least tolerate one another because to do otherwise would be to deny the standing that each of their subjects has conferred upon them. Toleration entails that an authority do nothing to undermine or exclude another authority or otherwise allow its own activities to interfere with that other authority's ability to serve its subjects.[7] Reason would require toleration, for instance (and in either overlapping or interactive domains), if the activities of the authorities are compatible, or if there is conflict but there is no undefeated reason to avoid conflict. The point is that the moral significance of conferring standing upon an authority, and the substantive legitimacy of that authority, are together sufficient to make any interference with it unjustified, even if it comes at the hands of a separately justified authority. The moral standing that a legitimate authority has earned thus acts as a side-constraint upon the legitimacy of another authority with which it has an interactive or overlapping domain.

Governance reasons then come into play to determine whether the relationship between the authorities needs to be coordinated and, if so, whether hierarchical or dialogical coordination is more desirable. Governance reasons about the advantages and disadvantages of various kinds of relationships between authorities are infinitely variable, as they depend upon all the circumstances of the relationship and the context within which it occurs, so cannot be detailed in the abstract. I have already noted some recurring examples of governance reasons (centrality/monism is often linked to better coordination, and plurality linked to the expression of value pluralism), but these are contingent on actual circumstances, and there are other common (and sometimes opposing) arguments. For instance, a hierarchical system may create a system of checks and balances

---

[6] Just as the value of autonomy continues to constrain the justification of authority (by requiring a justified selection procedure, see Ch 7.1.a), it also requires that an authority must not interfere with the autonomy of non-subjects.

[7] This might look like an argument in defence of external state sovereignty with its principles of non-intervention and comity, but it does not take these principles (or sovereignty itself) as starting points or prima facie holders of value. For recent contributions to the literature debating the value of sovereignty and the principles applying to relationships between sovereigns, see Timothy A Endicott, 'The Logic of Freedom and Power', in S Besson and J Tasioulas (eds), *The Philosophy of International Law* (Oxford University Press, 2010), 246; Anne Peters, 'Dual Democracy', in Jan Klabbers *et al.* (eds), *The Constitutionalization of International Law* (Oxford University Press, 2009), 513–544.

in which each authority is subject to review by another. Or, both compatible and conflicting authorities in dialogical relationships may generate positive developments in governance through responding to each others' trials and errors.[8] Even conflicts of authority can generate positive developments in governance, as authorities respond to each other and are forced to justify their divergences. Conflicts of authority might also be valuable in giving recognition or expression to different ethical (including cultural or religious) systems that are inconsistent but reasonably justifiable. In contrast, plurality (and particularly conflicts of authorities) might be linked to uncertainty, confusion, and unfairness.

Although the relativity condition itself does not fill in the details of the reasons applying to the evaluation of actual relationships between authorities, it is a tool to explain how they can have legitimate authority despite (and sometimes because of) their plurality, via an interaction which accords with the balance of all of these reasons for decision and which allows them to help subjects comply with the balance of applicable reasons for action. The relativity condition thus alters both the procedural and substantive parts of the conjunctive justification of authority. On the procedural side, relative authority requires that authorities must not only have standing conferred by procedures, but they can also be required to engage in appropriate relationships with other similarly procedurally valuable authorities. Substantively, it requires that authorities help their subjects conform to reason in a way that also respects (by supporting or not detracting from) the conformity to reason of shared subjects or non-subjects with whom subjects interact.

In the following chapters I draw illustrations of these arguments from constitutional and international/transnational theory—the fields in which inter-authority relationships are most significant. The important abstract point, however, is that the relativity condition places the onus *upon the authorities* to interact appropriately so that subjects can rely upon those authorities to realize their own justifications, and so that any values attaching to particular authorities are not cast aside by the presence of other authorities which simply wield more or better resources. According to the relativity condition, authorities have a reason to fulfil their required relationships with one another, or else they will not be legitimate authorities.[9]

---

[8] The most discussed examples are those dialogues that occur between courts and legislatures through the practice of judicial review, although theorists dispute the extent to which that dialogue is constructive or damaging, and to what end. The literature here is vast; for examples see Ch 3, n 33.

[9] In Ch 9 I will argue that claiming legitimate authority generates a special commitment to pursue legitimate relationships, and that this is crucial to understanding the relative authority of law. Saying that there is a reason for authorities to seek out such relationships does not, of course, explain the political or behavioral motivations that might lead them to do so. That remains a subject for separate

2. A Pluralist Theory of Legitimate Authority (Why it is Preferable to a Monist Account)

The complete justification for pluralist authority therefore takes the five conditions of the conjunctive justification offered earlier, and adds a sixth, the relativity condition. It holds that authority is justified if:

(1) there is an undefeated reason to have authority rather than private decision-making;
(2) the standing of authority is conferred upon a person or body through a justified procedure;
(3) that authority is supported by or is consistent with the balance of governance reasons;
(4) that authority is supported by or is consistent with the balance of side-effect reasons;
(5) its exercise would better enable subjects to conform to the reasons for action that apply to them; and
(6) any overlap or interaction between the domains of prima facie authorities is managed through a relationship that:

   (a) improves or at least does not diminish the prospects of conformity to reason for subjects of either authority;
   (b) is consistent with the values protected by the justified procedures that confer standing upon either authority;
   (c) is consistent with the balance of governance reasons applying in the circumstances; and
   (d) is consistent with side-effect reasons generated by the overlap or interaction.

This pluralist justification of authority does two things. First, it provides a device for evaluating the legitimacy of relationships between authorities. Taken together, the modified conjunctive justification and the relativity condition allow us to determine whether or not authorities should cooperate or coordinate, whether conflicts between them should be tolerated, or whether one ought to exclude another. This analysis is best played out with reference to actual examples, as will be offered in Part IV of this work.

---

inquiry, which may invoke much of the debate about states' pursuits of legitimacy surveyed in Harold Hongju Koh, 'Why Do Nations Obey International Law?' (1997) 106 *Yale Law Journal* 2599.

The second contribution of the pluralist theory is more abstract and fundamental. It enables an explanation of authority in circumstances of plurality by replacing confusion and collapse in the face of conflict with toleration, cooperation, or coordination. It takes care of the identification and rankings problems by re-imagining the authorities to which they attach as relative rather than independent, so that purported authorities must work together or in harmony if they are to be legitimate, rather than creating confusion over their identification or rankings.

It remains to be seen how all of this can be operationalized into actual decision-making by authorities, and for that we need a detailed account of particular concrete relationships between authorities of the sort offered in the following chapters. It is however important to reiterate here, as a general observation, that the pluralist conception's relativity condition does not always require that authorities be ordered into conjunctive or coherent hierarchies, or that they must achieve singular or harmonized outcomes. Relationships might be hierarchical or heterarchical; and on some matters degrees of difference and even conflict can remain without upsetting the legitimacy of authority. Furthermore, my account does not seek to derail decision-making altogether by requiring cooperation on each and every issue that arises between relative authorities. Rather, the pluralist test for legitimacy should be applied as a general matter, to see whether, in general, an authority's directives and decisions are legitimately authoritative by virtue of an appropriate relationship with other relative authorities. Sometimes a particular directive or decision may depart from the ideal that is set by the pluralist test for legitimacy, but the overall relationship between the authorities preserves their general legitimacy. What remains, in that case, is a standard against which commentators can criticize the straying directive and advocate its reform.

It remains to argue that the complete pluralist account of authority—the conjunctive justification plus the relativity condition—is a better explanation of the contemporary practice of authority. I have already made the negative case against rival interpretations which, I have argued, are subject to either or both the identification and rankings problems. Those problems either make it impossible or very difficult to explain the possibility of plural authorities, particularly if they are in conflict, or make it impossible or difficult to explain how, if authorities can be plural, they should interact with one another. I have shown in this chapter how the relative authority account addresses those concerns, but there is a further normative case to be made for it in contrast to rival interpretations.

The first benefit of the relative authority account is simply tied to the normative value of a more accurate description of what is going on in practice. For instance, the relative authority account preserves the possibility of conflicts of authority not for its own sake or as some intellectual curiosity, but because conflicts seem to be a key feature of the contemporary practice of authority. Conflicts thus seem to be the sort of thing a theory of authority should be able to explain, as do cooperative/coordinated relationships between non-integrated authorities, tolerant relationships between overlapping authorities, and other particular configurations of plurality of authority, all of which can be explained through the structure offered by the relative authority account.

A stronger normative argument for the relative authority theory is that it avoids the pitfall of a default starting assumption about who has (or can have) legitimate authority. The (typically statist) monist accounts of authority cannot defend their choice of starting point once we adopt an awareness of the overlap and interaction of domains of authority, or even simply claims to authority. The problem is not that they are statist; it is that they are monist. Thus, the same criticisms apply to theories that begin from the default assumption that authority is claimed by/located in a particular international or tribal or sub-federal body. Reconceiving authority as relative can avoid a starting assumption about the location of the authority being explained, instead explaining a kind of authority without reference to its location.

The strongest normative case for a conception of relative authority, and a pluralist theory of legitimacy built upon a relativity condition, is tied to the value of plurality. After all, one response to the puzzles posed by plurality would be simply to deny the possibility of legitimate authority altogether, and argue instead that an explanation of plurality should focus upon coercive power or any kind of de facto power in order to explain and evaluate inter-authority relationships. The argument for holding on to both a conception of and justification for legitimate authority in circumstances of plurality is connected to two other arguments: one regarding the centrality of authority and the other regarding the value of plurality. I have already defended the reasons for this work's focus upon authority (and will go on to discuss the special importance of law's claim to authority in later chapters). The case for pluralism is different but equally critical. The normative attraction of an account of relative authority enlists the support of the same arguments about the value of plurality that appear in any particular instance of relative authority. In particular, those arguments turn upon whether governance reasons can support having plurality rather than turning inter-authority relationships into hierarchies of centralized or even monist arrangements.

3. The Case for Pluralism

The set of values associated with plurality, or, in other words, the case for pluralism, provides reasons for preferring the relative authority account over other contenders. That case is more directly important, however, in providing a set of reasons to be weighed up in any particular assessment of relative authority. The legitimacy of any particular instance of relative authority will be directly parasitic on a justification of plurality, because we can only start down the road of assessing whether a particular inter-authority relationship of conflict, cooperation, or dialogical coordination is justified, if the reasons favouring plurality in that instance outweigh the reasons against it. If plurality itself is unjustified, then the appropriate relationship between overlapping authorities must be coordination into centralized hierarchies or, if that fails, exclusion of one by the other.

Proponents of pluralism—the normative defence of plurality—have offered various arguments in its favour. One is that there is normative appeal in having an accurate description of the current landscape of competing constitutional claims and authorities. The appeal lies not simply in descriptive accuracy, but also in clearer insights and better proposals about the policies needed to deal with the challenges of overlaps and contest.[10] Second, and more substantively, pluralism (particularly constitutional pluralism) can be seen as the highest level of recognition for the politics of difference; the idea is that pluralism respects the different claims and relationships between sites of authority in a way that avoids making one subject to another.[11] Krisch for instance argues that pluralism can be consistent with the values of equal respect and self-determination, and with respect for political and affiliative differences within or among communities.[12]

Third, and relatedly, is the argument that contest can be preferable to finality. This argument is found in all the defences of dialogical decision-making or interpretive developments that appear in analyses of the relationship between judiciaries and legislatures, or defences of customary, unwritten, or conventional constitutional development. To take just one, Walker suggests that there may be 'productive possibilities in thinking of law in terms that cannot be resolved by some sort of final authority', rather as a kind of public reason; and that high constitutional questions should be decided 'in a context of dialogue

---

[10] Matev Avbelj and Jan Komárek, 'Four Visions of Constitutional Pluralism—Symposium Transcript' (2008) 2 *European Journal of Legal Studies* 325, 342–343.

[11] Avbelj and Komárek, 'Four Visions of Constitutional Pluralism', 342–344. On the politics of difference, see Iris Marion Young, *Justice and the Politics of Difference* (Princeton University Press, 1990).

[12] Nico Krisch, 'The Case for Pluralism in Postnational Law' in De Búrca and Weiler (eds) *The Worlds of European Constitutionalism* (Cambridge University Press, 2012) 203–260, arguing that if individuals are regarded as self-legislating equals, then unities and hierarchies are impositions upon those individuals. Krisch qualifies his endorsement of pluralism with the condition that any one institution deserves respect only if it and the polity it represents have a satisfactory deliberative pedigree.

where no court and no political body can finally just stop listening because they get the final word'.[13]

Arguments against pluralism also take on familiar patterns. First, there is the argument from disorder, which attributes to pluralism a failure to resolve disputes, or to solve common/coordination problems. The concern is that, at some point, decisions must be taken, and pluralism leaves unclear channels of decision-making which can hamper or even prevent solutions to common problems, or which, at worst, generate conflict without means for dispute settlement. Second, and relatedly, are concerns about the rule of law, and the worry that plurality of legal orders generates unpredictability, unevenness, incoherence, and inconsistency, which leave subjects unable to plan as autonomous and rational agents should be entitled to do.[14] Third, there are arguments that would limit justified self-determination to political communities comprising sovereign states, or which at least give independent and greater value to bounded political communities, ahead of cosmopolitan or cross-boundary or other political associations. These are sometimes, but do not need to be, nationalistic; the value of state-based political communities has also been linked with voluntarism, principles of fair play, or associative obligations among those susceptible to a common coercive power.[15]

There are many responses to the criticisms. One response denies that centrality and hierarchy necessarily do any better in achieving conformity to the rule of law or in establishing order and stability, particularly if they generate resistance from parts of communities or whole communities which feel unrepresented or even excluded from the centralized decision-making process. Disorder and failure to coordinate are not exclusive to pluralism. A second response disputes the benefits or at least the primacy of order itself, arguing that the formal rule of law values of integrity, consistency, and so on are not obviously more important than others; for instance, having a multiplicity of orders acting as checks and balances upon each other can generate more protection for individuals against the power of each of these publics.[16] Third is a cosmopolitan defence of the value of persons, quite apart from their

---

[13] Avbelj and Komárek, 'Four Visions of Constitutional Pluralism', 342–344.

[14] Pavlos Eleftheriadis, 'Pluralism and Integrity' (2010) 23 *Ratio Juris* 365.

[15] This diversity of opinions is represented by a comparison of: Michael Blake, 'Distributive Justice, State Coercion, and Autonomy' (2001) 30 *Philosophy & Public Affairs* 257; Robert E Goodin, 'What Is So Special About Our Fellow Countrymen?' (1988) 98 *Ethics* 663; David Miller, *On Nationality* (Clarendon Press, 1995); John Rawls, *The Law of Peoples: With 'the Idea of Public Reason Revisited'* (Harvard University Press, 2001); Jeremy Waldron, 'Special Ties and Natural Duties' (1993) 22 *Philosophy & Public Affairs* 3.

[16] Krisch, 'The Case for Pluralism in Postnational Law'.

roles as members of nation-state polities, and/or arguments that any valuable polity must be consistent with the rights of others to self-determination (and that conventionally understood nation states can be inconsistent with those rights).[17] A fourth response is to deny that order and plurality are in counterpoint; rather, that there can be a kind of 'ordered pluralism' through either institutional reform or the spread of ordering values, and which preserves the benefits of both order and pluralism.[18]

These debates are often formulated in the abstract, and the arguments from each side simply do not seem to resonate with the other no matter how well-formulated or well-supported or widely repeated they are. This may be due simply to the nature of political disagreement, in which these highest order questions—of how to organize people in communities and how to balance inclusion and exclusion within and between social groups—will resonate differently with people of different political persuasions and personalities. This basic variability of political and personal beliefs may, in the end, be the strongest reason to support Walker's suggestion that high constitutional questions could be best left without a final arbiter and left open to dialogical and incremental developments, but this can occur in a more principled fashion if armed with an account of legitimacy that can be used to evaluate the various authorities involved and the details of their relationships. That then creates a way to work out when leaving things open is not a justifiable option.

In the abstract, disagreements about the value of plurality are intractable. Instead, concrete examples are required to see whether the relative authority theory can be used to help explain and assess particular inter-authority relationships. The following three chapters take up this task by considering the significance of relative authority for both legal and constitutional theory, both within and outside of the state.

---

[17] On varieties of cosmopolitanism, see Thomas W Pogge, 'Cosmopolitanism and Sovereignty' (1992) 103 *Ethics* 48; Samuel Scheffler, 'Conceptions of Cosmopolitanism' (1999) 11 *Utilitas* 255; and for an example of a cosmopolitan defence of persons excluded by many state-centric accounts, see Seyla Benhabib, *The Rights of Others: Aliens, Residents, and Citizens* (Cambridge University Press, 2004).

[18] For one detailed account of this argument, see Mireille Delmas-Marty, *Ordering Pluralism: A Conceptual Framework for Understanding the Transnational Legal World* (Hart Publishing, 2009).

9
The Relative Authority of Law: 'Pluralist Jurisprudence'

I have so far said very little about how the relative authority theory might help us understand, explain, and evaluate the interrelationship of legal systems or orders. Yet part of the impetus for this project was to seek to explain legal authority in circumstances of overlapping and interacting legal orders, institutions, and systems; and to consider the impact of such legal pluralism upon conventional jurisprudential understandings of the nature of law. The foregoing account of relative authority explains authority as a power that is plural and relative rather than singular and exclusive; and entwines the conditions of plural authorities' legitimacy for their subjects, so that each can be legitimate only if they coordinate, cooperate, or tolerate one another as the particular balance of procedural and substantive reasons requires. Is this plausible as an account of the authority of law? Can legal authority be relative? Or is there something special about law that would deny such relativity? What, if anything, does the relative authority account tell us about law itself?

These questions take the inquiry away from the study of authority to the study of law; away from the study of a kind of normative power, to the study of an institutionalized normative system or, in the context of plurality, the study of institutionalized normative systems/orders/rules. Can an account of authority play any role in executing a turn towards pluralist jurisprudence— a jurisprudence that takes law's plurality as one of the features to be explained by a theory of law? One way to make that turn is by focusing upon borders and boundaries between legal systems and institutions, which are clearly important given that boundaries generate the very practices of interaction and overlap that make plurality of law interesting; and institutions are the ones doing the actual interacting. As discussed in Chapter 4, several scholars in jurisprudence have sought to account for law's plurality from this starting point. Some apply the idea of systemic borders so that they include multiple levels of law within a single system, or multiple systems in a single order. Others argue that plurality upsets the systemic view of law and instead seek to explain legality as something that is inter-systemic or inter-institutional.

With these approaches, I share an interest in plurality of law but, instead of focusing upon the institutional/systemic side of the explanation of law's plurality, I focus upon the normative element of law's authority. That is, rather than attempting to explain plurality's impact upon a theory of law, I think the answer might lie elsewhere, in an account of law's authority or, in other words, in the question when does law bind, rather than the question of what is law. This is not to deny the significance of the institutional side of the story, but to augment it with a consideration of how plurality might impact law's normativity via its authority. A full pluralist theory of law—which cannot be offered here but which must be seen as the eventual target of pluralist jurisprudence—must then grapple with how the normative and social/institutional explanations interact, to generate a full explanation of law as some kind of institutionalized normative system.[1]

This chapter explains how law's authority can be relative, and considers whether law necessarily or contingently makes a claim to relative authority. It then draws an implication to consider what law must be like if it is to claim relative authority in good faith. In section 1 I explain why authority matters to an account of law, and why we should care about the characteristics of law's authority. Section 2 argues that law claims, and may have, relative rather than independent authority. Section 3 considers whether the relative authority account implies any changes to conventional wisdom about what law is like, while section 4 concludes by integrating an account of law's relative authority into a growing body of 'pluralist jurisprudence'.

1. Why Care about Authority?

The relative authority theory is a theory of authority, not of law. What relevance does it have, and how can it help explain anything about law, let alone law's plurality? Two widely debated ideas are central to showing that authority matters for an account of law, and that a theory of authority can help explain plurality of law. The first is the idea that law makes claims that are best understood as claims about what, from the law's point of view, is morally required.[2]

---

[1] This characterization of the dual social and normative elements of a theory of law comes from Jules L Coleman, *The Practice of Principle: In Defence of a Pragmatist Approach to Legal Theory* (Oxford University Press, 2001). In different terms, Alexy makes a related point about the social and moral natures of law, explored as real and ideal elements in a theory of law: Robert Alexy, 'The Dual Nature of Law' (2010) 23 *Ratio Juris* 167.

[2] Joseph Raz, *The Authority of Law* (2nd edn, Oxford University Press, 2009), 29–33. For a discussion of the diversity of claims about law's claims, see John Gardner, 'How Law Claims, What Law Claims', in Matthias Klatt (ed), *Institutional Reason: The Jurisprudence of Robert Alexy* (Oxford University Press, 2010).

The second, related, and more relevant idea is that law claims to have (or to be a) legitimate authority.[3]

If we accept the idea that law makes claims about moral requirements, and that law claims legitimate authority, then an analysis of 'legal authority' should not simply treat 'legal' as an adjectival modifier of authority—that is, legal authority is not a distinctive kind of authority whose explanation is divorced from the explanation of authority simpliciter.[4] We do not throw out everything we know about authority in order to understand the authority of law, or reduce it to a technical device akin to jurisdiction.[5] The concept of 'legal authority' can then be understood as shorthand for moral authority 'from the law's point of view'.[6] Or, put a different way, when law claims authority, it tells us what, from the law's point of view, is morally required.[7] If that claim is justified, then legal authority can give its subjects reasons for action, which add to or differ from those of morality, precisely because it is operating as a perspective on what morality requires. In turn, that claim invites the use of (non-legal) moral standards as tools for evaluating that perspective and its claims to authority.

Each of these steps in the argument can be contested, and has been subjected to substantial jurisprudential debate. Some doubt that law can make claims at all;[8] others doubt that law's claims are moral claims.[9] The character of law's claims generates disagreement between those who think law's claims are of a technical, non-moral, or even uniquely 'legal' character, and those who think the claims are claims about what is morally required. In other words, between those who treat law's claim to impose obligations as a claim to impose obligations of a special, legal sort, and those who treat law's claims to impose obligations as a claim to impose moral obligations.[10] As Coleman explains,

---

[3] See, eg Coleman, *The Practice of Principle*, 26: 'like Raz and other positivists, I hold that normative concepts that figure prominently in law—obligation, right, duty and so on—are employed in their moral sense'. For clarity, it also bears repeating that, in this work, I use the term 'authority' to mean legitimate authority rather than de facto authority.

[4] See also Scott J Shapiro, *Legality* (Harvard University Press, 2010), 184–188.

[5] Another possibility would be to treat 'legal authority' as a description of the de facto authority that the law has, and to set aside questions of its legitimacy. Under that interpretation, law's authority would be whatever de facto authority law has, qua law. I will not follow that approach in this work, which is focused upon the question of legitimate rather than de facto authority. See also comments at n 9.

[6] On the law's point of view, see Shapiro, *Legality*, 184–188.

[7] Coleman, *The Practice of Principle*, 22.

[8] See, eg Ronald Dworkin, 'Thirty Years On' (2002) 115 *Harvard Law Review* 1655, 1665–1668; and Kenneth Einar Himma, 'Law's Claim of Legitimate Authority', in Jules L Coleman (ed), *Hart's Postscript: Essays on the Postscript to the Concept of Law* (Oxford University Press, 2001), 277–279.

[9] Matthew H Kramer, *In Defense of Legal Positivism: Law without Trimmings* (Oxford University Press, 1999), 78–112.

[10] Coleman, *The Practice of Principle*, 26; John Gardner, 'How Law Claims, What Law Claims', in Matthias Klatt (ed), *Institutional Reason: The Jurisprudence of Robert Alexy* (Oxford University Press, 2010), 15.

the latter view holds 'that legal directives are best understood as claims about what those to whom they are directed are morally required, authorized, or permitted to do'.[11] Following Coleman, Gardner, and Raz, this work is committed to the notion that law makes moral claims; and that this is not some mysterious anthropomorphic suggestion, but rather shorthand for saying that legal officials, in their capacity as legal officials, make moral claims on behalf of the law.

The question then is whether these moral claims made by the law are claims to authority. Much has been written about the coherence, contingency, or necessity of law's claim to legitimate authority.[12] Put more precisely, the question is: does law necessarily claim to give rise to content-independent moral obligations to obey the law? Those who argue that it does, or accept others' arguments that it does, make the notion of authority central to understanding law and therefore to the tasks of jurisprudence.[13] Many others hold that a theory of law need not include or even join an account of authority, because they either reject the necessity of law's claim to authority or reject that it makes such a claim at all.[14] A lot turns on the answer to this question because of its implications for analytical jurisprudence.

Claims to authority are, of course, just that. They can be true or false, and they can be made in good faith or disingenuously. The significance of claiming is, I think, twofold: it has significance for the insight it offers into what law is like, but it also has significance in its own right because of the commitments that accompany a claim. First, the significance of claiming, as an insight into what law is like, turns upon whether or not law's claims are necessary ones. If any of law's claims are necessary features of law, then the claims become jurisprudentially interesting because they provide a clue to the nature of law. Both an account of law's necessary claims, and/or a theory which rejects their necessity, are devices for debating what law is like. That analytical inquiry is quite different from a normative inquiry into the conditions under which

---

[11] Coleman, *The Practice of Principle*, 26.

[12] This is due to its centrality to debates within positivism about the possibility of moral criteria for legal validity. For a rejection of the conceptual necessity of law's claim to authority, see Himma, 'Law's Claim of Legitimate Authority'. In Raz's formulation: 'though a legal system may not have legitimate authority, or though its legitimate authority may not be as extensive as it claims, every legal system claims that it possesses legitimate authority': Joseph Raz, *Ethics in the Public Domain* (Oxford University Press, 1994), 215. Compare Kramer, *In Defense of Legal Positivism*, 78–112, eg at p 101: the law claims authority but does not necessarily claim moral authority.

[13] In addition to the Raz, Coleman, Shapiro, and Gardner works cited, see A Marmor, *Philosophy of Law* (Princeton University Press, 2011), 58; Coleman, *The Practice of Principle*, 144; L Green, 'Positivism and the Inseparability of Law and Morals' (2008) 83 *NYUL Review* (2008).

[14] Compare Kramer, *In Defense of Legal Positivism*, 78–112; although at 101, noting that it would be an unusual legal system that did not claim moral authority.

law's claims are justified, but in both the analytical and the normative inquiries, the actual practice of claiming is not the target; rather, it is the trigger for analysing what the making of those claims reveals about law itself, including the question of whether law can live up to its claims.

The analytical and normative inquiries are distinct but related because any claims that law necessarily makes spawn theories about what law must be like if it is to make those claims in good faith—and this in turn requires an account of what might justify making those claims. For instance, if it is necessary to law that it claims to have legitimate authority, then a theory of law needs to explain what law must be like in order that those claims could be true. Raz argues that such a claim to legitimate authority is a necessary feature of law, and, as Coleman summarizes, the implication of Raz's argument (with which he agrees on this point) is that the 'nature of law is constrained by the account of the conditions of legitimate authority; for whatever law is, it must be the sort of thing that could be a legitimate authority, whatever consists in being a legitimate authority'.[15] A claim to authority is not the same thing as having authority, but in order to understand what the claim to authority reveals about law, we need to examine the conditions under which that claim is true or justified. In so doing, we cover some of the same ground as a purely normative analysis of law's claims to authority, one which does not particularly care whether those claims are necessary or merely contingent features of law, and one which does not address at all the question of whether law (necessarily or not) claims authority.

For now, then, this section can set aside the dispute over the claim's existence/contingency/necessity, because some of the implications of my relative authority theory apply whether or not claiming authority is a necessary or merely common feature of legal systems, and they apply similarly to the claiming of authority and to its existence. In section 2.b I will address the significance of the necessity/contingency dispute for a pluralist account of law's authority.

The second significance of claiming authority is the matter of what such a claim entails. If law does make a claim to legitimate authority (ie to be able to generate moral requirements for its subjects), then by the act of making that claim, law holds itself out as a legitimate authority in a way that also commits law to a good faith pursuit of legitimacy. In this regard the subjects of law are entitled to rely upon law's claim to legitimate authority, and indeed it is rational for them to do so. This seems the most attractive way of understanding the claim to authority—that it is made in good faith, not in bad—and this means that entailed within a claim to legitimate authority is a commitment to

---

[15] Coleman, *The Practice of Principle*.

try to be legitimate. This view, in which claims to authority are seen to entail commitments to the pursuit of its legitimacy, is particularly important for considering the prospect of law's relative authority.

2. Relative Legal Authority[16]

The authority of law might simply be reconceived as the relative authority of law, and law's claims to authority understood as claims to relative authority. I will end up arguing for those conclusions, but that argument is more difficult than simply slotting in relativity at convenient points in an otherwise untouched story of law's (claimed) authority. To say that law claims relative authority rather than independent authority is to say that law claims authority that is conditional upon appropriate relationships between its legal institutions and others with which it shares authority. Then, in turn, if law has authority at all it has only this relative, interdependent kind of authority. Although a little awkward to express, I think that this is a plausible and attractive account of law's (claimed) authority. To see why this is so, however, we first need to consider the interaction of law's claimed authority with law's claimed supremacy. Significantly, if law's (claimed) authority is relative, it sits uneasily with the idea that law claims supremacy—a claim which Raz, for one, argues is entailed by the claim to authority.[17]

a. Law's claim to supremacy

Raz suggests that our 'general knowledge about the law and human society' reveals that law makes a claim to supremacy, and that this claim is one of the existence conditions for a municipal legal system.[18] The claim to supremacy takes two forms: (i) a claim to supremacy over non-legal systems, including an

---

[16] This section and the following include some material that appeared in Nicole Roughan, 'The Relative Authority of Law—A Contribution to Pluralist Jurisprudence', in Maksymilian Del Mar (ed), *New Waves in Philosophy of Law* (Palgrave Macmillan, 2011); reproduced with permission of Palgrave Macmillan.

[17] Raz argues that central to 'the uniqueness of law', and constituting necessary features of a legal system, are law's claims to comprehensive authority and supremacy, and law's systemic openness to norms from other normative systems: Raz, *The Authority of Law*, 117–120. These claims are related and all will be challenged by the pluralist analysis I will provide, but while the claim to openness has generated discussion about the precise character of potential inter-systemic interaction in circumstances of plurality, it does not unsettle the core of the Razian account of law's authority.

[18] Raz, *The Authority of Law*, 120. Raz argues that 'every legal system claims authority to regulate the setting up and application of other institutionalized systems by its subject-community'. He argues that the claim to supremacy is one aspect of law's claim to comprehensively regulate any area of its subjects' activities.

entitlement to regulate, exclude, or otherwise control their operation through recognition or incorporation of their norms; and (ii) a claim to supremacy over other legal systems or at least other instances of law. The first form of the claim seems straightforwardly coherent, although there are disputes about whether the claim is a necessary feature of law itself, or merely a contingent feature of legal systems in modern sovereign states.[19] The second form of the claim is more difficult; it is much less clear whether law's claim to supremacy includes a claim to supremacy over other systems of law. Raz thinks that it does, and that, significantly, 'since all legal systems claim to be supreme with respect to their subject-community, none can acknowledge any claim to supremacy over the same community which may be made by another legal system'.[20]

There is an obvious empirical objection to this line of argument: even if law claims supremacy over (for instance) the rules of voluntary associations or family life, it is simply not true that all prima facie legal systems claim supremacy over others, nor even that all modern municipal legal systems make this claim. Both the necessary and the contingent views of the supremacy claim run counter to the phenomena of constitutional and legal pluralism (particularly but not exclusively in Europe), which feature many prima facie legal systems, including those of municipal states, that do not claim supremacy over all others, or even claim subjection to others.[21] This list also includes some federal and quasi-federal states, and states with other complex divisions of sovereignty, that do not straightforwardly have single legal systems claiming supremacy, but rather feature domains of overlap or concurrent activities in which neither or both systems claim supremacy.[22] Furthermore, even a straightforwardly unitary state's legal system does not claim to exempt members of its subject-community from being subject also to any extraterritorial rules

---

[19] Raz himself limits his discussion of the claim to supremacy to a theory about municipal legal systems, leaving open whether other instances of law might also (or might necessarily) make the same claim. Andrei Marmor suggests that the claim to supremacy is an incorrect implication from the concept of supreme political sovereignty, and not a necessary feature of law. Marmor argues that we can conceive of possible legal systems that do not make a claim to supremacy over non-legal systems. See Andrei Marmor, *Positive Law and Objective Values* (Oxford University Press, 2001), 39–42.

[20] Raz, *The Authority of Law*, 119.

[21] Marmor, *Positive Law and Objective Values*, 40–41. Examples include constitutions that give supremacy to international law. See, eg M Claes and B de Witte, 'Report on the Netherlands', in A Sweet, A-M Slaughter, and J Weiler (eds), *The European Court and National Courts* (Hart Publishing, 1998), 171. In reverse, the scope claimed by some international legal regimes is subsidiary to that of some municipal laws, for instance the subsidiarity principles operating in international criminal court jurisdiction. The other core example is the supremacy of EU law (both formally, and to the extent that supremacy is accepted).

[22] For discussion of examples, see Keith Charles Culver and Michael Giudice, *Legality's Borders: An Essay in General Jurisprudence* (Oxford University Press, 2010).

that other states enact—such as rules regulating cross-border commercial, criminal, or tortious activity. The legal system of the 'home' state does not always claim supremacy over these other prescriptions, or even supremacy of jurisdiction, even though executive enforcement authorities in that state may elect not to engage in extraditions or other processes that would give effect to another state's law. Arguably, even when such enforcement is refused, all that is claimed is supremacy of enforcement authority, not supremacy of the law itself. If the supremacy claim is a necessary condition for a legal system, we would have to either limit it to a claim about the enforcement of laws in a way that runs counter to the contemporary jurisprudential emphasis on normativity rather than sanction, or deny that any of these systems were legal systems, despite their meeting all other existence conditions and/or displaying other necessary of even ordinary features of legal systems.

There are, of course, many further examples to be drawn outside of the municipal state context to which Raz expressly confines his analysis. These would not be relevant if the goal here were solely to object to Raz's own theory, but that is not my aim. The examples are important for considering arguments about what law is like, in the context of plurality of law. Many examples are historical, including those medieval legal systems which, despite being surrounded by others, did not claim supremacy over them.[23] International law is another example over which scholars disagree; some deny that it makes a claim to supremacy (then argue over whether this matters to its status as law); others think that it does, often citing Article 27 of the Vienna Convention on the Law of Treaties, which denies that national law can be used to justify failure to comply with international law.[24]

Although I think that the basic truth of the empirical objection to the supremacy claim is important—indeed, it captures the very practice of plurality that the core of jurisprudence can no longer ignore—it is not entirely successful as a response to Raz's point. Raz accepts that claims to non-supremacy and multiplicity of legal systems can exist in fact; his point is not that no systems in fact acknowledge each other's claims to supremacy, but that, 'as a matter of law', they cannot.[25] Although Raz does not elaborate an argument for this explanation, it seems to be derived from his monist conception of authority, which entails the supremacy claim. If that is right, then Raz's argument may be that a legal system cannot acknowledge another's supremacy because this would vitiate its authority by forcing the subject—in order to determine

---

[23] Marmor, *Positive Law and Objective Values*, 40–41.
[24] 'A party may not invoke the provisions of its internal law as justification for its failure to perform a treaty.'
[25] Raz, *The Authority of Law*, 118.

which legal system to obey—to revisit the reasons authority is supposed to pre-empt.[26]

Thus, the empirical objection to the supremacy claim needs to be matched with an analytical account of law that explains how different supremacy claims can be integrated and mutually recognized while upholding the authority of law, and/or that denies the necessity of a legal system's claim to supremacy.

The account of relative authority can do both. The way to avoid Raz's concern—that legal systems cannot recognize the supremacy of another—is to substitute supremacy for relativity, so that even if a legal system cannot recognize another system's claim to supremacy, it can recognize the relativity of its own claim to the claims of others, and of their claims to its own. If law's claim is to relative authority, not supreme authority, then it is straightforward to see these claims as integrated rather than competing claims to supremacy. Furthermore, no claim to supreme authority over other legal systems could be justified wherever it turns out that legal authority is relative, and therefore no claim to supremacy could be made in good faith, and nothing would follow about the nature of law or legal systems from the fact that some systems actually make such a claim.[27] In short, if we can show that under some conditions legal systems have relative and not supreme authority, then we deny that a claim to supremacy is a necessary condition of the existence of legal systems—municipal or otherwise.

In this way the relative authority account makes it possible to hold on to the idea that law claims legitimate authority, even when so much pressure is coming on the idea that it claims supremacy.[28] As an empirical matter, it also better captures the claim that many legal systems make over their subjects, in regards to their legitimate authority, including many municipal states. Yet in order for that full potential to be explained, it is necessary to consider how to understand law's claim to relative authority, and under what conditions law's authority can be relative.

---

[26] This argument echoes the argument Raz makes for exclusive legal positivism.
[27] This remains consistent with legal systems making the stronger claim to supremacy over non-legal systems applying to the same subjects.
[28] An alternative reading of law's claim to supremacy treats it as a claim to a monopoly on justified coercion within a particular community, rather than a claim about supreme legitimate authority. This is relevant for my interest here because law might still claim enforcement supremacy even while claiming relative authority. As argued in the preliminary chapters of this book, coercion and authority (and claims thereto) exist and should be explained separately. If law claims coercive supremacy, this may be an important element for a pluralist theory of law to explain, but it does not diminish the need to explain law's pluralistic authority as well.

b. Law's claim to authority

The relative authority theory argues that, when there are multiple prima facie legitimate authorities in interacting or overlapping domains, and there is no outweighing reason to have just one singular authority, then those prima facie legitimate authorities can have only relative authority and must coordinate or cooperate or tolerate one another in order to be legitimate for their subjects. In these circumstances, law can still claim to possess legitimate authority; indeed, claiming legitimate authority remains an important part of law's having authority (because it can have authority only if it can, as a matter of fact, secure a degree of respect for its directives, and claiming legitimacy presents a powerful image that might attract such respect). That claim, however, is best understood as a claim to relative authority.

A claim to relative authority is simply a claim to have legitimate authority through appropriate relationships with other authorities. The claim is a special kind of claim to legitimate authority, which includes an awareness of its relativity to other authorities with which it overlaps or interacts. It links the legitimacy of authority with its interdependence. In more precise terms, the relativized claim is a claim to change the moral reasons applying to the subject by working with other authorities which share or also have this normative power, and whose cooperation or coordination is needed for the authority to be legitimate. It is important, however, that a claim to relative authority is different from a claim to reduced authority; rather, is a claim that acknowledges the conditionality of one's authority upon appropriate interaction with others.

Thus, embodied within a claim to relative legitimate authority is a commitment to pursuing the appropriate relationships with other authorities that are required by the relativity condition. This is important, and it arises out of the argument, set out earlier in this chapter, that law's claim to legitimate authority is a claim about what, from the law's point of view, is morally required. If law does make a claim to be able to generate such moral requirements, then, by the act of making that claim, the law is holding itself out as a legitimate authority in a way which also commits the law to a good faith pursuit of legitimacy. When there is plurality of legitimate authority, such that any one authority must engage appropriately with others in order to be legitimate, then any claim that such an authority makes entails a commitment to the pursuit of those appropriate relationships.

Interpreted in this way, a claim to relative authority is a more credible and nuanced claim which is to be preferred to the more sweeping claim to independent authority which, it turns out, cannot be sustained when facts support relativity rather than supremacy. In other words, claims to authority are only plausible when made in conjunction with recognizing the interdependent authority claims of those other legal authorities with which they must cooperate or coordinate. Crucially, a claim to relative authority also avoids triggering the identification problem that plagues any monistic view of authority. It does so by building in the condition (of justified interrelationships) that would remove the uncertainty and doubt over which (of multiple) authorities should be followed. This makes it easier for subjects to follow, and indeed rational for them to do so. Consider this in relation to the alternative—it would be irrational for a subject to follow a legal authority which claims independent legitimate authority, but which, in fact, is unable legitimately to do most of the things it claims to be able to do because of the presence of other authorities and the need for coordination, cooperation, or toleration.

As an empirical matter, legal systems in situations of plurality do make claims to authority, but the question remains how we should understand them. As explored in section 2.a, there are problems with interpreting these as claims to independent authority, as many supposedly straightforward examples turn out not to be so straightforward. There are, instead, examples of claims to relative authority among legal institutions at different levels of law. The most obvious involve claims to subsidiary or complementary jurisdiction, which can be seen as claims to relative authority in which one body's legal authority is conditional upon the non-action of another—a type of coordination of their authority.[29] Other examples include arrangements of overlapping, concurrent, or shared jurisdiction, which occur not only within the much-discussed setting of the European Union, but can also feature in self-government claims by groups within states and states' responses to those claims.[30] Such examples of jurisdictional arrangements, along with arrangements of concurrent, overlapping, or joint jurisdiction, are complex and cannot be detailed here, but it is important to note that where such concurrency or complementarity or overlap of authority is expressly claimed, these should be understood as claims to relative authority.

Finally, it remains to ask whether a claim to relative authority is a necessary feature of law. If Raz is right, and it is of the nature of law that it claims legitimate authority, and if we accept that there is plurality of law, then this claim is best interpreted as a claim to relative authority; one which is made in interaction with the claims of other legal systems. Even if Raz is wrong, and law does not necessarily claim any authority, let alone relative authority, we

---

[29] Examples include the subsidiary (or 'complementary') jurisdiction of the International Criminal Court; and the much-discussed subsidiarity principles governing EU interactions with Member States.

[30] For analysis of an example in the context of indigenous-state relationships, see Korey Wahwassuck *et al.*, 'Building a Legacy of Hope: Perspectives on Joint Tribal-State Jurisdiction' (2009–2010) 36 *Wm Mitchell Law Review* 859.

can still ask about the character of claims to authority that law does make, and from those claims we can learn about important contingent features of law (albeit not necessary ones), including its relativity.

A Razian response might argue that, if legal systems must only claim authority, and it does not matter (for purposes of thinking about law) that they may fail to have legitimate authority, then there is no conceptual problem posed by plurality. So long as a legal system still claims authority, it fits the Razian explanation of law. This seems unconvincing, for the trouble stirred up by plurality is not simply a question about whether authority is justified, but about whether authority can exist at all. The bigger issue is that we need to revisit what can actually be claimed, in good faith, by a legal system that has unclear boundaries and overlapping borders with another legal system. If it turns out that in situations of plurality there cannot be the kind of authority that is typically claimed by a monistic municipal legal system, then it is hard to see a claim to such authority as a necessary condition of such a legal system. The argument could still be made, but it becomes unattractive and far less convincing.

It is tempting to leave open the question of whether law necessarily claims relative authority, but equally tempting to see if the idea of relative authority might actually help answer the question of the necessity of law's claim to any authority whatsoever. In his argument for the necessity of law's claim to authority, Raz maintains that law's claim to authority can be false, and indeed may very often be false, but that it cannot be necessarily false.[31] If we adopt the context of plurality of law, then it seems that a claim to independent, monistic authority is necessarily false. Put the other way, the claim to independent authority cannot be true if facts generate relative authority. This is obviously tautologous, but it serves to highlight the real crux of the issue over the necessity of claims to relative authority; ie that it turns upon the necessity of circumstances of plurality rather than singularity of law.

Is it possible for law to exist in isolation from other instances of law? Such isolation seems conceptually plausible, for one might imagine a customary legal system of an isolated community whose members have no interaction with members of outside communities (or at least no interactions involving legal questions); which does not participate in any policy projects involving outside communities; and which applies only its own rules which are not in any way designed to replicate or be compatible with the rules of outside communities. The conceptual plausibility of this account would seem to deny that plurality is the condition in which all law operates, and therefore also deny that law necessarily claims relative rather than independent authority.

---

[31] Raz, *The Authority of Law*.

Yet although such a monist account remains a conceptual possibility, it is practically questionable. Although there are, undoubtedly, normative systems (and some may say legal systems) of such isolated communities, they must be an endangered species of law, due to the dominance of the state as a political structure imposing 'official' state law onto such customary legal systems, or even simply claiming superiority over them and thereby creating plurality between the official and the customary systems along with overlap or interaction with subjects of other states.[32] It is arguable that in the post-Westphalian practice of law, plurality is always present to greater or lesser degrees, and if that is the case, and plurality is marked by overlap or interaction between legal authorities, then any particular legal authority can only make a credible claim to relative and not to supreme authority.

c. The interaction of legal systems

A pluralist theory of law would be incomplete if it failed to explain the features of law that the claim to relative authority entails, whether they are necessary or merely contingent. The key feature is a capacity to be responsive to other instances of law, not merely open to them.[33] More precisely, legal systems, through the officials who make claims and act on law's behalf, must be capable of being responsive to one another.

Here, a distinction can be drawn between two possible types of responsiveness between legal systems—'associations' and 'interactions'—which can both satisfy the demands of legitimate relative authority, although in different ways. Elsewhere I have discussed unilateral 'association', where one system incorporates rules from another system, or elects to apply the rules of the other system in order to achieve coordinated, compatible, or harmonized outcomes.[34] Association via incorporation involves a unilateral outreach by one system, of which the target system need not even be aware, and involves borrowing content from another system by replicating it in one's own system. It does not necessarily involve acknowledging the authority of the system from which the content is borrowed; merely that its content is desirable. Similarly, giving direct effect to rules of a different legal system might involve recognition of its separate authority, but this separate authority is then subsumed under the

---

[32] The relationship between customary and official law is, of course, much more complex than a simple 'overlay'. See Nicole Roughan, 'The Association of State and Indigenous Law: A Case Study in "Legal Association"' (2009) 59 *University of Toronto Law Journal* 135.

[33] Compare Raz, *The Authority of Law*, 119–120.

[34] Roughan, 'The Association of State and Indigenous Law'. In that work I suggested in passing that interaction was a more general type of contact between systems, without indicating what it entailed. This passing claim is misleading—interaction is better understood as a bilateral or two-way contact which is a special type of association between systems.

control of the host legal system and, specifically, its law-applying institutions. Both these kinds of associations between systems are unilateral, operating under the authority of just one of the systems, yet both can still be paths to securing authority in situations of relativity. For instance, where reason is equally or incommensurably balanced between the options proposed by the two different systems, and there are reasons to coordinate their content, one system's unilateral decision to adopt, incorporate, or directly apply the option chosen by the other has the effect of securing the authority of both. Relative authority makes each system's authority conditional on the conduct of the other authority, but this does not necessarily mean they need to cooperate to come up with a joint solution. They may simply need to be made compatible, and this may be achievable through the unilateral conduct of either system.[35]

By contrast, 'interactions' involve multiple legal systems engaging in cooperative activity or dialogue, which harmonizes or makes compatible their respective content and its application, or which arranges their content and application to achieve some outcome to which they both contribute.[36] Cooperation pursues this directly and entails joint mutual commitments; dialogue pursues it through mutual responsiveness with incremental adjustments that may be less overt. Neither process requires strict harmonization of laws, but both require either working out procedures to adjudicate if there are conflicts that need to be resolved, or otherwise finding ways to ensure that the rules of the overlapping/interacting systems are not so confusing or inconsistent for subjects that they cannot use them as reliable guides for practical reasoning and planning. This might mean arriving at rules that are consistent or compatible, or at least applying those rules in ways that are compatible. In this the roles of courts and legislatures are both important. For instance, where courts in two systems are aware of a potential conflict between their respective laws, and of the importance of coming to compatible decisions, then they may engage in a dialogical coordination by rendering compatible decisions. Similarly, legislatures can enact laws giving effect to cooperative bilateral or multilateral commitments, or which make dialogical gestures aimed at

---

[35] The most straightforward examples appear in the ratification and incorporation of treaty provisions harmonizing rules among treaty parties, such as the International Convention on the Sale of Goods.

[36] On the subject of dialogue between legal institutions, particularly courts, there is an extensive literature which includes extra-judicial publications from leading judges. See, eg Rosalyn Higgins, 'A Babel of Judicial Voices? Ruminations from the Bench' (2006) 55 *International and Comparative Law Quarterly* 791; Michael Kirby, 'Transnational Judicial Dialogue, Internationalisation of Law and Australian Judges' (2008) 9 *Melbourne Journal of International Law* 171. Dialogue can include both formal communications in the form of judgments, and the informal dialogues that occur through transnational judicial networks.

encouraging another system's law-making institutions to do likewise and eventually achieve compatibility.[37]

In both the unilateral and multilateral forms of association, legal systems are not simply open to other systems, they are responsive to them. When different systems have relative rather than independent authority, this responsivity is crucial to their having authority at all.

3. The Value of Relative Legal Authority

It appears, from the foregoing, that law's legitimate relative authority is parasitic upon a normative defence of plurality of law. Normative arguments determine when plurality of law and the interaction of relative authorities might be valuable, or when the need for singular or hierarchically centralized law outweighs any value in plurality. Arguments about plurality also indicate whether justified relationships between authorities must be hierarchical or heterarchical; as well as determining whether on some matters, degrees of difference and even conflict can remain without upsetting the legitimacy of authority.

The advantages and disadvantages of plurality of law have been analysed in detail elsewhere.[38] Suggested advantages sometimes tie the presence of multiple, fragmented, and disordered systems of law to principles of political pluralism; arguing that a plurality of systems of law can give effect to competition or simple co-existence between different eligible conceptions of the good, between the practices and beliefs of different communities, and even between different kinds of affiliations that individuals share.[39] At other times, plurality is linked to a particular value, such as individual autonomy or community self-determination.[40] Others argue for plurality as a type of check or balance on the use of public power, in which one level of law can keep other levels in check.[41]

Arguments on the other side challenge the consistency of plurality with the formal and substantive versions of the rule of law. The formal objection is concerned with the ability of law to guide conduct in a way that treats subjects

---

[37] Paul Schiff Berman, 'The New Legal Pluralism' (2009) 5 *Annual Review of Law and Social Science* 225.
[38] See, eg Nico Krisch, *Beyond Constitutionalism: The Pluralist Structure of Postnational Law* (1st edn, Oxford University Press, 2010).
[39] Michael Rosenfeld, 'Rethinking Constitutional Ordering in an Era of Legal and Ideological Pluralism' (2008) 6 *International Journal of Constitutional Law* 415.
[40] Edward McWhinney, 'Self-Determination of Peoples and Plural-Ethnic States' (2002) 294 *Recueil des Cours—Academie de Droit International* 167.
[41] Robert M Cover, 'Nomos and Narrative' (1983) 97 *Harvard Law Review* 4.

with respect, by meeting the formal requirements of the rule of law which enable subjects to plan their lives around clear, consistent, and coherent rules. The substantive objection is concerned with any of a range of substantive principles. One candidate is the principle of integrity, which is thought to be threatened by the overlap, conflict, or even simple diversity of different legal orders, and the resulting confused or inconsistent content and application of laws.[42] The value of integrity can also be attached to a belief in the law's value as a clear, hierarchically organized dispute-resolution system, which is an artificially blunt but necessary instrument given the plurality of moral authority; ie law offers a way to adjudicate between competing moral claims. Another substantive worry concerns the principle of equality, and the need to ensure that a plurality of legal orders does not mean that some members of a community are worse off than others because of their subjection to different rules. For instance, Waldron has argued that the principles associated with the rule of law 'are actually quite hostile to pluralism'.[43] These principles:

> regard it as a matter of concern and dismay when people are subject to disparate and incompatible legal demands, vulnerable to the cross-cutting administrative, judicial and enforcement efforts of rival groups of 'official[s]', and dealt with unequally on the basis of disparate norms and procedures that make a mockery of generality, legal equality, and the idea that like cases should be treated alike.

Often, the contest over these substantive and formal values is framed as a contest between singularity or centrality of legal orders, on the one hand, and plurality, on the other. Yet that framing is misleading, for neither monist nor pluralist arrangements are necessarily better at serving their supposedly respective values.[44] Pluralist arrangements might in fact be stable, certain, and predictable, yet fail to really give effect to values of pluralism or self-determination or, worse, magnify the risk of oppression. On the other hand, monist arrangements might be changeable, incoherent, or unevenly applied, and so lack the virtues associated with the rule of law, even while having content that supports political pluralism or self-determination in forms that are more successful than simply having separate legal systems.

The response to Waldron's worry—that under a plurality of orders, like cases may not be treated alike—is not the obvious retort that there is sometimes good reason to treat like cases differently, because the real concern is the case where not only is there no good reason to treat like cases differently, but doing so is

---

[42] Pavlos Eleftheriadis, 'Pluralism and Integrity' (2010) 23 *Ratio Juris* 365.
[43] Jeremy Waldron, 'Legal Pluralism and the Contrast between Hart's Jurisprudence and Fuller's', in Peter Cane (ed), *The Hart-Fuller Debate in the 21st Century* (Hart Publishing, 2010).
[44] Krisch, *Beyond Constitutionalism*.

actually contrary to reason. This concern directly targets the kind of plurality in which minority, ethnic, or religious communities have their own legal standards that are contrary to reason in a way that outweighs any value associated with that community's self-determination.[45] Yet this is no objection to plurality of law per se, rather an objection to legal standards that have such immoral content. The moral problem is not that some people are treated differently than their neighbours under different legal systems, but that some people are treated badly and such treatment should not be tolerated in the name of preserving pluralism.

An account of relative legal authority would reframe these debates by linking plurality with the normative account of legitimate authority. It shows that both the value and the danger of plurality are instrumental; tied to its success or failure in securing legitimate authority. Any values that plurality can carry are dependent upon whether pluralist arrangements can secure authority that is effective and also justified. Thus, plurality itself is justified only where the justification of authority requires or permits it. On this view, any pluralist arrangements which fail to serve their subjects due to inconsistencies or any other formal defect are not authoritative, but the defect is in their authority, not in plurality itself.

In a very important sense, therefore, the relative authority account can be distinguished from a normative case for pluralism. Pluralism is comfortable with or even supportive of unresolved conflicts and overlaps between legal orders, but the relative authority account makes it possible to work out if, and then when, one order should prevail over others. The justificatory conditions within the relative authority account will sometimes find that monist arrangements are preferable to pluralist ones, and sometimes generate monism out of pluralism by requiring authorities to coordinate themselves into hierarchies. None of this, however, is predetermined.

The theory of relative authority also makes it clear that such legal orders whose content is, independently, contrary to reason, cannot be contenders for sharing in legitimate authority. To have authority, they must be capable of meeting the conjunctive justification for authority, conditional upon appropriate interactions with other legal orders similarly qualified. Thus, a legal order that instantiates requirements contrary to reason is not legitimately authoritative, and even if its officials do cooperate or coordinate with authoritative legal

---

[45] This position is consistent with moral pluralism, although it rejects moral relativism. It rests upon a commitment to the universality of moral truth, alongside what Raz has called a 'new sensitivity to the facts which establish this moral truth': Joseph Raz, *Multiculturalism* (1998) 11 *Ratio Juris* 193, 195. It also allows that different reasons can apply to members of different communities, without giving up the objectivity of moral reasons.

orders, that interaction does not make them authoritative unless they actually remove those rules that are contrary to reason. In such contexts, there is no relative authority from the outset because there is only one legitimate authority in play. This has the effect of highlighting the true location of the value and danger of plurality, and demonstrating that concerns about the consistency of plurality with the rule of law are no greater than they would be for any singular legal order.

The theory of relative authority also indicates how any defects of plurality in securing the formal rule of law can be overcome. The requirements of relative authority impose a burden on legal actors in pluralist arrangements to cooperate or coordinate to achieve authority that can serve subjects and avoid the harms caused by instability, opacity, or unevenness. It is the responsibility of the legal authorities to avoid placing their joint or interactive subjects in situations of problematic practical conflict, uncertainty, or confusion over their legal rights and obligations. To succeed *qua* authorities, legal officials (on behalf of their systems) must be responsive to other systems with which they share subjects or domains of activity. If they are not, in respect of problems that require an authoritative resolution, the legal officials and the legal systems lack authority. Of course this is an aspirational goal; sometimes they will not be able to avoid some degree of contradiction or incoherence, just as independent authorities can fail in this regard. The stringency of the requirements of the relative authority condition should therefore be read to require that the purported authorities must always try to coordinate or cooperate on common problems, and, if they are generally successful in doing so, this is sufficient for them to share legitimate authority. Occasional failures can be tolerated up to the point at which they obscure the visibility of the shared authority for the subjects and/or remove its reliability, for if subjects cannot identify or trust that authority, they cannot be guided by it, and this in turn triggers the identification problem that plagued the independent justifications of authority. The importance of visibility also means that purported authorities must not only try to interact appropriately, they must be seen to try, so that the subject can rely on following one authority and trust that that authority will work out any contradictions which could otherwise cause conflicts for the subject.

Finally, the theory of relative authority establishes grounds for evaluating the interactions of legal officials with one another. Relative authorities which fail to realize their authority through cooperation or coordination can rightly be criticized. When they do engage in such relationships, that is cause for celebration. Imagine for a moment that there is a dispute between a Member State of the European Union and an EU institution involving questions of national and EU constitutional interpretation, which could be determined equally well by two procedurally-justified courts: one national court applying national law, and the Court of Justice of the European Union. (Here, the different courts are relative authorities.) Suppose that this same issue arises not just in one Member State, but in many, and suppose there is a governance reason to want a coordinated or cooperative settlement of these questions.[46] In that context, legal actors within those systems must either cooperate to enact a clearer demarcation of who should resolve the conflict of authority, or engage in the kind of dialogue that can, incrementally, arrive at coordinated or consistent results through devices of deference or consistent interpretation.

Interestingly, some practices of judicial notice of foreign law can also be seen as moves to realize relative authority. The role of foreign legal norms in judicial reasoning will often be driven by courts simply wishing to learn from each other's solutions, but sometimes a system's legal content will need to be aligned with foreign law in order to meet the substantive conditions of legitimate authority, including the relativity condition. We can use the relative authority theory as a tool for analysing when such alignments are required, not merely desirable, and as a way to respond to arguments that the practice of alignment is unprincipled.[47] Instead of searching for a theory about the authority or influence of foreign law, it offers a theory of the relative authority of laws and legal institutions, in relation to one another.

None of these practices are the subject of this study, but it should not be surprising that many legal officials are, on behalf of their systems, already engaged in realizing their legitimate authority in the way that is required by the relativity condition. After all, the account of relative authority is simply designed to explain—using the tools of legal philosophy and in a way that shows its importance for that field—the phenomenon of plurality that has become a staple feature of the contemporary practice of law. My account offers one piece of the explanation that a new 'pluralist' jurisprudence must give for the facts of overlapping and interactive legal systems; and one response to the challenge of integrating theories of legal pluralism into the jurisprudential canon. In so doing, it offers a step towards a pluralist theory of law.

---

[46] Many of the real cases that have come before the European Courts have this structure—they raise the same issues in different Member States, and there are reasons to want a consistent outcome. However, not all cases have this structure; not every point of conflict within the system must have a consistent resolution. Indeed, the EU system itself permits a margin of appreciation and divergence between members.

[47] See, eg Justice Scalia's dissent in *Roper v Simmons* 125 SCt 1183 (US, MO, 2005) and, for analysis, Jeremy Waldron, 'Foreign Law and the Modern Ius Gentium' (2005) 119 *Harvard Law Review* 129.

4. The Place of Relative Authority amid 'Pluralist Jurisprudence'

In Chapter 4 I indicated that jurisprudence has arrived relatively late to the pluralist party, and that analytical and normative analyses of plurality of law are only recently being taken seriously within the jurisprudential canon. This section, in brief, examines how the relative authority account might aid that process of integration, and how it interacts with other leading jurisprudential ideas about law's plurality. Although it cannot answer all the questions that a pluralist theory of law must address, the account of relative authority serves as a crucial building block for such a theory. It offers an explanation for law's normativity, in circumstances of plurality. What remains, then, is to consider the implications for, and content of, other aspects of a theory of law. If a theory of law must explain both law's institutional and normative character, then the relative authority account seems to do only half the job of a pluralist theory of law.

The task of explaining institutionality in a context of plurality of law is perhaps more complicated than offering an account of law's authority. Candidate explanations have come from Culver and Giudice, who emphasize that legality can reside in relationships between institutions, rather than being limited to separate institutions and their associated sets of sources of law; and Von Daniels' search for a transnational concept of law, which explores how linkages between systems weave legal systems together.[48] Both works use inter-institutionality/linkages between systems as a way to explain the institutional element of legality, but, in doing so, as Halpin has criticized, neither fully explores the implications for distinguishing legality from non-legality.[49] I cannot resolve that puzzle, or give it due attention here, but it is worth noting the nexus with the relative authority account's argument that law's normativity can also be explained through understanding and evaluating the connections between legal authorities. There are two possible results of the synergy between my work and these other relational/inter-institutional approaches. The first is that there may be a way to offer a coherent theory of law which uses relativity as the key to explaining both law's institutional and normative elements. The second, however, would see relativity become a pathology of a pluralist theory of law, which would be insufficiently clear or precise to do the juristic work that a concept of law needs to do. As Cotterrell

---

[48] Culver and Giudice, *Legality's Borders*; D Von Daniels, *The Concept of Law from a Transnational Perspective* (Ashgate Publishing Co, 2010), 163.
[49] Andrew Halpin, 'Conceptual Collisions' (2001) 2 *Jurisprudence* 507.

has cautioned, a concept of transnational legality should not simply accept some sociological jurists' comfort with legal pluralism and a plurality of concepts of law; instead, it should remain a juristic concept which nevertheless can 'adopt criteria of the legal that are sufficiently flexible to recognise many different forms of law in currently indeterminate but potentially developing relations with each other'.[50]

My suggestion here is that, of the many different elements of a theory of law with which pluralist jurisprudence must wrestle, the element of authority is perhaps most easily conceived as relational and/or relative. This leaves the way open for a robust juristic account of legality itself, while simply treating law's authority and/or its claimed authority as relative. It is then open for a theory of law to develop any other criteria for legality, or account of the grounds of law, which are consistent with law's claiming or having relative authority. Although the relative authority theory is offered here as an account of law's (claimed) moral authority, a resulting theory of law might draw upon positive or non-positive explanations. On the one hand, there are several reasons to think that a non-positivist explanation of plurality might be the most promising way forward. The first is that plurality of law generates significant discord among legal officials as to its significance. Importantly, this problem of disagreement is not, in Dworkin's terms, mere 'empirical' disagreement over what satisfies the criteria for legal validity. Instead, it seems to be a particularly complex theoretical or even ontological disagreement between those legal officials who insist that legal norms can only be authoritative within the particular system to which they attach, then treat their system as closed to the norms of other legal systems, and others who treat at least some legal norms as semi-independent, perhaps even inter-institutional or inter-systemic, or even having relative authority, and therefore applicable within their own systems. On the other hand, the practice of plurality of law seems to slot neatly into explanations of the social foundations of law upon which any positivist legal theory relies. The plurality of law, for instance, reflects coordinated, cooperative, or other forms of joint activity among officials across the boundaries of legal systems and between different levels of law.

Regardless of the direction a full pluralist theory of law might take, however, it remains the case that an account of law's relative authority does not, by itself, address the challenges of dealing with colliding legal regimes in practice.

---

[50] Cotterrell's own suggestion is that a notion of 'relative legal authority' could be linked to 'Degrees of legality': Cotterrell, 'Transnational Communities and the Concept of Law' (2008) 21 *Ratio Juris* 1, 15. Cotterrell's own work, however, emphasizes the connection between transnational communities and the concept of law, and puts that topic on the agenda for legal theory, rather than focusing upon an explanation of relative authority associated with degrees of legality.

As Cotterrell argues, a notion of relative authority linked with 'degrees of legality', 'will not solve jurisdictional disputes or conflicts over authority and legitimacy claims but it may offer a slowly emerging template in terms of which these can be judged'.[51] The relative authority template offers to do just that; providing a way of evaluating competing claims to authority, by looking through them to assess the authority with which they are invoked, and which they in turn can achieve. In this way I hope to add something to the existing detailed explanations of ways in which legal systems, orders, and doctrines respond to their own plurality, across fields of international, transnational, and constitutional law.

---

[51] Cotterrell, 'Transnational Communities and the Concept of Law', 15.

PART IV

RELATIVE AUTHORITY IN INTERNATIONAL, TRANSNATIONAL, (AND) CONSTITUTIONAL LAW

10
Relative Authority in Public International Law and Transnational Law

Part IV aims to show how the relative authority approach can be used to suggest new insights into the relationships between authorities that characterize international law, constitutional pluralism, transnational regulation, national constitutional practice, and indigenous-state relationships. These fields share common and interrelated interests in the limits of authority and its location or distribution, and seek to explain the presence of contending, overlapping, and interacting authorities. Their targets include relationships between states; relationships between EU institutions and members; relationships between international legal authorities (and states); relationships within federal or other forms of intra-state devolution of authority; and relationships between non-state or other transnational authorities. If these are seen as examples of overlapping or at least interactive authorities whose legitimacy depends upon their interaction, they can be evaluated to see if the relationships work to uphold the legitimacy of the participants. Relative authority is a tool enabling those evaluations to move beyond vague notions of comity, dialogue, or deference.

1. Relative Authority in Public International Law

Although it is now fashionable to explore the field of 'transnational' rather than international law when theorizing about the range of legal phenomena beyond state borders, some of the most interesting implications of relative authority concern the more traditional relationships between states and the international legal regimes to which they are subject. Relative authority illuminates three of the most intractable topics in international legal theory: (i) how to conceptualize international law and its key elements; (ii) how to assess the authority of international law; and, relatedly, (iii) how to explain and evaluate practices of dualism and monism in the relationship between state and international law. This chapter addresses each of these in turn, before considering what, if anything, is different about an analysis of transnational law.

The relative authority idea here is a modest but far-reaching addition to the existing literature on each of these questions. It is modest because international legal scholarship already displays a sophisticated and direct awareness of issues closely related to relative authority. This includes the wealth of literature on the fragmentation of the international system and resulting overlaps or conflicts between international regimes; on the constitutionalization of international law and/or the merits of constitutionalism in international law; on specific problems of inter-institutional relationships within the international legal system; and on international authorities relations with subjects. I do not mean to add relative authority as another contending vision of what the international legal sphere looks like, or another programme for how it should develop. Rather, relative authority exposes an idea which is persistent but either implicit or obscured in almost all of the leading contemporary international legal scholarship, and, for this reason, its implications are, I hope, far-reaching.

The relative authority theory generates three recurring themes for analysing international law. First, it offers a revised conception and justification of the very kind of authority that is under discussion in international legal theory, regardless of whether that authority is then subjected to a constitutionalist or pluralist analysis. Whether we think fragmentation or constitutionalization best characterizes international authority, that authority, I will argue, is best conceived as relative; and so too the conditions of its legitimacy.

The second contribution is potentially more potent, and more practical. Relative authority offers a tool for analysing and evaluating actual arrangements and relationships of legitimate authority within the international sphere. It offers a way to look beyond disputes about creeping jurisdictions and mandates of international regimes in order to question their actual authority; and to organize all the competing grounds for legitimacy with which they are typically associated.

Third, the relative authority account is relevant for conceptual and ontological debates over whether international law is properly considered law. These debates will not be subjected to lengthy discussion here, and the chapter will proceed as though the legal character of international law, its obligations, and its authorities, are well founded, but in the end it does not matter for my inquiry into the authority of international law, which is, after all, not an inquiry into legality in international law. However, the relative authority account does seem to make it easier to answer questions about the character of international law qua law affirmatively, because if authority is conceived as relative, then any argument that international law fails to claim supreme authority loses its bite.[1]

---

[1] This argument relies upon the discussion in Ch 9 of relative authority's jurisprudential implications, all of which remain important for analysing relative authority in international law.

If the arguments in Chapter 9 are convincing, and law can claim or have relative rather than supreme authority, then international law, as law, need only claim relative authority, and may only have relative authority.

These three broad and recurring contributions of the relative authority theory serve to frame the more specific contributions discussed in this chapter. For now, however, I will focus upon four conceptual difficulties troubling contemporary international legal theory.

2. Conceptualizing International Law

a. States as subjects and authorities

The first is the way in which to conceive of subjects and authorities in the international system. In the international order, states that are themselves purported authorities become subjects of purported international authorities constituted to sit over them, such as judicial, tribunal, or other rule-applying bodies. These juridical bodies, as well as the quasi-legislative, quasi-executive United Nations Security Council, all have powers to impose legal obligations upon those states subject to their jurisdiction (all states in the case of the Security Council).[2] If these arrangements turn out to reflect legitimate authority, and not just technical jurisdiction, then the state authorities are simultaneously subjects of the international system. This is confusing for an account of authority. Matters are further complicated by the fact that international institutional authorities are often collections of state representatives, including states that are subjects of those very institutions. This becomes even more confounding as a matter of legitimate authority, because the identity of subjects and authorities would seem to render impossible the role that authority is supposed to play for its subjects. Then, separately, there is the matter of relationships between international authorities and individuals who may be directly or indirectly subjects of international law. Direct subjection of individuals, such as occurs in international criminal law, is not conceptually problematic; but it becomes difficult to conceive of the relationship

---

[2] Indeed, all the seminal examples of international institutional authorities in international law are authorities over other authorities (mostly, but not exclusively, states), while the direct authority of international institutions over private or individual subjects is a more recent development. For a recent examination of the manner, form, and content of the public authority exercised by international institutions, as well as detailed essays examining particular authoritative regimes, see Armin von Bogdandy, 'General Principles of International Public Authority: Sketching a Research Field', in Armin von Bogdandy (ed), *The Exercise of Public Authority by International Institutions* (Springer, 2010).

between an individual whose state represents her and incurs obligations upon her behalf, and the international authority imposing those obligations.

To test whether (and where) there is authority in these relationships, conventional authority theory would first have to find a way to differentiate the office of authority from the office of the subject, to avoid conflating authority (as a normative power to change the reasons that apply to others) with autonomy (as the power to generate reasons for oneself). Otherwise, we would simply be dealing with autonomous states making certain promises or committing themselves to certain policies, without any notion of authority entering the picture.

Besson has one suggestion, arguing for an interpretation that there is 'unicity of subjects between the national and the international legal orders'.[3] Besson argues that if individuals are treated as the ultimate subjects of both international law and their states, then individual autonomy becomes the measure of the legitimacy of both international and national authorities. Following a broadly Razian conception, Besson argues that the different legal orders can then be compared by their service of these individuals' autonomy, relying upon a principle of subsidiarity so that the national level is only constrained when doing so would provide better protection for autonomy.[4]

Besson's is a highly persuasive account, yet there does seem to be a sense in which states may be subjects of international law, independently of the reasons that apply to their individual subjects. That is, states may be subjects of international law *qua authorities*, and this changes the character of their subjection as well as the reasons (and therefore the potential authorities) to which they are subject. When a state acts as an authority over individual subjects, and when that authority is grounded in an ability to coordinate subjects' activities or to provide a settlement between incommensurable reasons applying to those subjects, then the state itself is subject to reasons for action and reasons for decision quite different from those of an individual subject. Specifically, the state has reasons to settle disputes or choose among different, perhaps equal or incommensurable reasons, in order to provide the coordinative service that only it can provide. Sometimes, an international body will be in a position to help states (alone or in combination) to provide this service. More significantly, however, an international authority may help states to do things that subjects have no reason to do. States have reasons to place constraints upon their own powers in order to secure, for example, human rights or rule of law virtues. These are reasons that only apply to states, and if international bodies/

---

[3] Samantha Besson, 'The Authority of International Law—Lifting the State Veil' (2009) 31 *Sydney Law Review* 343, 374.
[4] Besson, 'The Authority of International Law', 373–374.

regimes/norms can help states satisfy those reasons, they will have authority. In these situations, although the international authority might be able to help states act in their subjects' best interests, it does not make analytic sense to link the international authority to the individual subject's conformity to reason. The reasons applying to the states qua authorities (and which may render them subjects of legitimate international authorities) are not all derivative of the reasons applying to the subjects.

This is a minor quibble, as many of the situations in which there is international authority will be able to be analysed through Besson's conception of the individual as the subject of both international and domestic authority. However, to capture those occasions in which the reasons come apart or are simply distinct, I think that the relative authority account, which treats states as (potential) subjects and authorities, but makes their authority relative to that of the international actors, may be a more useful way to characterize this complexity. Conceiving of the domains of states and international institutions as overlapping or interactive, in service of the same or interactive subjects, better explains the practices in which states are both subjects and creators of international institutional authorities while remaining authorities over their own subjects. It also better explains how international authorities can have authority over the subjects of the state despite not claiming an exclusive right to rule over them.[5] The various bodies are simply relative authorities whose legitimacy partly depends upon their interaction, and whose claims to authority are interdependent. In the case of states, legitimacy in part depends upon cooperating with, obeying, or otherwise acting in coordination with international authorities whenever those relationships are required in order to satisfy the relativity condition; and vice versa. On this model we do not need to, nor can we, identify a final, ultimate, or superior authority, because the authority of states and international institutions is not independent; it is relative.

Furthermore, the relative authority account offers insights for thinking about authorities and subjects that are not overlapping, but rather interactive. The difference between overlapping-domain relativity and interactive-domain relativity turns out to be important for how subjects and authorities are conceived. Unlike Besson's argument, which treats the individual as the ultimate subject of both levels of authorities (ie there is an overlap of domains, in my terminology), relative authority leaves room to say that an individual may be

---

[5] On the connection between international authorities and the ultimate subjects, see Besson, 'The Authority of International Law', 343. As Buchanan also notes, international legal institutions do not claim the right to rule exclusively: Allen Buchanan, 'The Legitimacy of International Law', in Samantha Besson and John Tasioulas (eds), *The Philosophy of International Law* (Oxford University Press, 2010), 84.

a non-subject of a particular international authority, yet that international authority must still work with the state of which the individual is a subject if their domains are interactive. Focusing on the interdependent character of authority, rather than the question of who is subject to which authority, enables the analysis to move on from the conceptual difficulty of separating subjects and authorities.

b. Sovereignty

A second and related conceptual revision concerns the idea of sovereignty. The relative authority account suggests that in circumstances of plurality, sovereignty should not be conceived as entailing ultimate authority, whatever else it entails. If sovereignty is instead thought to entail relative authority, then sovereign states, by themselves, will very frequently have to cooperate with, tolerate, or even subject themselves to other authorities if they are to both serve their subjects and respect the standing of these other authorities. This should have significant implications for debates about the nature of post-national sovereignty.

However, the relative authority account does not challenge the prospect that sovereignty may have an independent value separate from its relative authority component. For instance, it remains open that there may be some expressive, affiliative, or other identity-protective element of sovereignty, which may be valuable quite apart from the location of authority. There may be reasons to respect sovereignty even when it is inconsistent with legitimate international legal authority.[6] This is particularly likely whenever sovereignty is understood as 'popular sovereignty', namely a power that resides ultimately in the people of the sovereign state. Notably, however, ultimate popular sovereignty remains compatible with any state, which exercises that sovereignty on behalf of its polity, having only relative legitimate authority, because the conditions of that legitimate authority remain ultimately responsive to the reasons that apply to its subjects—the people. Furthermore, the separation of justifications for sovereignty and legitimate authority cannot be total, as any reasons to promote any identity-based sovereignty, or to by-pass it in favour of cosmopolitanism, will be part of the landscape of reasons that go into the substantive part of the test for the legitimacy of any authority seeking to enact sovereignty-promoting or restricting policies.

---

[6] On the inconsistency of sovereignty and international legal authority, see Besson, 'The Authority of International Law' 343, 343.

c. International law's fragmentation/constitutionalization

A third key re-conception involves the interrelationships of norms or norm-regimes in the international system. As outlined in Chapter 4, existing work on inter-regime relationships in international law, which divides into constitutionalist and pluralist camps, treats independent regimes and their norms as though they have independent authority. The relative authority account instead conceives that although these institutions might be functionally distinct, separately constituted, and independently authorized by their subjects, the legitimacy of their authority is interdependent and conditional upon their justified interrelationships. This has significant implications not only for the question of how to deal with conflicts between regimes, which I examine in the following section, but also for how we conceive of the international legal landscape. It shows that it does not matter whether international law is treated as a system or as a series of discrete regimes from which scholars, practitioners, and law-users can cherry-pick rules and institutions. If we treat all these subject-specific regimes as having interdependent, relative legitimate authority, we are effectively treating them as inextricably linked even across different subject areas. On this conception, for instance, although the World Trade Organization (WTO) and the World Health Organization (WHO) are constitutionally, functionally, and institutionally separate, they are interdependently legitimate (or not, as the case may be). This approach thus reveals the common element between different types of regime interactions, some of which involve single institutions applying norms from different subject areas; others which involve multiple institutions applying a single shared norm; or others which see the same legal or policy issue being addressed by multiple institutions across different regimes, sometimes with different results.[7]

d. Legitimacy

Finally, the relative authority account offers a way in which to conceive of legitimacy, which enables one concept of legitimacy to travel between domestic and international law without altering its content. This has the advantage of removing the need for a water-tight demarcation between international and domestic law (to say nothing of the more murky areas of transnational

---

[7] For a discussion of types of regime interaction, see Jeffrey L Dunoff, 'A New Approach to Regime Interaction', in Margaret A Young (ed), *Regime Interaction in International Law: Facing Fragmentation* (Cambridge University Press, 2012); and for a comprehensive analysis of interaction, including empirical analysis of interactions, see S Oberthür and T Gehring, *Managing Institutional Complexity: Regime Interplay and Global Environmental Change* (MIT Press, 2011), 83.

law that are simultaneously neither domestic nor international while retaining elements of both). A concept of legitimacy that can be applied regardless of the level or character of a legal system is particularly important in light of the basic premise of this project, namely that legal systems, regimes, and purported authorities are in overlap or deep interaction and have divergent procedural and/or substantive qualities.[8] In that pluralistic context, there is little hope of assessing respective legitimacy. The best hope is, I think, through assessing relative legitimacy.

3. The Relative Authority of International Law

Perhaps the most significant implication of the relative authority account is, unsurprisingly, its ramifications for testing the legitimate authority of international law. In my account, the justifications for domestic, regional, and international legal authority are simultaneously substantive, procedural, and relative. This has two key implications for the authority of international law. First, it means that state consent, although insufficient alone to establish legitimate authority, remains part of the justification as one procedurally valuable input into the overall equation, particularly when that consent is supported by valuable democratic processes internal to the state. Non-consent, however, does not bar an institution from having authority if there is sufficient justification elsewhere, either on the substantive side or the procedural; or through the relativity condition. The second key implication of the relative authority account is that it means that any one institution, at any level of law, can only be authoritative when it is appropriately related to others with which it intersects or overlaps.

a. The significance of consent

The orthodox account of international law's authority has it resting upon consent; treaties are explained as express contracts between states, and customary international law is thought to rest upon an implied consent with an opt-out mechanism through persistent objection. Across the range of law-making institutions, including international organizations, regimes, and the institutions of treaty and customary law, state consent is a necessary condition for the existence of a legal obligation.[9] In many cases, the international institution

---

[8] For similar and further arguments on the importance of a single concept of legitimacy see Besson, 'The Authority of International Law'.
[9] This list of international institutions matches Buchanan's characterization, which broadly describes such international law-making institutions as 'a persisting pattern of organized, rule-governed, coordinated behaviour': Buchanan, 'The Legitimacy of International Law', 80.

is not really the law-maker at all; rather, law-making authority can only be understood as resting in the states which are party to the institution and which consent to the precise laws that are enacted. A consent basis for international law makes sense if states are regarded as ultimate authorities with supreme (sovereign) autonomy, and thus immune from any legal obligations that they have not chosen. However, as has now become uncontroversial, consent cannot explain the binding character of *jus cogens* or *obligations erga omnes*, while consent's role in the authority of customary international law also turns out to be difficult to explain. It is still possible to hold on to a consent-based account of international legal authority, but this requires minimizing (or even denying) the significance of *jus cogens* norms and/or distinguishing between the authority of different sources of international law, so that some are consent-based and others are not.[10] That strategy, however, makes it difficult to see consent itself as having any special value.

Once again, however, it is important to reiterate the distinction between a descriptive account of where legal authority, or law-making authority, lies in the international system, and a justification of the legitimate authority to which it lays claim. My question is not whether there can be a legal obligation without consent; it is what can justify legitimate authority in international law. Consent in international law is vulnerable to the weight of jurisprudential arguments which suggest that consent itself is insufficient to provide a normative foundation for law's authority.[11] Any moral authority that international law has cannot simply derive from the consent of the states which make it.

Besson's contribution to a non-consent-based account of the authority of international law again goes a long way towards a persuasive account of international authority in circumstances of plurality, via its focus upon the individual as the subject of both national and international authorities, and its singular conception of their legitimacy. When it comes to relationships between authorities, however, the account relies upon a subsidiarity principle which risks running roughshod over the procedural element of the conjunctive justification; and a conception of legitimacy which still treats authorities as though they are independent in service of their subjects, rather than interdependent. Besson specifically suggests that in a pluralist context, where competing claims to legitimacy are made in respect of the same subjects, there are 'necessary connections among the justifications for the legitimacy of domestic, regional

---

[10] See, eg Matthew Lister, 'The Legitimating Role of Consent in International Law' (2011) 11 *Chicago Journal of International Law* 663, adopting both strategies.

[11] For a full account of the problems with using consent as a foundation for the authority of international law, see Besson, 'The Authority of International Law'.

and international law'.[12] I think that we need to spell out exactly what those necessary connections are, and that, when we do, we see that they are interdependencies.

Both the significance of consent/non-consent and the question of appropriate inter-authority relationships can best be considered through testing potentially authoritative international institutions and norms. One of the richest sources of examples is the field of international environmental law, which features a complex matrix of governance organizations (both governmental and non-governmental), treaties, and customary rules, as well as a complex relationship with the institutions of international trade law. Here, I do not want to examine all the substantive and procedural reasons that go into the conjunctive justification for the authority of various international environmental regimes. For now, my interest is in their relativity and the way in which the relativity condition alters the test for their legitimate authority. So, for purposes of examining the relativity condition, I will assume that a particular environmental regime (such as the Framework Convention on Climate Change and the Kyoto Protocol, the International Tribunal for the Law of the Sea, the International Seabed Authority, or any of the myriad specialized agencies, multilateral or bilateral treaties, or customary environmental laws) better enables states subjects to comply with reasons to protect the environment (through reduction of carbon emissions, minimizing pollution, protecting resources, etc) compared with leaving them to their own devices.[13] This should be instinctively plausible, given the classic coordination problems involved in meeting environmental goals, coupled with the fact that environmental problems very often have a transboundary and/or global character, making it difficult for individual states to act effectively by themselves. Under those circumstances, a regime will satisfy the substantive elements of the conjunctive justification test: there is both an outweighing reason to have authority rather than private action, and following authority will better enable subjects to conform to reason. The regime is thus substantially justified, but does it have standing? If a state has consented to be part of a regime, and if that consent is representative of a reasonably liberal internal political system and can therefore be taken to carry some value, then that regime will have the standing of authority. The interesting question is whether there are other, non-consent

---

[12] Besson, 'The Authority of International Law', 380.
[13] This is clearly going to be controversial in many cases: eg some non-Kyoto states claim that their own independent reduction systems are better and more effective than those established by the Treaty. A full analysis of any regime's authority would require a much more detailed assessment of all the competing arguments about its substantive merits and procedural propriety. The point here is to illustrate how that analysis would work, rather than to conclude upon its results.

procedures that can also confer the standing of authority on an international environmental regime.

One candidate might be the inclusion, in the law-making process, of direct participation from non-governmental actors, both private individuals and industry representatives. For instance, imagine that a particular state has not committed itself to (eg) a regime for reducing carbon emissions, but citizens of that state have been active as NGO participants in the formation and/or ongoing evolution of that regime. If we accept that the standing of authority can be conferred upon any international regime by any potential subjects, not just states, then the direct and substantial participation of individuals should be sufficient to confer the standing of authority on an international regime. Other potentially valuable procedures might include indirect consent, for example a regime's subjection to review or supervision from an authority which is itself participatory or consent-based.

The most common process conferring standing, however, is probably the process of customary norm formation. If we follow Postema in regarding custom as the discursive normative practice of a particular community, in which participants (mostly, but not only, states) engage in both giving and acting upon reasons as they go about their multiple interactions, in full awareness of the interdependency of their goals and interests, then in my terms that very process of engagement should be sufficient to satisfy the procedural element of the pluralist justification.[14]

This potential for international authority, even in the face of non-consent, offers a way to explain the authority of *jus cogens* norms. *Jus cogens*, typically understood as peremptory norms from which no derogation is permitted, and which apply regardless of a state's consent to them, can be re-imagined here as norms that are authoritative according to the relative authority test. These are norms which, on the balance of both reasons for action and reasons for decision, require a relationship of subjection on the part of states. They are norms that subjects are supposed to coordinate around because they protect those most important substantive reasons. They are norms about matters so important that they should not be entrusted to horizontal, dialogical coordination among states, or to margins of appreciation, or to conflicting practices; rather, the appropriate relationship is one of hierarchical authority—the norm is authoritative over all subjects, and this authority exists regardless of consent. One implication of understanding *jus cogens* through a relative authority

---

[14] For Postema's full account, see GJ Postema, 'Custom in International Law: A Normative Practice Account', in A Perreau-Saussine and JB Murphy (eds), *The Nature of Customary Law* (Cambridge University Press, 2007); G. J Postema, 'Custom, Practice, and the Law' (forthcoming, *Duke Law Review*, 2012).

analysis is that, on any matter of *jus cogens*, states (as a matter of their relative authority) should consent to any effective and procedurally proper regimes that are put in place to enforce *jus cogens*. This analysis also provides a justification for the use of universal jurisdiction to prosecute violations of *jus cogens*.

The core point from all of this is that the standing of authority can be conferred upon an international regime despite the non-consent of states; and these states may still end up subject to that authority if it passes the other elements of the conjunctive justification test. However, there are a number of hurdles to finding that a purported international authority has procedural standing, quite apart from the issue of consent. The procedural propriety (or otherwise) of international institutional authorities is widely debated and remains troubling for any conception of international public authority. The attempt to develop principles for global administration to enhance such procedural standing—through greater transparency, tighter accountability, better participation, and more concrete review or appeal practices—will be pivotal for bolstering the legitimacy of international authority.[15] Bearing in mind, however, that many domestic authorities are also imperfect on these measures, a defect in this area is to be expected, and indeed the procedural defects of one level of relative authority may be ameliorated if there are procedural strengths in another authority with which it appropriately interacts. Furthermore, if the substantive value attaching to international authority is particularly strong, then a state cannot legitimately isolate itself over a problem (such as climate change or shared resource protection), which would be best solved by coordination among states and with other international or domestic public and private actors.[16] The reverse is also true. A particularly strong substantive justification for a state's autonomy, or exemption from an international regime (for instance if an imposition of an environmental regime would generate critical problems for a nation's food supply), will be sufficient to render that state's authority relatively independent. A particularly strong substantive justification (favouring either level of authority) can make up for a procedural deficit and can establish authority—crucially, however, in my account this authority is relative authority.

It should be clear that the relative authority idea does not simply anoint international authorities in the hope that they might be able to coordinate states in pursuit of shared solutions to common problems. On the contrary,

---

[15] A Bogdandy, *The Exercise of Public Authority by International Institutions* (Cambridge University Press, 2010); Armin Bogdandy and Philipp Dann, 'International Composite Administration' (2008) 9 *German Law Journal* 2013; Benedict Kingsbury *et al.*, 'The Emergence of Global Administrative Law' (2005) 68 *Law of Contemporary Problems* 15.

[16] For a similar view, see Mattias Kumm, 'Democratic Constitutionalism', in Sujit Choudhry (ed), *The Migration of Constitutional Ideas* (Cambridge University Press, 2005).

international authority in general is constrained by its interaction or overlap with national and local authorities, and any particular international authority is also constrained by its overlaps and interactions with others. This is a long way from an account that is purely substantive and/or procedural, which treats authorities as independent, and which anoints a single or hierarchical authority as the best/most fair authority to deal with a problem.[17] It also does not depend upon adopting any presumptions about the authority of international law and/or the importance of subsidiarity.[18] Relative authority does not prejudge the respective strengths in the legitimacy of national, international, or other authorities—rather, the point is that their legitimacy is relative rather than respective.

b. Inter-authority relationships

According to the relative authority account, the authority of an international regime is relative to the authority of other interacting or overlapping authorities. These include consenting states, non-consenting states, and other international or transnational regimes engaged in overlapping activities. The relativity of the regime's authority requires that it engage in appropriate relationships with each of these other authorities. What is appropriate will depend upon circumstances, but there will be some common elements in each category of related authorities. The trickiest category is that of the non-consenting state. The interplay between substantive and procedural elements of the conjunctive justification can lead to a non-consenting state being nevertheless subject to an international authority, but for this to happen without simply running roughshod over any standing of the non-consenting state—conferred by its own subjects—the international regime and the state must work out some relationship to minimize that interference. One possibility might be a relationship that tolerates a margin of appreciation or even exemption from some legal obligations for the state, in relation to those aspects of the international regime which are most difficult for a state to commit to, provided this can be achieved without defeating the purpose, goals and substantive value of the regime itself. Another, less formal possibility might be a dialogical

---

[17] For a purely substantive, 'functional', and outcome-focused account of legitimacy in the global administrative law context, see MS Kuo, 'Between Fragmentation and Unity: The Uneasy Relationship between Global Administrative Law and Global Constitutionalism' (2008) 10 *San Diego International Law Journal* 447.

[18] See, eg Kumm's four moral concerns within a constitutionalist model of engagement between international and national law. In addition to procedural and outcome concerns, which are similar to my own, Kumm argues for a presumption of the authority of international law, and for the special importance of subsidiarity: Kumm, 'Democratic Constitutionalism'.

relationship that, over time, coordinates the activities of the state with that of the international regime, without overt establishment or enforcement of obligations. However the specific circumstances require, the responsibility is on all the authorities involved to manage the relationship appropriately. A non-consenting state cannot simply cast aside any responsibility for solving a shared problem or isolate itself from a collective regime (whether in the name of exceptionalism or otherwise).

In the case of consenting states, the relationship of moral authority sits parallel to the set of legal obligations to which those states have committed themselves. It does not alter the legal obligations themselves, but it adds a morally based reason for their existence and for their realization. It ensures that coordination is morally based and not simply legally organized. As Buchanan has suggested, such morally based coordination may be desirable for an institution's ability to sustain successful functioning when 'there are lapses in its ability to coerce and during periods when there is reason for some to doubt that it is indeed advantageous for all'.[19] As for the relationship between the authorities, their relativity means that each ought to operate as a kind of check or balance upon one another, and that they share responsibility for maintaining their relative legitimate authority. An international regime can lose its legitimate authority either by failing to provide its substantive benefits or by losing its standing. The latter might occur, for instance, if a regime becomes dominated by particular groups of like-minded states which exclude others from effectively participating in a regime's ongoing operation or development. For instance, so-called 'Green Room' and other meetings in which self-selecting delegates determine outcomes without the participation of representatives of all subjects can threaten the procedural propriety of an international organization. The former might occur if blocks or even individual states stall the activities of the regime by failing to join consensus when consensus is required, through withholding promised funds, or through failing to meet their legal obligations. When any of these failings occurs, the impact is upon the authority of both the international regime and the state authorities. As the relative authority account puts the onus upon these interacting authorities to ensure this does not happen, there are grounds to criticize those who let it or make it happen.

Finally, the category of interrelationships with other overlapping and interactive international regimes raises a special set of issues. If the domain of one international regime overlaps with another international regime (as can often occur between multiple international environmental regimes, given the interconnected nature of many environmental problems), then a minimum

---

[19] Buchanan, 'The Legitimacy of International Law', 81.

of toleration is required, and regimes will probably need to coordinate if not cooperate in order to best meet their substantive goals and/or to preserve their standing. If there is a risk of conflict that could defeat either regime's authority, then the best relationship might be one which compels both regimes into a dispute-resolution mechanism or even subjects them to a common superior authority, so that there is a procedure in place to manage these conflicts. The exact requirements of the relationship will also be generated by any defects in their respective procedural and substantive qualifications. For instance, where there are deficits in the standing conferred upon an international institution—eg the Security Council might be structurally too beholden to powerful state interests and as a result have weakened standing—then that institution will need to cooperate more closely with others which are authorities for those less powerful and/or have more valuable standing.

Implications are similar but more difficult in the case of interactive regimes, where the domains are not overlapping and subjects are not shared; rather, authorities are distinct but come into contact through the activities in which they or their subjects engage. In the case of environmental regimes, such interaction occurs most obviously with international economic regimes. Both are concerned with resources, but they are not often in agreement about whether or how those resources should be used or protected. The WTO regime, for instance, frequently interacts with local or international environmental regimes, and the WTO's dispute-settlement system is rich in examples of disputes which are, at least at face value, contests between regimes for environmental protection, and regimes for free market access.[20] My question asks about the appropriate relationships for the WTO (or any other international trading regime), with the environmental regimes with which it interacts.

In the case of the WTO, the institutionalization of the dispute-settlement process creates the opportunity for conflicts between regimes to be weighed up and the balance of reasons assessed. If that occurs, then there is likely to be sufficient toleration (for the interactive regime) to establish legitimate relative authority—although, again, this will depend on the precise circumstances. However, the legal character of this process means that assessment is limited to what, as a matter of law, can be assessed. In a strictly legal sense, there will not always be room for a WTO dispute or appellate body to take into account

---

[20] See GATT Dispute Settlement Panel Report, *United States—Restriction on Imports on Tuna*, GATT Doc DS21/R, 16 August 1991 (not adopted), GATT BISD (39th Supp) 155 (1993); GATT Dispute Settlement Panel Report, *United States—Restrictions on Imports of Tuna*, GATT Doc DS 29/R, 16 June 1994, reprinted in (1994) 33 *ILM* 839; WTO Report of the Appellate Body, *United States—Import Prohibition of Certain Shrimp and Shrimp Products*, WT/DS58/AB/R, 12 October 1998, reprinted in (1999) 38 *ILM* 118. For a full account of the trade-environment nexus, see, eg DC Esty, 'Bridging the Trade-Environment Divide' (2001) 15 *The Journal of Economic Perspectives* 113.

substantive reasons that might be only weakly supported in the law, or which come from another regime and are thought to be outside the WTO's legal jurisdiction. Those bodies are required to determine a legal outcome from the available law, yet as any student of adjudication practice and theory realizes, there is frequently room for moral judgments to play a deciding role between balanced (and sometimes even imbalanced) legal reasons. There is therefore a potential mechanism for coordination between trade and environmental norms, through legal dispute-resolution, in order to generate legitimate relative authority.

Using the relative authority account also enables a test for the authority of particular norms that are in conflict. So, when there is conflict between two subject-specific regimes both seeking to govern a particular practice overlapping the two, or between an international norm and a national/local norm, the question is not which regime should win out, or even which is the best regime to govern that conflict; rather, it is: what is the authoritative norm to be applied? We then get an answer to this by asking which norm can meet the conjunctive justification and the relativity condition. There is an obvious tension, however, in that any particular regime is likely to be most concerned (and will have a responsibility) to apply and prioritize its own norms. Legitimate relative authority does not require that interactive regimes sacrifice their own norms, if these are part of what makes it a contender for legitimate relative authority. Instead, if there is a genuine conflict between norms that are equally important to their respective regimes, the required relationship may simply be one of toleration for that difference; and in that case both norms are authoritative. Sometimes one may prevail, sometimes another.[21] If, however, there is a strong governance reason to coordinate, then those authorities applying the norms from each regime have a responsibility to either directly or dialogically shift the norms closer together or at least generate harmony between them.

The foregoing sketches the structure of the required relationships between international legal regimes and those bodies/norms/regimes with which they share relative authority. Even without seeing all the details of particular instances of these relationships, it is evident that this view of inter-authority relationships would have significant implications for the way in which courts, in particular, regard international legal authority.

---

[21] This is precisely the sort of pluralism that Eleftheriadis criticizes in Pavlos Eleftheriadis, 'Pluralism and Integrity' (2010) 23 *Ratio Juris* 365.

4. Monism and Dualism about the Relationship between International Law and Domestic Law

Orthodox descriptions of the relationship between international and domestic legal systems typically divide into monist approaches, in which international law is considered part of domestic law, and dualist approaches, in which the systems are considered separate so that international law only has authority if it is incorporated or otherwise authorized by state law. That depiction is somewhat oversimplified, and on a more subtle analysis, it appears that any approach which permits the domestic system to determine the relationship that exists between it and the international system is inescapably dualist.[22] As Kumm notes, however, the search for a sound theoretical model to explain the growing body of doctrinal practices in which international law is incorporated or applied domestically has largely taken a backseat in favour of more pragmatic theorizing.[23]

The relative authority account might suggest a new model that can be applied in order to determine the relative authority of international and domestic law, in relation to specific legal questions. That model is neither monist nor dualist. It does not give controlling or determinative status to the national level, nor does it conceive of the international and domestic legal systems as entirely distinct. Rather, it makes their authority interdependent and in the process provides a tool for evaluating any particular court's practice of international norm application.

The contribution of the relative authority theory in this area can be seen as a response to Kumm's call for a normative framework with which to guide analysis of the international law/national law relationship. Kumm himself argues that the justification for national courts' engagements with that law depends upon weighing up four moral concerns. First is the formal legitimacy of international law (Kumm argues for a prima facie duty to obey international law); second is jurisdictional legitimacy (in which Kumm gives special weight to a principle of subsidiarity); third is procedural legitimacy (including

---

[22] As Kumm argues, 'the very idea that the national constitution is decisive for generating the doctrines that structure the relationship between national and international law is dualist. Law is part of the law of the land': Kumm, 'Democratic Constitutionalism', 258. A great deal of literature seeks to make sense of the interaction of international and domestic law, exploring either or both questions about the legitimacy of that interaction, and its theoretical or doctrinal explanation. For leading analyses, see Karen Knop, 'Here and There: International Law in Domestic Courts' (1999) 32 *NYU Journal of International Law and Policy* 501; Eyal Benvenisti and George Downs, 'National Courts, Domestic Democracy and the Evolution of International Law' (2009) 20 *European Journal of International Law* 59.

[23] Kumm, 'Democratic Constitutionalism', 257.

participation and accountability); and fourth is substantive legitimacy (or, to allow space for reasonable disagreement, achieving substantively reasonable outcomes). Kumm uses these in the place of constitutionalist principles, to be applied in order to determine how national courts ought to engage with international law.[24]

Like my relative authority account, Kumm's framework seeks to balance procedural and substantive concerns, and finds that imperfections in one element can be made up for in one of the others. Similarly, Kumm also requires the authorities (in this case, courts) to engage in appropriate practices of applying or otherwise incorporating international law, where the balance of reasons requires it. However, Kumm's account conceives of this assessment of reasons as a way to generate a constitutionalist model to guide and constrain the use of international law in domestic courts. He presumes the authority of international law, which is the very point that the relative authority theory calls into question. Furthermore, the legitimacy at stake in Kumm's account is constitutional legitimacy, rather than legitimate authority. In that respect Kumm's approach invites the raft of concerns that attach to constitutionalist models, not least of which are the concerns generated by pluralism and the possibility of overlaps and interactions between constitutional orders which seem to undercut the very values that constitutional models can offer.

In contrast, the relative authority idea is smaller, for its focus is upon a specific power and the conditions of its legitimacy, rather than the broader idea of legitimacy per se. It nevertheless allows for evaluation of the authority of international law without being committed to offering a constitutionalist model to govern its relationship with national law. Just as relative authority is neither a monist nor dualist theory, neither is it pluralist or constitutionalist.

5. The Relative Authority of Transnational Law

Many of the same insights can apply to transnational law more broadly, which, for all its complexity, theoretical difficulty, and normative controversy, is also often simply used by legal actors as though it has relative authority. The processes of 'uploading' and 'downloading' law between different international, national, supra-national, or non-national locations might be seen to reflect the relative authority that these different levels of law can have, in their relations with one another.[25]

---

[24] Kumm, 'Democratic Constitutionalism', 261–273.
[25] Harold Hongju Koh, 'Why Transnational Law Matters' (2005) 24 *Penn St International Law Review* 745, 745–746.

The question, however, is whether specific transnational legal phenomena can be contenders for relative authority. The biggest challenge here is that many transnational legal (or purportedly legal) phenomena do not clearly have the kind of public authority that my account conceives as relative. Some are voluntary codes that are adopted by corporations, industries, or other groups of private actors in order to serve their own interests (eg through improved efficiency or contractual certainty) rather than to serve subjects in the way that public authority is required to do. They are organized, managed, and sustained by non-state bodies, and the governing institutions they create are governors of private actors such as financial institutions or corporations. How, in that context, are we sensibly to conceive of these agents as 'subjects' of an authority rather than simply interest groups which have organized their own 'clubroom' with its own house rules?

One answer is simply to say that these authorities (such as they exist) are private authorities just like those of private societies anywhere, and they do not correspond to public authorities with a community of subjects. Then, regardless of whether or not those transnational phenomena are properly legal, they are not contenders for legitimate relative authority because they do not generate overlapping or interactive subjects in the way that public authorities do. They may obligate and bind those who sign up to them, and in this sense a legal characterization might be appropriate in the same way that a domestic contract is a legal instrument; but this is not sufficient to bring those practices themselves into contention for having relative public authority.

Another answer is to reject a sharp private-public distinction and place a particular transnational legal phenomenon (such as *lex mercatoria*) somewhere in between, or even in both models. From a functional perspective, many norms and regimes that are privately constituted end up filling very public regulatory tasks. From a relational perspective, they might also end up having very close relationships with public institutions and share or even independently provide public services.

For my purposes here, the characterization is not critical, for, even if there are forms of strictly private transnational authority, which on their own do not feature overlapping or interactive subjects so as to trigger relative authority, these can still interact with uncontroversially public authorities in ways that will generate relativity. That is, states or international or sub-national public authorities might be required to recognize, coordinate, or simply tolerate the rules and obligations that such private authorities generate for their members. Here, the analysis is no different, in structure, from the analysis applying to the relative authority of public authorities. The content of reasons, however, will differ, to include the value of having such voluntary, private, or quasi-private authority, in cooperation or even in conflict with the public authority or authorities.[26] The matter of standing might also be complex, if the procedures that bring about these private or quasi-private or hybrid authorities are not sufficiently fair as to be valuable, or not sufficiently valuable as to confer standing akin to that of a public authority. The substantive arguments may then go in either direction, depending upon context. For instance, in matters concerning corporate governance and the status or obligations of multinational corporations operating within a particular state, there will be some matters (such as tax obligations, environmental or labour standards etc) over which the state may have independent legitimate authority, but others (such as organizational structuring and operations, or transnational/foreign contracts) that the state may have no authority to manage but which might be appropriately subject to the authority of a transnational regulatory body or set of rules. Other areas will be more contested; for instance, in the realm of dispute-resolution or matters of transnational liability, there may be fairly evenly divided arguments for the authority of local or transnational mechanisms. If so, there will be relative authority and the implications of relativity are the same as they are for any finely balanced relative authorities—the authorities must cooperate or coordinate in order to achieve legitimacy.

---

[26] On the legitimacy of private regulatory governance, for instance, see Zumbansen, 'Transnational Private Regulatory Governance'; A Claire Cutler, *Private Power and Global Authority* (Cambridge University Press, 2003); and, on the private-public nexus, or interrelationship, see Rodney Bruce Hall and Thomas J Biersteker, 'Theorizing Private Authority: The Emergence of Private Authority in the International System', in *The Emergence of Private Authority in Global Governance* (Cambridge University Press, 2002).

11

Understanding Europe: From Constitutional Pluralism To Relative Authority

In Chapter 4 I examined existing contributions to theories of European constitutional pluralism and suggested that although they emphasize the centrality of plurality and relationships between authorities for the tasks of constitutional theory, they do not fully explain what authority is or the implications of non-exclusive, overlapping, sub-ultimate, or shared authority. Advocates of constitutional pluralism in Europe instead typically do one or both of two things: first, they argue that constitutional pluralism provides the most accurate explanation (including an accurate description) of the manner in which Members and the European Union itself all have *constitutional* authority; second, they argue that such pluralism is not only the best way to understand what is actually going on, but that it is also normatively desirable.[1]

The idea of constitutional pluralism has been described as a 'third way' between hierarchical integration and radical pluralism.[2] Yet within the rich constitutional pluralist literature, one underexplored issue is the character of the authority being discussed. In some works, constitutional pluralism is expressly conceived as the conflict of (claims to) final or ultimate authority.[3] In other works, constitutional pluralism is framed as a response to the impossibility of final or ultimate authority; indeed, the acceptance of that impossibility is what makes constitutional pluralism the leading explanation for prevailing practice. Sometimes, the authority that is being contested is thought to be strictly constitutional in character—that is, it is the authority arising from the constitutions rather than the authority upon which the constitutions are themselves grounded. Sometimes the reverse seems to be the case.

---

[1] Miguel Maduro, 'Three Claims of Constitutional Pluralism', in Matej Avbelj and Jan Komárek (eds), *Constitutional Pluralism in the European Union and Beyond* (Oxford University Press, 2012), 70, discussing 'respective claims of final authority', illustrates that the empirical claim need not lead to the normative claim, and that the normative claim itself can be made to different degrees. Maduro himself favours a stronger normative claim than many of his fellow advocates of constitutional pluralism.

[2] Mattias Kumm, 'Conflicts of Authority' (unpublished, 2012) (draft paper on file with author).

[3] Maduro, 'Three Claims of Constitutional Pluralism'.

This all leads me to think that a key contribution of the relative authority account might be to tidy up the understanding of authority and see if all this work is indeed talking about the same thing. In this chapter, section 1 asks what exactly is the authority at issue in all the talk about constitutional pluralism? More importantly, however, this section examines whether the authority at issue might be relative, not final or ultimate, authority. Section 2 offers a relative authority framework as a 'fourth way' for explaining authority, which is not constitutionalist, pluralist, or 'constitutional pluralist'. In doing so, it engages directly with the work of Kumm, whose own approach is seemingly closest to one of relative authority. Finally, in section 3 I place relative authority head to head with constitutional pluralism to consider whether relative authority can outdo the empirical and normative claims that Maduro has ascribed to constitutional pluralism.

1. Characterizing Authority: Plurality or Constitutionality?

Constitutionalism and pluralism offer two approaches for explaining and justifying arrangements of authority in European practice. Maduro neatly makes the case for constitutional pluralism as both a tool for explaining constitutional practice and a normative response to that practice. Maduro's starting point is that, in a post-national context, it no longer makes much sense, nor offers much insight, to conceive of unified political spaces subject to an ultimate source of political authority. In his words, such a conception would require:[4]

artificially closing and insulating national polities under a self-referential notion of political authority that extends so far as the legal hierarchy and claim of supremacy of the constitutional order itself claims to extend. But this is a purely circular reasoning. More importantly, trust in political integrity will gradually erode as the purported coherence and universality of any particular legal order is increasingly challenged, in practice, by its interaction with other legal orders.

Maduro sees constitutional pluralism as a necessary adaptation to the post-national character of authority, which can make sense of and indeed justify the presence of competing claims to final authority. Along with others, ranging from Walker to Kumm, Besson, Cruz, and Krisch, Maduro's work acknowledges that, in European practice at least, there is something basically pluralistic about authority, which cannot be grounded upon a single constitution or other single legitimating ground. Instead, the challenges are to explain how the authority

[4] Maduro, 'Three Claims of Constitutional Pluralism', 82.

of different constitutional orders interacts; when (if ever) one might trump another; and/or how any resulting conflicts might be managed.

As Maduro has noted, an interest in constitutional pluralism typically begins from the need to address the presence of conflicts between different locations of constitutional authority, and the core insights of constitutional pluralism are typically focused on ways to tolerate and normalize such conflicts.[5] Conflicts are the bread and butter of the field, and can be illustrated with reference to a number of cases in the constitutional practice of the European Union and its Member States. These include conflicts over constitutional rights,[6] interpretive and allocatory authority,[7] and conflicts over the nature of distinct legal obligations or the relationships between legal orders.[8] The focus of the constitutional pluralists upon conflicts also takes us, once again, to the observation that in the presence of a constitutional conflict, there are orthodox responses, at different ends of the constitutional pluralist spectrum. One is the constitutionalist response, which seeks a way to render one of the constitutional claims superior to the other. The other is the pluralist response, which is happy to live with conflict and accept the benefits plurality might offer while tolerating its drawbacks.

A constitutionalist framework offers different ways to test for legitimate constitutional authority. One way is to trace the legitimacy of the constitution itself back through the polities or communities to which constitutions attach. This search for a 'source' of constitutional legitimacy builds upon the ideas of political or popular constitutionalism—ie that 'the people, in community', can authorize a particular constitution to claim supremacy over the others, and indeed give legitimacy to that claimed supremacy. This core idea can also be developed with reference to a specific principle or set of principles, which are thought to be critical for determining where legitimacy lies. For instance, the idea that democratic credentials matter to the legitimacy of a polity's constitutional order makes procedural, participatory principles key to the question of legitimate authority. In the EU context, such an approach generates debate over whether/how far an EU constitutional claim can be justified, given that the character of the EU polity is only 'potential' or 'emerging', in contrast to the more established (although still contested) character of the polities in respective Member States, given the imperfect democratic credentials of some EU institutions, and the overlap or

---

[5] Maduro, 'Three Claims of Constitutional Pluralism', 68.
[6] Compare BVerfGE 37, 271 (1974) ('*Solange I*'); and BVerfGE 73, 339 (1986) ('*Solange II*').
[7] Compare BVerfGE 89, 155 (1993) ('*Maastricht*') and BVerfGE 123, 267 (2009) ('*Lisbon*').
[8] See, eg Case 6/64 *Costa v Enel* [1964] ECR 585; Case 106/77 *Amministrazione delle Finanze dello Stat v Simmenthal* [1978] ECR 629; and Case C-402/05P *Yassin Abdullah Kadi v Council of the European Union and Commission of the European Communities*, 3 September 2008 ('*Kadi*').

multiplicity of the valuable identities of subjects who are both 'nationals' and also 'Europeans'.[9]

That multiplicity of identities and loyalties within and among polities in Europe grounds the strongest arguments for pluralism. Pluralism leaves open, and is comfortable with leaving open, conflicts of authority.[10] Yet that need not be read as a descent into disorder or chaos of conflicting claims interfering with one another. In Krisch's sophisticated pluralist argument, for instance, each system legitimately defines its own interactions with others, but subject to the substantive conditions that are necessary for each right of self-legislation to be consistent with the same right of others.[11] Yet even the richest pluralist arguments run out at the very point at which evaluations of those claims and relationships might be made, and this is the point at which the constitutionalist end of the constitutional pluralism spectrum seems once again attractive.

The constitutional pluralists who try to meet in the middle of the spectrum tend to see the pivotal connection between constitutional and pluralist approaches, and indeed national and European levels of authority, as being institutional,[12] principled,[13] pragmatic,[14] or even deviant.[15] They try to hold on to some aspect of both pluralist and constitutionalist ideas. It is at this point that, despite the wealth of important lessons to be learned from the constitutional pluralist literature, my relative account departs.

---

[9] On the idea of a European demos, or demoi, see JHH Weiler, 'Does Europe Need a Constitution? Demos, Telos and the German Maastricht Decision' (1995) 1 *European Law Journal* 219. A rich account of contending factors in legitimacy equations between European and national constitutional orders, and a survey of theorists advocating different factors, appears in Mattias Kumm, 'Jurisprudence of Constitutional Conflict: Constitutional Supremacy in Europe before and after the Constitutional Treaty' (2005) 11 *European Law Journal* 262.

[10] See the analysis and discussion of examples in Maduro, 'Three Claims of Constitutional Pluralism'.

[11] Nico Krisch, *Beyond Constitutionalism: The Pluralist Structure of Postnational Law* (1st edn, Oxford University Press, 2010), 99–103.

[12] See Maduro, 'Three Claims of Constitutional Pluralism', 74: 'different orders can be construed as normatively autonomous but also institutionally bound by the adherence of their respective actors to both legal orders'.

[13] See Mattias Kumm, 'Democratic Constitutionalism', in Sujit Choudhry (ed), *The Migration of Constitutional Ideas* (Cambridge University Press, 2005); and Maduro, 'Three Claims of Constitutional Pluralism'.

[14] Neil Walker, 'The Idea of Constitutional Pluralism' (2002) 65 *MLR* 317, 337. Walker suggests that relationships among pluralist orders can be managed with an appropriate 'ethic of political responsibility'.

[15] J Baquero Cruz, 'Legal Pluralism and Institutional Disobedience', in M Avbelj and J Komárek (eds), *Constitutional Pluralism in the European Union and Beyond* (Hart Publishing, 2012).

2. Relative Authority in Europe: A Fourth Way

The relative authority account does not purport to replace constitutional pluralism as a framework for analysis, insofar as constitutional pluralism is an analysis of the pluralism of constitutions rather than the plurality of authority. However, much of the leading constitutional pluralist scholarship invokes questions about the legitimate authority of interacting constitutions, and thus requires some account of legitimate authority from which to assess the interacting claims and practices of constitutional pluralism, quite apart from a constitutional pluralist theory.[16] The relative authority theory is offered here as a candidate for that role, and in that respect is in contention with constitutional pluralism. Relative authority offers a new tool for answering the question of where authority is located amid practices of constitutional pluralism; and it is a device that rejects the constitutional pluralists' premise that their task is to explain and evaluate conflicts of ultimate (or claims to ultimate) authority. Instead, it treats the authority at stake as relative authority, and the conditions of its legitimacy as dependent upon relationships between authorities at the EU and Member State levels.

The first departure from the constitutional pluralist framework is a denial that constitutions themselves settle the question of authority, or even that interpreting constitutions can settle that question. To reiterate arguments offered in the discussion in Chapter 5 of the Raz–Waldron debate, my position is that, although a constitution can, tautologically, determine *constitutional* authority, it cannot alone determine a constitution's legitimate authority. Even with an expansive notion of a de facto, 'small c' constitution, assessments of the legitimacy of constitutional rules themselves must still proceed with reference to some external standard. This is even more true in the context of conflicts of authority between, and not just within, constitutions. Just as one constitution cannot determine the legitimate authority of inter-constitutional relationships, two constitutions are even less helpful in determining legitimate authority in their inter-relationship. Instead, whenever there is conflict, but even where there is not, we should turn towards an assessment of legitimate authority, including legitimate relative authority, to work out the appropriate interrelationships between institutions at EU and Member State level, and including law-making, adjudicatory, and executive institutions.

---

[16] Maduro, 'Three Claims of Constitutional Pluralism', 69: 'any debate on how to solve or regulate constitutional conflicts of authority inherently involves a debate on the nature and legitimacy of the competing constitutional claims of final authority. As such, it always requires a broader understanding of the nature of European and national constitutions and their relationship with constitutionalism in general'.

The relative authority thesis also takes issue with the search for a constitutional legitimizing source within an authorizing polity. It is one thing to assess the legitimacy of a political constitution by reference to its embeddedness in a particular polity or polities, or by its satisfaction of constitutionalist principles such as democratic inclusiveness, transparency, and accountability of governing institutions, or justifiability of the polity's public practices and values. It is a different question to ask, as I am asking, whether a constitution or constitutions has/have legitimate authority in the sense of being able to change the normative situation for subjects of that authority. Some of my enquiry will touch upon the same material as the search for a political constitution. For instance, when investigating the procedural aspect of the conjunctive justification, the relevant procedures must ensure fair participatory (and probably democratic) opportunities for people in a polity. Similarly, the substantive standards that are conditions for having legitimate authority under the conjunctive justification will also be standards constraining any plausible theory of what can be authorized by 'the people'. However, the whole point of the relative authority thesis is that such a direct line of authorization from a specific polity is not enough to establish legitimate authority, *because of* the interaction and overlap that occurs between purported authorities claiming authorization from interacting and overlapping polities. That overlap and interaction is what generates a relativity condition in addition to the procedural and substantive elements of the conjunctive justification for authority.

A third point of departure then questions the need for the constitutionalist model itself. This point distinguishes my account from Kumm's, which is in many other respects similar. Kumm's work also takes seriously the idea that a theory of legitimate authority must be used to evaluate choices between a plurality of constitutional orders and their rules. In his extensive analysis of possible contending normative defences of either European or national constitutional authority, however, Kumm maintains the view that, given the diversity and inconsistency of various principles that might support the legitimacy of one constitutional level over another, the best normative grounds for authority entrusts courts with the task of choosing a conflict rule to determine authority in the particular instance. Kumm finds that, as 'the jurisprudential idea of an ultimate legal rule provides no guidance to the question of what it is a judge should do (in situations of constitutional conflict), a normative account of an ultimate source of authority and legitimacy may provide the necessary guidance'.[17] Kumm then adopts a Dworkinian/Alexian jurisprudential account in which courts must reconcile competing principles 'to the highest degree

---

[17] Kumm, 'Democratic Constitutionalism', 274.

possible'.[18] Yet by using restrained legal decision-making to solve the problem of constitutional conflict, Kumm's solution preserves the possibility of constitutional authority by linking that authority with constitutionalism beyond the state, rather than abandoning the constraining characteristic of legal/constitutional decision-making as a source of authority in itself.[19]

The interesting question is: what does constitutionalism add that an account of authority cannot? Here, Kumm seems right to argue that, in order for constitutional pluralism to be convincing as an account of legal order rather than an opaque arena of dialogue, discourse, and negotiation, there must be some way to generate doctrinal structure and remain in 'the world of law'.[20] Kumm uses constitutional principles to remain in the legal world—the principles determine when there is legal authority and when disobedience of that authority is justified; and the principles ground the resulting doctrines of legal authority. The argument presented in this work, in contrast, is that any such constitutionalism that is so disconnected from a polity, and subject to such extensive interpretation, negotiation, amendment and indeed disobedience among different levels of authorities, does not constrain in the way that a constitutional model should. It is a form of constitutionalism that has value for its openness to diverse values, institutions, and even identities, but it is hard to see that it constrains ordinary legal plurality sufficiently to be viewed as a tool imposing order among disorder.

That difference, however, is mostly nit-picking, and in the end is less significant than the final point of departure, in which the relative authority account takes a step away from the constitutionalist model Kumm offers. The step beyond is the conception of relative authority, and the consequent addition of the relativity condition. To recap: the conjunctive justification I have outlined largely coheres with Kumm's account of the moral concerns that make up his constitutionalist model. These are: formal legality, jurisdictional legitimacy, procedural legitimacy, and substantive reasonableness. Kumm asks courts to weigh up these principles in their decisions about where 'graduated authority' lies, in respect of the particular issue they are required to address. My conjunctive justification looks similar, in that the kinds of reasons that go into an assessment of procedural legitimacy (including conferral of standing, governance, and side-effect reasons) and substantive legitimacy (which is outcome-dependent in much the same way as Kumm's, and acknowledges the prospect of disagreement and/or value pluralism) will likely match the

---

[18] Mattias Kumm, 'The Jurisprudence of Constitutional Conflict: Constitutional Supremacy in Europe before and after the Constitutional Treaty' (2005) 11 *European Law Journal* 262, 290.
[19] Kumm, 'Democratic Constitutionalism'.
[20] Kumm, 'Conflicts of Authority'.

reasons going into Kumm's principled balancing/interpretive assessment.[21] Within both the conjunctive justification and Kumm's cosmopolitan constitutional principles, there is room for the contest of reasons that divides advocates of constitutionalist order and pluralist diversity.[22] Sometimes reason will be balanced in favour of plurality or diversity, sometimes hierarchy or uniformity; sometimes the national order, sometimes the EU order.

From that point, however, the relative authority account parts company with Kumm's model. The conception of authority itself as relative, with legitimacy being partially dependent upon inter-authority relationships, is different from Kumm's conception of that authority as graduated, featuring comparative legitimacy. Kumm's approach treats the authority of different orders as though it is independent; mine treats it as interdependent. The difference is important. As I indicated in Part II, an independent conception of authority is vulnerable in circumstances of plurality, due to the challenges of identifying and ranking authorities. A relative conception seems the best way to avoid those problems. The upshot is that, as well as bringing both constitutionalist and pluralist allocations of authority into contest within the test for legitimate authority, the relative authority account also insists that the relevant authorities must engage appropriately with one another as is required by the balance of reasons. Then, I argue, it is *that relationship*, rather than any constitutional character of the substantive and procedural principles themselves, which constrains the authorities and avoids a descent into disorder. In practice, this means that authorities at both EU and Member State levels must at various times engage one another through cooperative review or supervision mechanisms, coordinated outcomes, consultations, interpretations, or even toleration via margins of appreciation. Therefore, and perhaps most importantly of all, an account of relative authority offers a tool for prescribing and evaluating the appropriate relationships between these different bodies sharing interdependent authority, something which neither the constitutionalist nor pluralist accounts, nor constitutional pluralist accounts, on their own terms, can provide for.

The question then is whether the relative authority account is persuasive as a contender to both the empirical and normative claims of constitutional pluralism. The best way to assess this is via an engagement with Maduro's important account of those two claims, and by reference to some of the key

---

[21] Kumm at times seems to suggest that the exercise if one of Alexian balancing, and at other times suggests that the court's task is Dworkinian interpretation. For analysis, see Kumm, 'Democratic Constitutionalism'.

[22] Kumm describes his conception as 'cosmopolitan constitutionalism' in Mattias Kumm, 'The Cosmopolitan Turn', in Joel P Trachtman and Jeffrey Dunoff (eds), *Ruling the World* (Cambridge University Press, 2009).

inter-authority relationships that have established, and will continue to drive, the practice of constitutional pluralism.

3. Relative Authority's Empirical and Normative Credibility

a. Relative authority in practice

Maduro argues that constitutional pluralism claims to offer the best explanation of what is going on in European constitutional practice, and that, importantly, it best captures the existing conflict between 'respective claims of final authority'.[23] Much of the early part of this work was aimed at showing that conflict between such respective claims can have the impact of collapsing any potentially legitimate authority, and that a conception of claims to relative authority might be more plausible while also keeping alive the potential for legitimate authority. As an empirical matter, however, we can assess whether the authorities in play do in fact make claims to final authority, or whether they might claim relative authority.

On the one hand, it is easy to find examples, sometimes express examples, of individual cases in which final decision-making authority is claimed by either the European Courts or a Member State's constitutional court.[24] On the other hand, the overall practice of these courts presents a subtler picture of their relationship. The claims made by the respective courts appear mindful of the claims to authority of each other. As Kumm notes, 'even where [national courts] resist the full-blown acceptance of EU law supremacy, they generally do so under a strong presumption that they should apply EU law'.[25] At the European level, and in the human rights context, the flexibility of the margin of appreciation doctrine represents a similarly reflexive approach to

---

[23] Maduro, 'Three Claims of Constitutional Pluralism', 70.
[24] Compare Case 6/64 *Costa v Enel* [1964] ECR 585 and Case 106/77 *Amministrazione delle Finanze dello Stat v Simmenthal* [1978] ECR 629, in which the ECJ declared the primacy of EU law over national constitutional law, with the German Federal Constitutional Court's recent affirmation that the primacy of EU law does not prevent a national court from determining whether a particular law is ultra vires: see BVerfGR 89, 155 (1993) ('*Maastricht*') and BVerfG, 2 be 2/08 (30 June 2009) ('*Lisbon*'). Among other findings, the Lisbon court found that the German Basic Law prohibits the transfer of competence to decide on its own competence (Kompetenz-Kompetenz): *Lisbon*, para 233. Thus, the question whether a particular EU law or regulation is ultra vires may be reviewed by the national court: *Lisbon*, para 240.
[25] Kumm, 'The Jurisprudence of Constitutional Conflict', 263.

the relationship between the authority of national and regional order.[26] The claims are responsive rather than being made in isolation. In this sense they appear to embody claims to relative authority—they acknowledge that the regional level may be better placed to secure such common concerns as uniform human rights protections, common market regulation, and/or standards; while also acknowledging that the national level is likely better placed to secure democratic processes and maintain any values that those procedures reveal to be important.

An insight in this direction can be found by comparing the different positions taken by the German Federal Constitutional Court in *Solange I* and *II*, where, in the first case, it asserted its authority to protect national constitutional rights against measures of EU law, due to the relative weakness of the EU's own rights-protective jurisprudence; while in the second case, that jurisprudence was thought sufficiently improved that rights protection could be entrusted to the institutions of the European Union.[27] Both decisions were clearly concerned with the degree of substantive rights protection, and used that substantive concern to formulate a principle for allocating judicial review powers. I think that these can also be read as decisions about the appropriate location of relative authority. The change between *Solange I* and *II* appears consistent with an approach in which the relative authority of the national court initially gave it greater substantive and procedural legitimacy, but the substantive and procedural legitimacy of the EU's rights-protective functions was then improved, via coordination with the level of protection offered by the national courts, so that it came to equal or even trump that of the national authority.[28] Importantly, the German court's recognition of that improvement gave effect to an appropriately deferential relationship in order to achieve relative authority.

A further illustration of relative authority might be found by looking at the much-analysed *Kadi* decision, which upheld the European Courts' power to review the rights-consistency of a European Community (EC) Directive giving effect to an international legal obligation relating to international security.[29] In *Kadi*, the ECJ looks to be making a strong claim to independent authority, by rejecting the Court of First Instance's monist approach to

---

[26] On the margin of appreciation in European human rights law, see, eg Eyal Benvenisti, 'Margin of Appreciation, Consensus, and Universal Standards' (1998) 31 *New York University Journal of International Law and Politics* 843.

[27] Compare BVerfGE 37, 271 (1974) ('*Solange I*') and BVerfGE 73, 339 (1986) ('*Solange II*').

[28] Similar reasoning was reflected in *Bosphorus Hava Yollari Turizm v Ireland* (2006) 42 EHRR 1.

[29] Compare the Court of First Instance decision, Case T-315/01 *Kadi v Council and Commission* [2005] ECR II-3649, and the opinion of Advocate General Maduro in Case C-402/05P *Yassin Abdullah Kadi v Council of the European Union and Commission of the European Communities*

the relationship between international and domestic law, and its finding that the Court could not review the EC directive because it was giving effect to international law. In doing so, the ECJ avoided answering broader questions about the relationship between international and European legal orders, and declined to confront the question over whether the EC was bound by the specific international rule, arguing instead, from within a European perspective only, that the European legal order is autonomous and the Court's constitutional role is to give effect to European constitutional principles and rules via review of EC directives, and notwithstanding any role those directives may have as applications of international obligations.[30] The Court found that European law constituted an 'internal and autonomous legal order', adopting a dualist approach in which EU law incorporates international legal norms only when such incorporation is expressly provided for by the Treaties.[31]

Yet, as Besson argues, in insisting on its autonomy from international law, the ECJ's reasoning is weakened by its failure to consider expressly the implications of that claimed autonomy for the integration of EU law with the law of Member States, and the resulting imposition of a dualist approach. In Besson's view, an assessment of the relationship between the international and EU legal orders, and the rank, validity, and effect of their respective norms, must be sensitive to the interaction of both those orders with the legal orders of Member States. The complexity of interaction means that, in Besson's words:[32]

in an integrated legal order like the European legal order, national law remains central to the reception of both EU law and international law; if the European legal order can be described as internal, it is precisely because there is a national legal order that integrates EU legal norms (and any international norm that has become part of EU law) and gives them primacy. The relationship between European and international law cannot therefore but affect the relationship between EU and national law, on the

---

(16 January 2008). The extensive literature discussing the decision includes a number of specific analyses of the EU international Member State interaction. See, eg the incisive analysis by S Besson, 'European Legal Pluralism after *Kadi*' (2009) 5 *European Constitutional Law Review* 237; Juliane Kokott and Christoph Sobotta, 'Constitutional Core Values and International Law' (2012) 23 *European Journal of International Law* 1015; Jan Willem van Rossem, 'Interaction between EU Law and International Law in the Light of *Intertanko* and *Kadi*' (2009) 40 *Netherlands Yearbook of International Law* 183; Grainne De Búrca, 'The EU, the European Court of Justice and the International Legal Order after *Kadi*' (2009) 51 *Harvard International Law Journal* 1.

[30] See *Kadi*, para 316, and analysis in Besson, 'European Legal Pluralism after Kadi'.
[31] *Kadi*, para 317.
[32] S Besson, 'European Legal Pluralism after *Kadi*' (2009) 5 *European Constitutional Law Review* 237, 255. Also at 256: 'The imposed monism and primacy of EU law within the domestic legal order and the forced dualism this implies vis-à-vis international law, may, however, create difficulties for those member states that have traditionally adopted a monist approach in their relationship to international law. The reverse may also be true'.

one hand, and that between international and national law, on the other. If this is the case, the 'ménage à trois' between the three legal orders ought to be taken into account whenever a bilateral relationship between either two of them is assessed.

Besson's analysis suggests to me that the different legal orders likely have relative authority in the *Kadi* situation, and indeed in other similar structural scenarios where international legal obligations might conflict with EU and/ or Member State law. Relativity might even be found within the apparently robust claim to independent authority. For, rather than emphasizing strong jurisdictional boundaries between the different orders, the ECJ's reasoning in *Kadi* appears to have been sensitive to the weaknesses of the international level's own review mechanisms, compared to the more robust substantive and procedural legitimacy of the available EU constitutional principles and processes of judicial review. It did not rule out that a different degree of rights protection at the international order might have led to a different outcome.[33] The Court's reliance upon constitutionalist and principled arguments to support its conclusions suggests that there was no technically determinative resolution to be found; indeed, there was at least an apparent conflict of authority and a need for an analysis of the relative authority of the different orders. Although none of this is expressed within the Court's judgment or vague reasoning, that vagueness may itself be suggestive of the Court's 'readiness to compromise' in the way that relative authority can require.[34] Weighing up that relative authority would offer a stronger foundation for the Court's eventual decision to choose a principle for determining the existence of a review power that could indirectly challenge the authority of an international legal obligation, as well as elevate the substantive and procedural legitimacy of the EU's own constitutional principles vis-à-vis its subjection to international obligations.

The conflict of authority between the orders at issue in *Kadi* could helpfully be interpreted as requiring a relative authority analysis, which weighs up the role of constitutional principles, the integration of EU and Member State law, and the claimed primacy of both European and international law, by reference to the procedural and substantive legitimacy of each order and the appropriate degree of cooperation, coordination, or deviation between them. This is an abstract and inevitably difficult exercise for any authority, not least a court, to undertake, but it is available, and there is some evidence from the *Kadi* judgments that courts are sensitive to the kind of reasoning it requires.

---

[33] For the argument that the Court did not rule out the appropriateness of a *Solange*-type argument, see Kokott and Sobotta, 'Constitutional Core Values and International Law', 1017–1019.

[34] Kokott and Sobotta, 'Constitutional Core Values and International Law', 1017.

Others have suggested that, despite the overlap and interaction of constitutional and legal orders throughout Europe, there are sufficiently robust principles or procedures that can be invoked so as to avoid, resolve, or tolerate conflicts.[35] These very principles and procedures, insofar as they are actually practised, might themselves be evidence of the nature of the claims to authority that are being made by the different interacting authorities. For instance, Weiler's suggestion that the principle of constitutional tolerance lies at the heart of European constitutionalism resonates with an interpretation of claims to authority as being claims to relative and not final authority. Again, these claims are not made in isolation or as an assertion of independence from the other orders; they are made in response to and interaction with those other orders.

b. Relative authority as a normative theory

As Maduro identifies, the basic normative claim of constitutional pluralism rests upon the idea that the different constitutional orders cannot be assessed for their comparative legitimacy, and for this reason questions of their final authority should be left open. There is then a thicker claim, which Maduro supports, that constitutional pluralism provides a closer approximation to the ideals of constitutionalism than either national or European constitutional orders could on their own. Thus, Maduro sees constitutional pluralism not simply as a response to conflicts of authority, but as the best representation of the values of constitutionalism.

Maduro's view, however, suggests that there is some sort of additive conception of legitimacy at stake, in which the EU's claim to authority can be justified by the value it adds to national constitutionalist practice, through the engagement that occurs between these different constitutional orders. This is important. In Maduro's hands, it is offered as a powerful argument for the normative claims of constitutional pluralism, in which neither Member States nor EU institutions have greater legitimacy or more authority. The argument could be even stronger if it included a conception of relative authority, and if legitimacy were assessed using a relativity condition.

The important difference here between a view of relative authority with its interdependent conditions of legitimacy, and Maduro's own view, is that in Maduro's view, the claims to authority made by members and European authorities are normatively separate—they are respectively legitimate; but are also institutionally interdependent—linked through the practices of their officials.[36] I take the opposite view, in which the authorities are normatively

---

[35] See, eg Joseph Weiler and Marlene Wind, *European Constitutionalism Beyond the State* (Cambridge University Press, 2003).
[36] Maduro, 'Three Claims of Constitutional Pluralism'.

interdependent—their normative force is constrained by their interactions or overlaps—but they are and can remain institutionally separate. In both Maduro's and my own view, processes of interaction and engagement between legal officials are critical to the practice of constitutionalism in Europe.[37] However, my argument is that the engagement between claimants of relative authority in Member States and EU institutions is significant not for the institutional and procedural bridge it provides between systems, but for the very normativity of those systems.

This distinction does make a difference to the normative claims being offered. For instance, Maduro argues that the justification for the EU's claim to authority lies in the value it adds to national constitutionalism—including enhanced constitutional discipline and consideration for out-of-state interests—and that the best values of constitutionalism are generated through the interplay of constitutions.[38] This seems to be an implicit argument for relative authority, insofar as the value added is dependent upon the way in which the national constitutional orders also engage and commit to cooperative, coordinative, or tolerant processes. If EU authority overstepped its legitimate boundaries, in a way that threatened the relative legitimacy of the national constitutional authority, then that would be illegitimate. Wherever the legitimacy of the relationship is critical to the legitimacy of each of its participants, a relative rather than an additive conception of legitimate authority is preferable. In Maduro's argument, pluralism is normatively attractive because of the processes of mutual correction that it can generate. However, I think that in order to explain when pluralism has that value and to work out the limits of its benefits, it is more helpful to conceive of authority and claims to authority as relative rather than treating one as opposed to another.[39] Relative authority can better capture the range of cooperative, coordinated, and tolerant relationships that are at least as valuable as conflicting ones. The notion of relative authority, unlike the additive conception, acknowledges that comparative legitimacy cannot always be determined, but, rather than being comfortable with pluralism as the end point, it seeks to integrate the conditions of legitimacy.

Perhaps most importantly, a conception of relative authority better accounts for the way in which individuals may be subjects of authority at both levels, and/or may interact with their co-subjects in interactive Member State communities. Relativity seems to offer a way to bridge the conceptual tension

---

[37] Miguel Maduro, 'Contrapunctual Law: Europe's Constitutional Pluralism in Action', in Neil Walker (ed), *Sovereignty in Transition* (Hart Publishing, 2003).
[38] Maduro, 'Three Claims of Constitutional Pluralism'.
[39] Maduro, 'Three Claims of Constitutional Pluralism', 15.

that Maduro identifies between a unitary conception of law and authority, and a pluralist conception of society and political space. Being neither unitary nor pluralist, a conception of relative authority treats individuals as potential subjects of overlapping or interactive authorities at both state and EU levels. It then uses that notion of the subject to generate a relative test for legitimacy which, in turn, can be used to examine the legitimate domains of EU law and state law, and/or to assess particular responses that relatively authoritative institutions make to one another. Here, all the work on constitutional pluralism is invaluable for examining the respective merits of plurality and centrality, hierarchy and heterarchy, monologue and dialogue—all the specific reasons applying to different inter-authority relationships which must be assessed to work out what relative authority requires. Yet the contribution of the relative account is not to declare one or other approach the winner, nor to identify doctrines or principles to resolve conflicts between legal norms or constitutions, but to require the authorities themselves to cooperate or coordinate or tolerate conflicts as the requirements of their relativity dictate.

In this respect the account of relative authority has much in common with Maduro's emphasis upon the promise of mutual engagement, rather than the dualist's conception of inter-systemic relations as being 'a simple function of jurisdictional power'.[40] However, as I argued in the discussion of the conjunctive justification in Chapter 7, the processes of mutual engagement (favoured by Maduro), which are so central to realizing legitimate authority, are no more nor less important than the principles which (in Kumm's work) provide a model for assessing the very direction that such engagement should take. The interplay of those two elements is reflected within the conjunctive justification I have outlined earlier, with the addition of the relativity condition to reflect the fact that sometimes the procedural and substantive elements can favour different or multiple authorities, whose relationship becomes critical to their legitimacy. That final contribution makes the relative authority view more attractive than those rich substantial and procedural accounts alone, or in combination.

---

[40] Maduro, 'Three Claims of Constitutional Pluralism', 24.

12
Relative Authority Inside the State

In addition to international and constitutional theory, the idea of relative authority offers insights for understanding and assessing relationships between authorities inside the state. There is obvious potential for relative authority in cases of federal, devolved, or multi-sovereign state examples, but even unitary states feature relative authority within familiar relationships such as those between branches of government. In all these scenarios, relative authority provides a way to analyse and evaluate relationships without being limited by their particular formalities (or lack thereof).

This chapter first examines the implications of relative authority for understanding and evaluating relationships between the judicial, legislative, and executive branches of government, and the important principle of separation of powers, before going on to consider relationships between overlapping or interactive governments within the state, including federal-state and state-indigenous relationships. These brief introductions will then be used to set up the detailed case study offered in Chapter 13.

1. Inter-branch Relationships

Relationships between branches of government provide an intuitive example of how the legitimacy of one authority can be constrained by its interaction with other authorities. Where authorities are integrated under a constitution—as legislatures, executives, and judiciaries typically are—we require that they give appropriate deference to or engage in cooperation with each other in respect of their mandated activities. If they fail to do so, we can criticize them just as readily as if they have failed to carry out one of their own independent activities. The interaction of authorities becomes a crucial element of their legitimacy. Indeed, it becomes straightforward to speak of the legitimacy of a whole integrated system of courts, legislatures, and executive offices as shorthand for the legitimacy of each, *given* its relationships with others, as well as the legitimacy of the relationships themselves.

Even the most straightforward-seeming relationships between branches of government can be treated as relationships of relative authority, in which there are overlapping or interactive subjects. For instance, one interpretation of intra-constitutional relationships between branches of government is that, in addition to the formal constitutional rules that govern their relationships, there are requirements of relative authority operating to substantiate the legitimate authority of courts, legislatures, and executives. These requirements include the appropriate operation of checks, balances, dialogue, review, and other forms of inter-branch interaction.

The relative authority account is most illuminating of two aspects of inter-branch relationships. The first is the principle of separation of powers, which justifies separating the institutions of legislative, judicial, and executive powers. The second is the possibility that one of these branches might be justified in reviewing, checking, or otherwise supervising one or both of the others.

a. Separation of powers

The very idea of the separation of powers is perhaps the most powerful illustration of relative authority inside the state, but one that must also be reinterpreted in light of that notion of relative authority. On its face, the idea of separation of powers seems to insist on independent rather than interdependent authority. This is especially true if the reasons for separating the branches of power come down to the function and value of each different power. Recent work from Waldron, for instance, explains that much of the value of separating powers lies in the different functions of the different organs.[1] Separation is not simply a division of power to avoid concentrating power in any one institution, nor another way of explaining a system of checks and balances. Instead, the separation of powers has a value beyond each of those principles, which is that, as part of the rule of law, subjects should be 'ruled by a process that answers to the institutional articulation that is required by the separation of powers'.[2] This entails that each branch must do its own specific kind of work, and that each function has its own integrity. As Waldron cautions, however, these functions should not be thought to carry their integrity independently. Rather, 'the integrity of each of these three operations of government is important precisely because they have to fit together into the general articulated scheme of governance'.[3]

To me, this looks like an argument resting upon a conception of relative authority. The principle requiring that powers be separated also renders those

---

[1] Jeremy Waldron, *Separation of Powers or Division of Power?* New York University School of Law, Public Law Research Paper No 12–20, 2012, available at http://ssrn.com/abstract=2045638.
[2] Waldron, *Separation of Powers or Division of Power?*, 25.
[3] Waldron, *Separation of Powers or Division of Power?*, 31.

exercising the powers relative authorities. Their legitimacy depends upon not only their exercise of their own functions, but their respect for the separateness of the others' functions. However, they are still authorities serving overlapping or at least interactive subjects, and thus are bound together into relationships of relative authority. The question of whether subjects are overlapping or interactive is not critical here, but it is interesting because it goes to the same point that Waldron makes about the value of articulated power. The interaction of the roles of law-making, law-applying, and law-administering clearly supports a view in which authorities fulfilling those functions are interactively in service of their subjects.[4] The same functional account which separates the branches also leads them into interaction. Alternatively, to treat the subjects of judiciaries, legislatures, and executives as being overlapping is to say that individuals are the subject of all three branches because each is prima facie procedurally justified and can also help the subjects conform to substantive reasons that apply to them. Their multiplicity then triggers the relativity condition and they need to interact appropriately.

If the idea of relative authority carries the normative force of the principle of separation of powers, it can also be used to test the legitimacy of particular manifestations of inter-authority relationships. The relative authority theory thus offers a way through debates about whether one institution is more justified than another, or where supreme authority should be located. Instead of pitting branches against one another, their legitimate authority is treated as relative, and their coordination, cooperation, or toleration is necessary to their legitimacy. A number of relationship practices might then be justified, or not, according to the relative authority requirements. For instance, a relative authority theory might be used to assess the value of the practice mechanism of judicial review.[5]

b. Judicial review and oversight

Separations and interactions between relative authorities must be supported by the balance of reasons for action and decision, and must satisfy the relativity condition. Judicial review will be justified if it is substantively required but also procedurally proper, and, importantly, it must be conducted with an appropriate level of cooperation or even deference to the relative authority of the legislature—insofar as it is also substantively and procedurally justified.

---

[4] See Fuller, who thought that there was 'reciprocal dependence' between law-makers and law administrators: Lon L Fuller, *The Morality of Law* (Yale University Press, 1964), 91.

[5] The core controversy is presented by Adrian Vermeule, 'Judicial Review and Institutional Choice' (2001) 43 *William & Mary Law Review* 1557; and Adrian Vermeule, 'Second Opinions and Institutional Design' (2011) 97 *Virginia Law Review* 1435.

The character or intensity of judicial review that is required will thus depend upon the character of the legislature under review. More intense review will be appropriate where the legislature is either substantively or procedurally deficient (or both). Where the legislature has strong procedural and substantive credentials, only a minimum of judicial review is justified. In this respect the argument is again close to Waldron's position, which sets out the procedural conditions of strong legislative legitimacy against which judicial review of legislation would not be justified.[6] However, unlike Waldron's position, the procedural balance of reasons must itself be weighed up against the substantive balance of reasons, which may sometimes generate an outcome-based preference for judicial review.

In further contrast to Waldron's position, however, the same principles, if not the same specific arguments, apply to judicial review of administrative action. In that relationship, difficult questions over the degree or character of judicial review will be just as constrained by the requirements of the relativity condition. The more important the substantive issue and/or the less procedurally justified the administrative action, the greater the intensity of justified review. In most contexts, for instance, this will support the use of proportionality review for administrative action that is restrictive of core individual rights.[7] Indeed, the practice of judicial review of both legislative and administrative action will most often be justified where there is an overriding substantive role for the judiciary as a protector of individual rights.[8]

Judicial review aside, relationships between the branches might be managed through a number of other tools. One that has drawn wide discussion is the practice of dialogue between branches of government. The dialogue model of constitutional relationships has been advocated as a sort of mid-point between legislative and judicial supremacy, and its precise application can either include or exclude judiciaries striking down legislation. The model—first detailed in explanation of Canadian constitutional arrangements but with its roots in American legal process theory and the work of both Fuller and Bickel—has gained

---

[6] Jeremy Waldron, 'The Core of the Case against Judicial Review' (2006) 115 *Yale Law Journal* 1346; and Jeremy Waldron, *The Dignity of Legislation* (Cambridge University Press, 1999).

[7] On the controversies in common law jurisdictions over proportionality review, and its appropriateness for matters (and sometimes only) matters of rights, see Michael Taggart, 'Proportionality, Deference, *Wednesbury*' (2008) III *New Zealand Law Review* 423; Paul Craig, 'Proportionality, Deference, *Wednesbury*: Taking up Michael Taggart's Challenge: Proportionality, Rationality and Review' (2010) II *New Zealand Law Review* 265; and other essays in that volume. See also Mark Elliott, 'The Human Rights Act 1998 and the Standard of Substantive Review' (2001) *The Cambridge Law Journal* 301.

[8] On the significance of the judicial role in rights protection, see analysis in Richard H Fallon, 'The Core of an Uneasy Case for Judicial Review' (2008) 121 *Harvard Law Review* 1693.

momentum in Commonwealth legal scholarship.[9] Importantly, however, under a conception of the relative authority of courts, legislatures, and executives, the dialogue must occur in pursuit of the legitimate relative authority of the different branches. Dialogue is not valuable for its own sake; it is valuable if, and because, it is required by the conditions of relativity. Thus, if a court is required to defer to a legislature, it cannot refrain from doing so in some supposed attempt at dialogue. Or, if it is required to scrutinize a legislative offering strictly, it must do so without attempting to soften the blow of its intervention by engaging in dialogue instead. Of course, the dialogue mechanism must also go in the other direction—legislatures and executives will also be required to engage in dialogue when that is necessary for securing their relative authority. The power of the relative authority account is that it opens up but also integrates the analyses in all these areas and, importantly, it indicates that such measures as judicial review or dialogue must be assessed within the context of the relationships that are required between all three branches of relative authority that make up the modern state.

2. The Relative Authority of Governments within the State

a. Federal-local relationships

Scholars of federalism are well-versed in the dynamics of relative authority. Indeed, the idea that the legitimate authority of state, local, and federal levels of government is partly constituted by their relationships might seem a banal statement when compared to the rich and detailed analyses of particular models of federalism around the world. These models typically offer different ways of allocating authority between levels of government, according to substantive and/or procedural concerns, which closely mirror the assessments made within relative authority's conjunctive justification. Some models favour strict separations between competencies and spheres of authority at each level, while some are more comfortable with overlap and concurrency.[10] Yet they could all be described in the terms offered by the relative authority theory,

---

[9] For analysis, see K Roach, 'A Dialogue About Principle and a Principled Dialogue: Justice Iacobucci's Substantive Approach to Dialogue' (2007) 57 *University of Toronto Law Journal* 449. See also, eg Alexander M Bickel, *The Least Dangerous Branch: The Supreme Court at the Bar of Politics* (2nd edn, Yale University Press, 1986), 70–71: 'in a Socratic colloquy with the other institutions of government'.

[10] For a discussion of cooperative models, see Michael S Greve, 'Against Cooperative Federalism' (2000) 70 *Mississippi Law Journal* 557.

as either cooperative, coordinative, or tolerant. There is, however, little to be gained here by rehearsing the connection between relative authority and each of these models, for those connections are obvious. Instead, I think that the relative authority theory makes a promising contribution towards explaining the legitimate authority of different levels of government as being interdependent—not in the sense that each level is separately answerable to some external theory of what makes a particular activity (eg torts, crimes, or commerce) a state, federal, or cooperative function, but rather as depending upon the very relationships in which these levels are engaged—both with each other, and with other relative authorities with which they overlap or interact.

There is a very important sense in which a focus upon relative authority, within practices of federalism, may enable a more detailed assessment of the legitimacy of the relative state/local and national governments. This contribution is similar to Resnik's offering of 'noncategorical federalism', ie an approach to federalism that does not seek to determine, in a binary sense, what should be a state function and what should be a national function, nor limit its analyses to relationships between state and federal levels engaged in cooperative or competitive practices. Instead, Resnik's work encourages a focus upon the range of relationship practices that occur outside of the ordinary channels of state-federal power. These can include relationships between states, which, through cooperation and coordination among themselves, can serve to change the very allocations of functions that traditional scholarship on federalism is concerned with justifying.[11] As Resnik analyses, states do, among themselves, engage in joint activities, adopt uniform legal standards, form organizations to manage common or shared problems and opportunities, and, as she has emphasized, they engage in relationships with foreign and/or international authorities.[12]

The insight of the relative authority account is to see all these relationships as critical to the legitimacy of the authorities involved, insofar as they are relative authorities. This means that questions over the appropriate character of relationships between state and federal levels of government must also be sensitive to other external relationships. Thus, the crucial question becomes the investigation into the actual relativity of local, federal, and international authorities. In order to be relative authorities, the different levels must have overlapping or interactive subjects. There must be substantive and/or procedural factors

---

[11] Judith Resnik, 'Afterword: Federalism's Options', Symposium Issue (1996) *Yale Law and Policy Review/Yale Journal on Regulation* 465.
[12] Resnik, 'Afterword: Federalism's Options', 473–475; and see Judith Resnik, 'Foreign as Domestic Affairs: Rethinking Horizontal Federalism and Foreign Affairs Preemption in Light of Translocal Internationalism' (2007) 57 *Emory Law Journal* 31.

that render individuals subject to these authorities at the same time, and over the same issues. There are some uncontroversial substantial matters that generate such relativity—including legal disputes between subjects of these different jurisdictions, commercial/environmental/criminal matters that require cooperative or coordinative action, and matters related to civil emergency measures or security. The more controversial issues arise when there are matters that are not, practically, trans-jurisdictional, but rather are issues involving rights or interests that are common to subjects either as citizens or simply as humans. For instance, if people are common citizens, they will be affected by practices that uphold or diminish civil and political rights; as humans, they will also be affected by any restriction or promotion of economic and social rights, and, more broadly, matters associated with human dignity. The application of the conjunctive justification could render federal, local, and international authorities as relative authorities in the service of their subjects in relation to all of these matters.

One implication of situating state-federal relationships within a broader context of other relative authority relationships within and outside the state is that the intra-branch relativity relationships discussed in section 1 will also be relevant to assessing the legitimacy of intra-federal relationships. For instance, relative authority may offer a new method for assessing the practice in which courts (and, most controversially, the US Supreme Court) and/or legislatures refer to international or foreign judgments.[13] On my account, trans-judicial dialogue and legislative borrowing may not simply be a convenient form of learning from others' experiences with similar problems; rather, it may be required if the borrowing authority is to have legitimacy. As a matter of legality, a court may be required to bar certain non-legal and/or non-local reasons from determining its judgments, but as a matter of legitimate authority, a court is unlikely to be able to be hermetically sealed off from other courts. That is all the more unlikely given the extent to which both international and foreign law interacts with federal and/or state law, whenever the participants in a dispute or criminal process have some transnational standing or affiliation, or the issue at stake has a transnational character. The relativity of their authority means that courts making decisions on such matters may be required to engage in dialogue with foreign or international law, or the law of other states within their federation, as part of realizing their legitimate authority. There may even be strong enough substantive and/or procedural reasons to require that the court's decision align with those other jurisdictions. Or, if the reasons

---

[13] On the US Supreme Court's use of international materials, see Sarah Cleveland, 'Our International Constitution' (2006) 31 *Yale Journal of International Law* 1; RP Alford, '*Roper v. Simmons* and Our Constitution in International Equipoise' (2005) 53 *UCLA Law Review* 53.

are less strong, so that the engagement with the law of those relative authorities ends up being a sidebar to the court's judgment, the process of engagement may still be a crucial element of their legitimacy.

b. Federal/state relationships with indigenous authorities

My discussion of relative authority within relationships between levels of government has much in common with an account of relative authority across different types of governments. Some complex and highly charged examples are relationships between indigenous tribal governments and governments of federations or states in which they are located. There are an enormous variety of formal arrangements between such authorities, including: formal shared sovereignty agreements; treaties establishing zones of separate authority, jurisdiction, or quasi-sovereignty; provisions for shared representative institutions; and, on the other hand, express exclusion of competition between authorities and a claim to unitary (usually state) sovereignty. In addition, there are a range of informal or de facto arrangements, which may leave certain geographic regions or policy issues to be dealt with by an indigenous authority, or involve a practice of cooperation or partnership in the management of a particular resource or issue, or which may deny such sharing of authority by either inadvertent or deliberate exclusion of indigenous authorities.

A relative authority test could be turned upon all of these relationships in particular contexts, to see whether they are in accordance with legitimate authority and therefore whether they can bind those who are the shared or interactive subjects of the authorities. Using a common tool for evaluating these relationships might also help us draw insights from their comparative study, noting that there are general reasons for action and reasons for decision that will bear upon many particular relationships, even when their actual circumstances add different or additional reasons to the equation. This work cannot do that comparative study, but will instead offer an in-depth case study in Chapter 13, in order to demonstrate the way in which a relative authority account might assist in identifying where legitimate authority lies between state/federal and indigenous governments, and which relationship structures can work to achieve relative authority.

13

A Case Study in Relative Authority: Crown–Māori Relationships in New Zealand

A thorough examination of the relative authority account must consider its operation in concrete circumstances, so that all the detail of the procedural, substantial, and relational requirements can be filled in. The insights then go in both directions. The theory of relative authority helps to make sense of actual relationships between authorities and evaluate their legitimacy, while setting the theory in a concrete situation demonstrates how actual reasons go into the determination of what relative authority requires. A case study illustrates the circumstances in which plurality, monism, or hierarchy are permissible or desirable, what sorts of reasons for action and reasons for decision can generate relativity between multiple authorities, and what sorts of arrangements between authorities can help them better serve their subjects and respect the standing each carries.

This chapter tackles one example of state-indigenous relationships, in isolation. Some of its insights, particularly in relation to substantive and procedural elements of indigenous self-determination, will apply to other instances of these relationships. Yet this work is not aimed at comparison. It does not consider whether its insights might apply to other instances of relative authority between indigenous peoples and the states with which they interact. Rather, it is necessary to isolate the precise features of the particular relationship, and to consider that in substantial depth, in order to show how it generates relative authority and assess its resulting legitimacy. Much of what appears here will be unfamiliar to scholars interested in other aspects of the relative authority thesis, but the explanation is offered in a way that tries to accommodate that foreignness without simplifying too much.

In section 1 I set out the background to the relationships that exist between the New Zealand state ('the Crown') and indigenous (Māori) authorities, including the difficult matter of identifying each of these authorities. Section 2 then examines whether these parties are candidates for relative legitimate authority, an analysis that necessitates consideration of justifications for self-determination, and the overlap or interaction of Māori and Crown authorities. Section 3 then examines what difference the relative authority account makes to the relationship, compared to similar 'relational' accounts of self-determination. Section 4 concludes by presenting Crown–Māori relationships as ones of relative authority, and assesses how those relationships perform both in the context of specific issues and in the wider constitutional picture.

1. Background to Crown–Māori Relationships in New Zealand

Any introduction to the relationship between Māori and the Crown must begin with the Treaty of Waitangi, which is now widely regarded as a foundational part of New Zealand's constitution, although it does not have the force of law.[1] This standing is reflected (and sometimes disputed) in the vast amount of academic, political, and legal effort that has gone into establishing the Treaty's meaning, application, and significance.[2] The briefest of introductions is that the Treaty itself, signed by the British Crown and many of the hapū (sub-tribes) that held authority over particular areas of New Zealand in 1840, is ambiguous and contradictory. It purports both to cede sovereignty to the British Crown and to preserve it for Māori (through a guarantee of 'tino rangatiratanga', which has been variously described as 'full authority', 'sovereignty', 'self-determination', or, in the more natural Māori term, 'mana').[3] The fraught question of the Treaty's meaning and interpretation has been brought within the jurisdiction of a special tribunal (the Waitangi Tribunal), which hears Māori claims of breaches of the Treaty and can recommend (but not usually require) that the government take action in response.[4] Alongside this claims process, governments engage in direct negotiations with various groups to reach settlements that can include financial compensation, restitution of land and resources, and symbolic satisfaction or apologies. Since the 1980s, Parliament

---

[1] For a comprehensive analysis of the historic and current role of the Treaty in New Zealand's constitution, and suggestions as to its future, see Matthew SR Palmer, *The Treaty of Waitangi in New Zealand's Law and Constitution* (Victoria University Press, 2008).

[2] It is impossible to engage here in the depth of analysis required to make sense of the Treaty itself, the breaches of Crown guarantees it contains, the revival of political and legal attention to the Treaty beginning in the 1970s, or the claims and negotiated settlement processes that have been pursued since that time. For an introduction, see Claudia Orange, *The Treaty of Waitangi* (2nd edn) (Bridget Williams Books, 2011).

[3] Rangatiratanga is the term used in the Treaty, but the more natural expression of the idea of authority/self-government in Te Reo Māori is mana—which can include mana whenua (land), mana tangata (people).

[4] The exception is the limited compulsory recommendation powers for the return of certain lands to Māori ownership. The exceptional category includes lands that are subject to a Crown forestry rental licence and certain lands owned by a state-owned enterprise, which have a notation on their title that the land may be returned to Māori ownership. See Palmer, *The Treaty of Waitangi in New Zealand's Law and Constitution*, 190–192.

has also passed a series of laws requiring administrative decision-makers to either have regard to, or respect, the 'principles of the Treaty', while imposing more specific obligations in areas ranging from conservation to education and resource management.[5] The judiciary has interpreted those principles to require, variously, 'partnership' in good faith, a duty of reasonableness, Crown duties of active protection, remedies for past breaches, and obligations to protect and preserve Māori property (and Māori control of that property).[6]

Here, I want to concentrate upon the totality of the relationship between Crown and Māori authorities—a relationship which includes but is not limited to what has been established by the Treaty. Elsewhere I have argued that in constitutional discourse, the Treaty is best regarded not as a statement of rights and duties but as an expression of differentiated citizenship, which includes a willingness to accommodate differences.[7] The Treaty can be read to give Māori status as tāngata whenua (people of the land), while still giving other New Zealanders historical grounds for their citizenship and the Crown a right to govern subject to the conditions of the Treaty. It also protects the practice of rangatiratanga, which is not subsumed under a singular conception of the subject. In this regard, the Treaty is fundamentally about citizenship—not of a homogenized nation state, but of a multinational state where differentiated political communities must work out their ongoing interactions.

Another key aspect of the relationship which is supported, but not driven or determined, by the Treaty, is the role of tikanga (Māori law) in New Zealand, and particularly the interaction it has with state law.[8] Recent developments

---

[5] One of the most frequently invoked is s 9 of the State-Owned Enterprises Act 1986. See also Public Finance Act 1989, Part 5A, s 45Q.

[6] The leading case is *New Zealand Māori Council v Attorney-General* [1987] 1 NZLR 641 ('*Lands*' case), according to which both parties have an 'obligation to deal with each other and with their Treaty obligations in good faith' (per Richardson J at 682). See also Cooke P at 664. The Supreme Court has observed that this case 'forms the basis of the approach of New Zealand courts to any subsequent legislation requiring that the Crown act consistently with Treaty principles. The judgment gives no support to narrow approaches to the meaning of such clauses': *New Zealand Māori Council v Attorney-General* [2013] NZSC 6, para 59. For further elaboration and application of the Treaty principles, including constraints on their application, see *Te Runanga o Te Ika Whenua Inc Society v Attorney-General* [1994] 2 NZLR 20, 21; *Taiaroa v Minister of Justice* [1995] 1 NZLR 513; *New Zealand Māori Council v Attorney-General* [1994] 1 NZLR 513.

[7] Nicole Roughan, 'Te Tiriti and the Constitution: Rethinking Citizenship, Justice, Equality and Democracy' (2005) 3 *New Zealand Journal of Public and International Law* 285. On differentiated citizenship, see Young, who argues that where there is or has been oppression of particular groups in society, the adoption of a universalistic and unified conception of citizenship 'tend[s] to reproduce existing group oppression': Iris Marion Young, 'Polity and Group Difference: A Critique of the Ideal of Universal Citizenship' (1989) 99 *Ethics* 250, 258–262.

[8] Nicole Roughan, 'The Association of State and Indigenous Law' (2009) 59 *University of Toronto Law Journal* 135. For much of New Zealand's history, the state has treated tikanga as a secondary system, having legal effect only through the device of 'customary law', in whichever limited domains the state allows. See, eg *Wi Parata v Bishop of Wellington* (1877) 3 NZ Jur (NS) 72 (SC), 73. For modern criticism

have given indigenous legal practice a place within the state's legal system.[9] Yet in contrast to the formal separations of jurisdiction that allow indigenous groups in parts of North America and elsewhere to live under their own systems of law, tikanga Māori has been left in a kind of limbo vis-à-vis state law, while remaining a powerful, active legal system for many Māori communities.[10]

The earlier chapters of this work argued that authority can be relative, and relationships between authorities a condition of their legitimacy, even in the absence of express rules governing their interaction. Thus, although the Treaty does not drop out of my analysis, the commitments made in the Treaty are not the only elements or requirements within the Crown–Māori inter-authority relationship. Instead, the relativity of the authorities is revealed by looking behind the Treaty to see what legitimacy requires of all parties.

a. Identifying the authorities

The first step is to identify the Crown and Māori authorities engaged in the relationship, but this is not straightforward on either side.[11] There are two ways of identifying authorities—one is descriptive and looks at the formal or informal arrangements that constitute de facto authorities; the other identifies subjects to see whether and where they are subject to legitimate authority. I will start with the former because it helps to give a fuller picture of the context in which the Crown–Māori relationship exists, but the second approach is the relevant one for the concerns of authority theory, which demand testing the legitimacy of authority for particular subjects, not simply accepting that arrangements purporting to establish legitimate authority over certain persons actually do so.

---

of this approach in the Supreme Court, see *Attorney-General v Ngati Apa* [2003] 3 NZLR 643, 663. For discussion, see David V Williams, 'Wi Parata Is Dead, Long Live Wi Parata', in Andrew Erueti and Claire Charters (eds), *Maori Property Rights and the Foreshore and Seabed: The Latest Frontier* (Victoria University Press, 2007), 31; and Nan Seuffert, 'Jurisdiction and Nation-Building: Tall Tales in Nineteenth-Century Aotearoa/New Zealand', in Shaunnagh Dorsett and Shaun McVeigh (eds), *Jurisprudence of Jurisdiction* (Victoria University Press, 2007), 102.

[9] Both the common law and specific legislation have allocated a domain to Māori customary law, most notably in relation to property. For analysis of the specific field of property law, see Richard Boast and Andrew Erueti, *Maori Land Law* (2nd edn, LexisNexis, 2004). Cases giving some status to customary law include *Attorney-General v Ngati Apa*. For discussion of this contemporary body of 'Māori jurisprudence', see PG McHugh, '"Treaty Principles": Constitutional Relations Inside a Conservative Jurisprudence' (2008) 39 *Victoria University Wellington Law Review* 39.

[10] Māori Custom and Values in New Zealand Law (2001), para 116.

[11] See Palmer, *The Treaty of Waitangi in New Zealand's Law and Constitution*, 307–309. On the New Zealand constitutional system in general, see Geoffrey WR Palmer and Matthew Palmer, *Bridled Power: New Zealand Government under M.M.P.* (3rd edn, Oxford University Press, 1997). On the difficulty of identifying the authorities, see Kirsty Gover and Natalie Baird, 'Identifying the

Formally, New Zealand is a constitutional monarchy, with a guiding constitutional principle of parliamentary sovereignty. Parliament includes the House of Representatives and the Sovereign (currently Queen Elizabeth II, but represented locally by a Governor-General and acting on the advice of 'Cabinet' Ministers in the New Zealand executive branch). What sounds complicated can be simplified in practice by explaining that the Queen, although the Head of State, has no independent legal authority; rather, that authority is held, for all practical purposes, by the House of Representatives, the executive, and, in a different form, the independent judiciary.[12] The electoral process is also an important part of the picture. An unusual feature of the New Zealand Parliament is the existence of special Māori electorate seats in Parliament, which are elected by Māori who choose to be registered on a separate Māori electoral roll instead of the general roll of electors.[13] In addition, New Zealand has had a proportional representation system since 1995, which consistently produces coalition governments and complex arrangements of support agreements outside of coalitions. Most recently, these have included arrangements with the 'Māori Party', whose Members of Parliament expressly aim to represent Māori individuals and communities.[14] The Māori seats and the proportional representation system are both important to the relative authority picture because they serve to entwine some Māori authorities with governmental authorities. Importantly, through these mechanisms, 'governmental' and 'Māori' authority can, in part, refer to one and the same thing.[15]

The third important aspect of Crown authority is the role of local government. Elected bodies in cities and regions have statutorily delegated authority

---

Māori Treaty Partner' (2002) 52 *University of Toronto Law Journal* 39; Janet McLean, '"Crown Him with Many Crowns": The Crown and the Treaty of Waitangi' (2008) 6 *New Zealand Journal of Public and International Law* 35.

[12] To simplify here, I will examine only the relationship between government and Māori authorities, where government is the collective group of Members of Parliament (not necessarily a majority) having the confidence of a majority of the House of Representatives.

[13] There are currently seven Māori seats out of the total 122 seats in Parliament, although both numbers can vary. The numbers here are important. In the most recent census in 2006, people identifying as Māori made up 14.6% of the population of New Zealand, or 565,329 people. At that time, the Māori electoral population of New Zealand was 417,081, of which 228,938 chose to be on the Māori electoral roll after the last option, offered in 2006. Māori are given the choice of electoral rolls upon their first registration to vote, then again shortly after every five-yearly census.

[14] On the mixed-member proportional electoral system and Māori political representation, see Andrew Geddis, 'A Dual Track Democracy? The Symbolic Role of the Maori Seats in New Zealand's Electoral System' (2006) 5 *Election Law Journal* 347.

[15] The identity is only partial because Māori authority is diverse and is located largely outside of the parliamentary process and the Māori Party.

and can make regulations on matters from environmental policy and planning to public health and traffic. With these powers come responsibilities, notably: to engage with Māori and respect the Treaty of Waitangi; to take account of Māori relationships with land and other resources; to establish processes for Māori to contribute to decision-making and to help foster capacity for such contributions; and to consult with Māori in the preparation or modification of regional plans and selected other resource management decisions.[16] The level of local government is often, in the words of a former Chief Judge of the Māori Land Court, 'where the rubber meets the road', for relationships among Māori and Pakeha individuals, communities, and authorities.[17]

The Māori side of the relative authority relationship is more complicated. There is no single Māori authority; rather, Māori authority is spread across different sites, which are often interwoven or interacting among themselves, as well as in relationships with different levels of government.[18] Traditionally, authority or mana in Māori communities is located in different hapū (sub-tribe/kinship groups) and/or iwi (tribal/common ancestral groups). Membership of an iwi or hapū is not elective; it is a consequence of whakapapa (genealogy) that can include spiritual and natural relationships as well as human kinship ties. Through their whakapapa, Māori individuals can have ties to more than one hapū or iwi. Today, hapū and iwi leaders retain a role as authorities in the lives of many of their members, but, for purposes of engagement with the government in Treaty settlement processes or asset management, or for purposes of consultation, there are also official bodies recognized as having a mandate to represent iwi and hapū, usually constituted as legal entities such as statutory

---

[16] See, eg statutory obligations in the Local Government Act 2002 and Resource Management Act 1991. For an analysis of Council–Māori engagement in the resource management sector, including case studies, see Te Puni Kokiri, 'Te Kotahitanga o te Whakahaere Rawa: Maori and Council Engagement under the Resource Management Act 1991' (Te Puni Kokiri, Wellington, 2006).

[17] Now Hon Justice Joe Williams, Judge of the High Court of New Zealand; in his capacity as Chief Judge of the Māori Land Court and Chairperson of the Waitangi Tribunal, in the keynote address for Local Government New Zealand's Annual Conference in 2005, and repeated in Local Government New Zealand's summary paper on Council–Māori engagement, available online at <http://www.lgnz.co.nz/library/publications/M?ori_Sheet_A4_02.pdf>. See also AJ Hayward, 'Local Government and Maori: Talking Treaty?' (1999) 50 *Political Science* 182.

[18] For analysis of the locations of Māori self-determination, see Mason Durie, *Te Mana, Te K Wanatanga: The Politics of Self Determination* (Oxford University Press, 1998); Kirsty Gover and Natalie Baird, 'Identifying the Māori Treaty Partner' (2002) 52 *University of Toronto Law Journal* 39; Andrew Sharp, 'Traditional Authority and the Legitimation Crisis of Urban Tribes: The Waipareira Case' (2003) 6 *Ethnologies Comparee* available at <http://recherche.univ-montp3.fr/cerce/r6/a.s.htm>; Andrew Sharp, 'Blood, Custom, and Consent: Three Kinds of Māori Groups and the Challenges They Present to Governments' (2002) 52 *University of Toronto Law Journal* 9; Wai 414: *Te Whanau O Waipareira Report* (1998).

Māori Trust Boards, incorporated societies, or charitable trusts.[19] However the legal entities are constructed, the key principle is that particular iwi and/or hapū are tāngata whenua in particular areas with a level of mana whenua/kaitiakitanga (authority/guardianship of the land).[20]

Yet there are also many Māori individuals who do not know or feel connected to their whakapapa. In recent times, new organizations that are not kinship-based have claimed authority to provide services and representation for so-called 'urban Māori' and their interests.[21] Examples are 'urban Māori authorities' which aim to build communities to replicate some of the structures, services, and support of traditional kinship groupings. Despite the large numbers of Māori individuals who, as Sharp describes, 'live their lives in ways scarcely distinguishable from their Pākehā neighbours', the extent of urban Māori authority is a subject of controversy.[22] Some insist that only iwi and hapū are legitimate sites of authority, but in a landmark and controversial decision, the Waitangi Tribunal thought otherwise, confirming that rangatiratanga (self-determination or authority) lies with Māori people and is not necessarily tied to kinship-based institutions.[23] Under the Treaty, the tribunal found, the Crown has a duty to protect rangatiratanga wherever it is located.[24]

2. Are These Parties Candidates for Legitimate Relative Authority?

All these different forms of Māori organization (whether or not kin-based, traditionally or statutorily constituted) and the formal constitutional arrangements in the New Zealand state, must then be investigated to see whether

---

[19] See, eg the list of 'Recognised Iwi Organisations and Mandated Iwi Organisations' in the Māori Fisheries Act 2004, and 'Iwi authorities' for the purposes of s 35A of the Resource Management Act 1991. For instance, Ngāti Whatua, one of the northern tribes whose tribal area includes much of greater Auckland, is represented by Te Runanga o Ngāti Whātua, which is a mandated iwi organization under the Māori Fisheries Act 2004, has a recognized mandate for Treaty settlement negotiations, and is an 'iwi authority' for the purposes of the Resource Management Act 1991.

[20] This principle recognizes tangata whenua rights of consultation or special standing to be involved in specified matters that impact upon their territories.

[21] 'Urban Māori' is a misleading term, for there are also many traditionally organized iwi and hapu based in urban areas.

[22] Sharp, 'Traditional Authority and the Legitimation Crisis of Urban Tribes'.

[23] *Te Whanau O Waipareira Report*. Compare the litigation over the pan-Māori 'Sealord's' fisheries settlement, in which a coalition of Treaty tribes successfully argued all the way to the Privy Council to confirm that urban Māori authorities were not 'iwi' for purposes of receiving a share of assets under the settlement: *Manukau Urban Maori Authority v Treaty of Waitangi Fisheries Commission* (Privy Council, Appeals 67–68/2000, 2 July 2001).

[24] For further analysis of Māori identities, see Manuhuia Barcham, *(De)Constructing the Politics of Indigeneity* (Duncan Ivison *et al.* (eds), Cambridge University Press, 2000).

they actually have legitimate authority, either alone or in interaction. Under the conjunctive justification set out in Chapter 12, this requires attention to the processes by which subjects and subject-communities confer standing upon these authorities, and the extent to which they help subjects conform to right reason.

The processes by which governments are elected in New Zealand are imperfect, but they are democratic and, particularly given the proportional representation system which aims to give minority views a worthwhile rather than 'wasted' vote, the processes are sufficiently justified to confer the standing of authority upon those Members of Parliament who can form a government. For argument's sake, I will assume that the criticisms made of the electoral process are not sufficient to deny its overall procedural justification.[25]

The different types of Māori authorities are differently justified. Kinship groups of iwi, hapū, and whanau share what Sharp describes as:[26]

> a legitimatory formulae... [in which] each fundamental group claims to be able to 'whakapapa back' to a certain ancestor; each claims a unique attachment to a certain portion of land; each refers to tikanga or custom, and to their own ways of proceeding in ceremony and deliberation (kawa) that point to their unique and exclusive rights to govern themselves and control their takiwā, or territories.

Although kinship groups are not voluntary associations, consent plays a large role within the justification of particular rangatira (chiefs). Chiefly authority has been described as having its foundations in an ongoing entrustment between leaders and subjects—a 'reciprocal relationship between leaders and members of a Māori community, kin-based or non kin-based'.[27] Positions of leadership are susceptible to 'continued community and individual judgment' so that consent can be withdrawn and standing conferred upon a new leader if that trust is broken.[28] Sharp's account of the justification of rangatiratanga relationships in New Zealand argues that they are '*in general justifiable* because they are precisely those relationships that are characteristic of a good

---

[25] Criticisms made of MMP include that it is inefficient, that it gives minority viewpoints disproportional weight when minor parties are left in the position of 'king-maker', and that the process of coalition talks can turn parties away from the platforms and commitments upon which they are elected. There are also democratic concerns about the presence of 'list' MPs who are not elected by a constituency but are appointed by the party and enter Parliament in proportion to the percentage of votes the party receives if that party is entitled to a greater number of members than the number of constituency seats won.

[26] Sharp, 'Traditional Authority and the Legitimation Crisis of Urban Tribes'.

[27] *Te Whanau O Waipareira Report*, §8.2.3. See also Ch 1.

[28] Sharp, 'Traditional Authority and the Legitimation Crisis of Urban Tribes'; Simon Hope, 'The Roots and Reach of Rangatiratanga' (2004) 56 *Political Science* 23.

community'.²⁹ The Waitangi Tribunal has found that these same principles attaching to trusting relationships could justify non-kinship-based authority, where the same values of rangatiratanga (essentially, values of good governance and community acceptance of that governance) are practised.³⁰

The real challenge, in the assessment of Crown–Māori relative authority, is not to defend the actual processes that legitimize these different authorities, but to establish that there are different subject-communities with the normative standing to do the legitimating. Although there are some small regions in New Zealand that are predominantly Māori and in which tribal control is equally as or more apparent than state control, most Māori and other New Zealanders have closely integrated social, economic, and, indeed, cultural ties.³¹ Many Māori also have and identify with non-Māori ancestry and culture, and many non-Māori identify with Māori culture more deeply than simply feeling pride in the All Blacks' pre-match haka or the Māori verses of the national anthem. Indeed, the social/economic interactions are so close and unremarkable that it would be easy to miss the political and sometimes cultural tensions in the relationship between the authorities, if they were not such a prominent feature of national political debate. Most Māori claims today are not for separate sovereignty, as they once were, but for shared sovereignty or shared authority.³² Both Māori and non-Māori mostly consider it impractical and/or undesirable to carve out separate territory for sovereign Māori self-government, partly due to the depth of integration and ties between Māori and non-Māori, and partly due to the array and diversity of tribes spread throughout the country. Yet, despite the closeness of interaction and integration between Māori and other New Zealanders, and the formally unitary New Zealand citizenship, many Māori individuals and groups have fought—in the political and judicial branches of government, and in the court of public opinion—for recognition of domains of self-determination. Although not

---

[29] Sharp, 'Traditional Authority and the Legitimation Crisis of Urban Tribes', 12–13 (emphasis in original). The 'idealised values [that] stand in judgement' as to the worth of the practice of rangatiratanga are 'a leadership dedicated to the good of the community; a community respecting its leaders; both committed in loving harmony to the preservation and flourishing of their joint enterprise'.

[30] *Te Whanau O Waipareira Report*, Chs 2 and 3. See also at § 5.8: 'The principle, or customary value, of rangatiratanga remains the same. All that changes is the way in which it is applied'.

[31] There are areas of New Zealand which are 60% Māori (including Kawerau (61.1%), Wairoa (60.7%) and Opotiki (59.3%) Districts). The north and eastern parts of the North Island average 25% Māori. Figures are from 2006 Census, which enables individuals to identify with more than one ethnic group.

[32] As Durie suggests, 'with the emergence of a bicultural jurisprudence, as well as a strategically placed presence in Parliament, Māori appear to be searching for a place within the nation state of Aotearoa New Zealand—rather than apart from it': Mason Durie, *Te Mana Te Kawanatanga = the Politics of Māori Self-Determination* (Oxford University Press, 1998), 238. See also FM Brookfield, *Waitangi and Indigenous Rights: Revolution, Law, and Legitimation* (Auckland University Press, 1999).

all Māori individuals wish to be involved in these processes or identify with particular Māori authorities, just as not all other New Zealanders strongly associate with the state or particularly care who runs it, there are enough who do, wielding sufficient political resources, to ensure that a degree of Māori self-determination, self-government, autonomy, or simply 'Māori control of Māori affairs' is now a widespread feature of the political landscape in New Zealand. Public policy often reflects this on both sides of the political spectrum. Although there are political parties that advocate 'moving on' from the difficult colonial relationships and/or ending any policies aimed at addressing the imbalances in social statistics that are colonialism's legacy, mainstream political discourse in New Zealand appears more focused upon managing the relationship in good faith, with the eye for fairness that characterizes New Zealanders' self-image.

The question is how much self-determination is feasible and justified, and how the inevitable interactions between Māori authorities and other authorities, communities, and individuals are to be managed.[33] Regardless of what other New Zealanders think, there are individuals and communities within the state who accept authorities other than or as well as the elected national government; who participate in processes that confer standing upon those authorities and credit them with a different kind of (and perhaps more) legitimacy than the national government.[34] Yet these authorities will only be legitimate if the community members themselves are able to confer that standing upon them, and the activities of the authorities are in service of those community members. This will depend upon the balance of reasons going into the procedural and substantive elements of the justification, including reasons about the value of independent Māori authority.

a. Justifying Māori authorities

The easy part is the strictly procedural assessment of the way in which particular Māori authorities are justified by their communities. This requires investigation into individual consent or participation by group members in the conferral of the standing of authority. The difficult part lies not in the procedural

---

[33] On the 'absorption' of the principle of self-determination into the New Zealand legal and political systems, see Palmer, *The Treaty of Waitangi in New Zealand's Law and Constitution*. Successive governments have committed to a policy that self-determination cannot include territorial separation. There is a similar repeated resistance to calls for separate justice systems, such as that proposed by Moana Jackson: *The Māori and the Criminal Justice System/He Whaaipanga Hou* (New Zealand Department of Justice, 1987–1988) (in two parts).

[34] As Durie argues, 'Māori in Aotearoa New Zealand want to remain Māori': Durie, *Te Mana Te Kawanatanga*, 4–5.

legitimacy of Māori authorities considered in isolation, but in justifying such self-determination when it is claimed from inside a larger community that has also conferred standing upon another, more general (state) authority.

There are both general and particular justifications for self-determination. The general test offers conditions for justified self-determination, wherever it is located and to whomever it is attached. The specific test then seeks a justification for indigenous (and sometimes other minority) communities governing themselves within a democratic multicultural state. Both the general and the specific questions then diverge into different justifications for self-determination, either with or without implications of statehood, sovereignty, or territorial self-governance.[35] These become tangled in arguments about: the value of individual well-being versus collective practices or collective well-being; the instrumental or intrinsic normative value of communities of various sorts; and even the differences between political and international legal conceptions of sovereignty, statehood, and self-determination. The specific question about indigenous peoples' self-determination then gets tangled in debates about the whole idea of indigeneity and the justification of indigenous rights as something distinct from minority rights.[36]

Within this broad literature on self-determination there are three rival approaches: liberal, communitarian, and critical, all of which derive arguments about self-determination from the perceived role and importance of culture. The 'liberal culturalist' approach values some degree of self-determination as an aspect of individual well-being, usually by finding instrumental value in collective manifestations of culture, which should be protected insofar as they support and enable individual fulfilment, provided cultural practices are consistent with individual freedom and include opportunities for exit.[37] If culture does play this role in its members' identities, lives, and well-being, there is reason to value that culture and, perhaps, depending upon other considerations

---

[35] The idea of statehood/sovereignty is simultaneously (and sometimes divergently) conceived under international law and political theory. The debate within the self-determination literature about the entitlements and conditions for statehood are not crucial for my purposes here. For coverage of some of the major theoretical puzzles of indigenous self-determination, see Duncan Ivison et al., *Political Theory and the Rights of Indigenous Peoples* (Cambridge University Press, 2000).

[36] See Claire Charters, 'A Self-Determination Approach to Justifying Indigenous Peoples' Participation in International Law and Policy Making' (2010) 17 *International Journal on Minority and Group Rights* 215; Benedict Kingsbury, 'Reconciling Five Competing Conceptual Structures of Indigenous Peoples' Claims in International and Comparative Law' (2001) 34 *New York University Journal of International Law and Policy* 189.

[37] For an account of this brand of liberal thinking, including its connection to earlier and more recent strands of multicultural theory, see Will Kymlicka, 'Liberal Theories of Multiculturalism', in Lukas H Meyer *et al.* (eds), *Rights, Culture, and the Law: Themes from the Legal and Political Philosophy of Joseph Raz* (Oxford University Press, 2003). Key works in this canon include Will Kymlicka, *Multicultural Citizenship: A Liberal Theory of Minority Rights* (Clarendon Press, 1996); Yael Tamir, *Liberal*

and without freezing or essentializing that culture, reasons to protect or promote it.[38]

Liberal culturalist arguments then become 'liberal multiculturalist' arguments by the addition of arguments for cultural pluralism. It is straightforward to infer that if culture plays the role in securing well-being that many liberals say it does, then all cultures playing that role for their members are valuable and cannot justifiably be repressed.[39] As Raz argues:[40]

> [W]e should recognise that [other cultures] realise important values, and that they provide a home, and a focus of identity which are entirely positive to their members, just as our culture realises important values, and provides a home and a focus of identity for us. This is why multiculturalism transcends what any principles of toleration can provide. Principles of toleration restrain us regarding what we may do in the elimination of error. Multiculturalism denies that the variety of cultures it enjoins us to protect and support are in error. They are seen essentially as different ways in which universal values are realised.

Although the exact terms of the support and encouragement of different cultures then differ between societies, which wrestle with different combinations of cultural groups and different societal challenges, the basic principle is that cultural plurality is to be protected for (and conditionally upon) the good it does the members of those cultures.

There are several steps between finding instrumental value in one's culture, finding instrumental value in others' cultures, and using those values to ground self-determination. Writing with Margalit, Raz has argued that self-determination is naturally understood to mean territorial self-determination, and can be grounded upon its instrumental value to individual well-being.[41] Self-determination is defined as the right of an 'encompassing group' to decide whether a territory should be self-governing, rather than a right to have others treat that group as self-governing.[42] An encompassing group is a group

---

Nationalism (Princeton University Press, 1995); James Tully, *Strange Multiplicity: Constitutionalism in an Age of Diversity* (Cambridge University Press, 1995). See also Raz's writings on this topic, including: Joseph Raz, 'Multiculturalism' (1998) 11 *Ratio Juris* 193.

[38] For example, Raz argues that the common culture into which a person is socialized can be crucial to their well-being because of its impact upon personal identity and its background role in constituting worthwhile social relationships: Joseph Raz, *Ethics in the Public Domain* (Oxford University Press, 1994), 162.

[39] Raz argues that multiculturalism is a normative commitment which is 'motivated by concern for the dignity and well-being of all human beings': Raz, 'Multiculturalism', 196.

[40] Raz, 'Multiculturalism', 204–225.

[41] Avishai Margalit and Joseph Raz, 'National Self-Determination' (1990) 87 *The Journal of Philosophy* 439, 440–441.

[42] Margalit and Raz, 'National Self-Determination', 448.

in which: members share a common culture shaping children's life choices, membership is based on mutual recognition using group-related symbols to overcome the lack of personal acquaintance between all group members; membership is based on 'belonging rather than achievement'; and is a central aspect of members' identities.[43] The authors argue that where an encompassing group is a majority within a territory, it may have a right to self-determination. Yet self-determination can still be unjustified if the majority encompassing group would be insufficiently cognizant of the interests of non-members or the individual freedoms of group members.[44] A right to self-determination can also be lost by prescription, where the claim of new occupiers is as good as that of the former group.[45] Or, if the group is in a minority, it does not have the right at all.[46]

The concept of an encompassing group is useful because it helps in working out what reasons apply to those group members. Not only does the significance of culture in group members' lives generate reasons for promoting that culture, which do not exist for non-encompassing groups, but culture can also affect the way universal reasons apply to participants in that culture, by determining the circumstances in which particular conduct is right or wrong. The obligations and rights applying between members can look different from those applying between non-members, and/or members of different encompassing groups or non-encompassing groups. Thus, the conduct of an individual from a non-encompassing community who (for instance) gathers a handful of shellfish from a public beach is different from the same action performed by a member of an encompassing group whose culture forbids collection from that beach. Different reasons can apply to different people, and the same reasons can apply differently depending on circumstances, including cultural circumstances.

None of this entails or requires a commitment to moral relativism, only moral pluralism. Even the most difficult questions about the different values to which different groups are committed can be explored through a position of moral pluralism in which there is incommensurability between different values held by different cultures, or in which there may be more than one objectively correct conception of right conduct, which nevertheless depends

---

[43] Margalit and Raz, 'National Self-Determination', 443–447. Compare Iris Marion Young's account of 'social groups': 'Though sometimes objective attributes are a necessary condition for classifying oneself or others as belonging to a certain social group, it is identification with a certain social status, the common history that social status produces, and self-identification that define the group as a group': Young, *Justice and the Politics of Difference* (Princeton University Press, 1990), 44.
[44] Margalit and Raz, 'National Self-Determination', 455–456.
[45] Margalit and Raz, 'National Self-Determination', 459.
[46] Margalit and Raz, 'National Self-Determination', 440, 458–459.

upon cultural practices for its specification.[47] The universality of moral truth is not threatened by introducing what Raz calls a 'new sensitivity to the facts which establish this moral truth'.[48]

Although I will retain the concept of an encompassing group and the moral pluralism that is embedded in the Raz–Margalit account, their account of self-determination is problematic. Even within its liberal framework, the emphasis on demographics is out of synch with the remainder of the authors' instrumental justification for self-determination.[49] On the instrumental approach, a minority encompassing-group should not be denied a self-determination right if, on balance, the result would be greater well-being for them and no loss for the majority. For instance, against a majority which persecutes, neglects, or persistently overrides the interests of a minority encompassing group, a benevolent minority encompassing group should not be barred from a right to self-determination simply on the basis of their smaller numbers. Even if numbers count for the purposes of justifying action that would be disruptive to individuals and expensive for communities (ie an encompassing group must be sufficiently sizeable to make its members' well-being a matter of sufficient public concern), there is no special magic to be had in reaching a majority.

More significant concerns come from the communitarian and critical responses to liberal multiculturalism, which, respectively, shift away from the focus on individual well-being to find inherent values in collective well-being, or reformulate conceptions of the individual and their well-being. The communitarian position emphasizes the intrinsic value of group cultures, sometimes in conjunction with their instrumentality to individual well-being, but also arguing that the value of groups themselves generates reasons to protect and promote their flourishing.[50] In contrast, critical positions reject what they see as an essentialization of culture and its constraining effects upon the lives and identities of individuals within them. Both critical

---

[47] For an example of such a position, see MC Nussbaum, 'Non-Relative Virtues: An Aristotelian Approach', in Martha C Nussbaum and Amartya Sen (eds), *The Quality of Life* (Oxford University Press, 1993). On incommensurability coupled with a rejection of ethical relativism, see Raz, 'Multiculturalism'; Joseph Raz, 'Comments and Responses', in Lukas H Meyer (ed), *Rights, Culture and the Law: Themes from the Legal and Political Philosophy of Joseph Raz* (2003).

[48] Raz, 'Multiculturalism', 195. Raz neatly summarizes: 'The universality of morality is rooted in the nature of moral thought: in the fact that generality is of the essence of all conceptual thought, that morality is necessarily knowable, and that moral principles are essentially intelligible, rather than arbitrary givens': Raz, 'Multiculturalism', 194.

[49] Raz confirms this aggregative approach to collective rights in Joseph Raz, *The Morality of Freedom* (Clarendon Press, 1986), 187, 209.

[50] This mixed position is found, for example, in Charles Taylor and Amy Gutmann, *Multiculturalism: Examining the Politics of Recognition* (Princeton University Press, 1994), 25–73.

and communitarian approaches can be combined in criticisms of specifically 'Western' liberal democratic/capitalist cultures, which are thought to constrain members of groups in which greater value is placed upon the collective. For instance, a critical approach could challenge the characterization of the significance of territory to the overall value of individual well-being. Margalit and Raz deny that territory has any intrinsic value in the process of organizing self-governing groups, and see territorial organization as contingent; a social fact generated by the current international practice of ordering peoples into states. This ignores the possibility that the territorial space in which a group is situated has significance for the group beyond a simple story about settlement or the formation of political units. A group—particularly of the encompassing type the authors describe—may have spiritual or ancestral ties to land which are part of group 'belonging'. Margalit and Raz's normal justification for self-determination is based upon a comprehensive view in which land is property to be owned, possessed, and transferred, and offers no room for comprehensive views in which land is part of the group members' visible public and self-identity—a feature which, on the Margalit-Raz argument, is one of the reasons for valuing encompassing group self-government.[51] To then deny a right to self-determination because that group is a minority within 'its' land moves too quickly over the damage that is done to those group members when their home is controlled (and perhaps even damaged or destroyed) by another group or the wider society. This argument is especially relevant to justifications for indigenous self-determination.

Various justifications for indigenous self-determination have been offered in the course of the battle for acceptance of the UN Declaration on the Rights of Indigenous Peoples, which, in the form eventually adopted by the UN General Assembly, preserves the right of self-determination.[52] These include reliance upon the general argument that there is instrumental or intrinsic value in encompassing group cultures, and that indigenous cultures are such encompassing groups; arguments from history—that indigenous peoples were not simply first occupants, but were first sovereigns and are distinct from other minority groups who cannot make that historical claim; and arguments

---

[51] Margalit and Raz, 'National Self-Determination', 445–446.
[52] See United Nations Declaration on the Rights of Indigenous Peoples, Adopted by General Assembly Resolution 61/295 on 13 September 2007, Art 3: 'Indigenous peoples have the right to self-determination. By virtue of that right they freely determine their political status and freely pursue their economic, social and cultural development'. See also Art 4: 'Indigenous peoples, in exercising their right to self-determination, have the right to autonomy or self-government in matters relating to their internal and local affairs, as well as ways and means for financing their autonomous functions'. See Claire Charters and Rodolfo Stavenhagen, *Making the Declaration Work: The United Nations Declaration on the Rights of Indigenous Peoples* (Transaction Publishers, 2009).

from contemporary injustices—that there are formal and cultural barriers to indigenous political participation or socio-economic injustices which can be addressed through self-determination.

b. The overlap or interaction of Crown–Māori authority

The point of traversing the arguments for self-determination here is not to settle the question in the abstract, but to try to establish when Māori are subjects of legitimate authorities other than or as well as the New Zealand state. Returning to the New Zealand case reveals that, in many circumstances of social and political life, different procedurally justified Māori authorities and the state can be overlapping or interactive authorities. Māori individuals are subjects of the state as a legitimate authority in respect of all those matters of common concern that affect the whole community and require state-wide coordination (including dispute-settlement) in order to help individuals better conform to reason, and remembering that Māori participate and have special participatory mechanisms in the process of conferring standing upon any particular state government in ways that may satisfy the procedural element of relative authority. Māori individuals are also subjects of any particular tribal or other authority with whom they have that standing relationship of rangatiratanga, when that relationship helps them conform to reason by practising the culture and values that are part of their personal identities and social relationships. They are shared subjects of these authorities.

However, if the existing procedures through which Māori participate in conferring authority upon state officials are not sufficient to confer that authority, then Māori would not be subjects of the state.[53] Nor would Māori individuals be subjects if, in general, trying to follow state authority would lead them to do worse in conformity to reason than they could on their own—as has been the case in the past when Crown actions towards Māori have included both forceful and insidious policies to oppress Māori identity and break down strong Māori communities.[54] In those cases Māori would not be shared subjects of the different authorities, but subjects of Māori authorities only. However, the degree of interaction with state authorities would still

---

[53] For example, some criticize existing procedures that use particular socio-cultural elements (language, structures, institutions, etc) that are not Māori and therefore are less inclusive of Māori people. See, for a specific analysis, Merata Kawharu, 'Local Maori Development and Government Policies' (2001) *Social Policy Journal of New Zealand* 1.

[54] The nineteenth and twentieth centuries offer many examples, including violence against peaceful protestors, scorched earth policies, land confiscation and privatization plans, language, and other assimilationist policies. A great deal of research on specific instances appears in the Waitangi Tribunal's reports, all available at <http://www.waitangi-tribunal.govt.nz/reports/>.

generate relativity between Māori and state authorities, which necessarily interact when there are common concerns or when the interaction of subjects forces the interaction of authorities.

Thus, the overlap or interaction is determined by who has conferred the standing of authority upon whom, the legitimacy of the conferral process, and the domains of activity in which the authorities can, separately or together, help people conform to reasons. The implications of the justification of self-determination are that only Māori authorities can help Māori individuals conform to those reasons that are bound up with expressing cultural (and therefore a key aspect of personal) identity. Yet there are other things that only the state can do. All New Zealanders are subjects of the democratic state's legitimate authority regarding any matters of common concern requiring state-wide coordination. All New Zealanders are not, however, subjects of tribal or other Māori authorities because, even if Māori authorities could also help them conform to reason by providing the service of coordination, non-Māori New Zealanders have not conferred upon Māori authorities the standing of authority over them.

Thus, it becomes necessary to work out what are the matters of common concern requiring coordinated, state-wide action. Some are obvious and uncontroversial, such as driving on the (left) side of the road or having a single currency and managing monetary policy, or providing an organized system of national defence. These are matters that either need to be organized on a large scale, are simply too expensive or impractical to organize in smaller units, or are necessary to the smooth interaction of peoples in such close proximity with one another. Others seem obvious but are actually controversial, such as having a centralized system of criminal justice which collectivizes punishment rather than leaving it in the hands of private individuals or distinct groups, and having a centralized system of distributive justice which collects taxes and distributes welfare so that no members miss out simply because of who they are or where they live. It is arguable that both criminal and distributive justice can be managed (and even managed better) by smaller and more close-knit communities sharing a common culture in which people actually feel their responsibilities to one another rather than being mediated by an impersonal state. The further one runs through examples of this sort—education, health, immigration policies, for instance—the more controversial they become and the more room for argument that these matters of 'common concern' can actually and justifiably be handled by self-determining authorities. Yet these more controversial issues are also the most important for those who claim self-determination; Māori self-determination claims are not claims to be allowed to drive on the right side of the road while the rest of the country drives on the left.

3. 'Relational' Self-Determination and Relative Authorities

The basic questions targeted by all these approaches, including perspectives of indigenous theorists, ask when a community is entitled to govern itself and what (if any) constraints this right to self-determination places upon other self-determining communities. In contrast to theories of multiculturalism per se, theories of self-determination are not interested in defending the value of supporting different cultural communities, but in justifying arrangements of separate authority in which communities defined in various ways govern themselves without interference from other communities.[55] The justifications for these different political authorities are made out separately—the justification of state authority is separate from the justification of (for instance) an authority in a self-determining indigenous community. Sometimes the justifications are not only separate from one another, but are also in opposition—ie an argument that democratic states are more justified than tribes or vice versa, or that cosmopolitan political arrangements would be more justified than states, and so on.

All of this gets tangled up, so that trying to separate between subjects or demarcate those matters on which individuals are subject to different authorities is an exercise fraught with vagueness, boundary problems, and value pluralism. In contrast to all these accounts, my relative authority approach integrates the justifications by starting from the interaction and/or overlap of different subjects, and doing away with the idea that the justification of one authority can be separated from others. It is easier to make sense of the complexities of inter-community relationships, and evaluate responses to them, using the relative authority theory, under which it matters less which authorities have authority over which subjects because we assess their interactive rather than independent legitimacy.

Under the theory of relative authority, instead of testing the justifications of different holders of authority, we ask about the legitimacy of each authority in its relationships with other authorities. On this view, territorial sovereignty, jurisdiction, or other formal bases of separation between subject-communities are not normatively decisive for the legitimacy of authority: if there is overlap or interaction between the domains of the authorities, which can occur across these formal lines of separation, then even if there is formal separation

---

[55] Indeed, this non-interference is often taken to be part of the very idea of self-determination. However, interference with a self-determining community which fails to allow self-determination to other qualifying groups could be justified: Young, *Justice and the Politics of Difference*, 37–38.

between the subject-communities, the interaction of their authorities will still become a condition of their legitimacy.

Applied to the self-determination context, the relative authority approach goes beyond the standard argument that self-determination must be consistent with others' equal rights to be similarly self-determining. It adds, first, the conditions imposed by reasons for action—that self-determination must be consistent with authorities helping subjects to conform to reason both separately and interactively; and also procedural reasons—that the self-determining and wider state authorities must not only have standing, but that the procedures conferring standing must be tailored so as to respect the subjects of other/shared authorities, while also engaging in relationships consistent with the balance of governance reasons and side-effect reasons.

The idea that interconnectedness between self-determining groups is crucial to the justification of self-determination is not new, nor is the idea that self-determination is conditional upon a balance of rights between those inside and outside self-determining groups. Young also argued for a 'relational' conception of self-determination, in which 'peoples can be self-determining only if the relations in which they stand to others are non-dominating'.[56] For Young, peoples stand 'in interdependent relations with others', and 'in so far as their activities affect one another, peoples are in a relationship and ought to negotiate the terms and effects of the relationship'.[57] Young notes that peoples' interaction with others can generate conflicts and collective problems, and thus a world of self-determining peoples requires institutions in which they can all negotiate terms of interaction and employ dispute-settlement to resolve conflicts.[58] In Young's account, the presence of self-determining peoples need not reduce the capacity for coordinated political action; it simply changes the makeup of the institutions which achieve such coordination by opening participation to diverse groups, without domination from nation states.

There are two differences between Young's relational account of self-determination and my account of relative authority. The first is that Young's account is procedural—it argues that in response to interconnected concerns or conflict between peoples, we need to ensure that there are institutions in which peoples can all participate, and which can regulate their interactions. In contrast, the account of relative authority is both procedural and substantive. On the procedural side it recognizes that there can be a plurality of procedural

---

[56] Iris Marion Young, 'Two Concepts of Self-Determination', in Stephen May *et al.* (eds), *Ethnicity, Nationalism, and Minority Rights* (Cambridge University Press, 2004), 177. See also Iris Marion Young, *Inclusion and Democracy* (Oxford University Press, 2002), 236–275.
[57] Young, 'Two Concepts of Self-Determination', 187.
[58] Young, 'Two Concepts of Self-Determination', 187–188.

reasons conferring standing upon different authorities; that those processes may need to be modified to reflect this fact; and that there can be governance reasons and side-effect reasons requiring cooperation, coordination, or other forms of interactive arrangements between authorities. Yet, it also adds a substantive requirement, in which interactions between authorities are measured not only by consistency with their procedural justification, but by their outcomes. As in theories of independent authority, a procedural justification is incomplete unless the substantive result is sufficiently valuable to confirm the normative value of the procedure. Procedures requiring participation of those with the standing to represent self-determining peoples are important, but the legitimacy of the authorities engaged within them still depends upon whether they produce outcomes allowing those peoples to conform to the reasons that apply to them.

The second difference is related and is also important. Accounts of self-determination emphasize peoples in the collective sense, and sometimes people in the individual sense, without exploring the significance of standing conferred by those people/s upon an authority over those people/s.[59] The point of bringing authority into the self-determination equation is to place the onus upon authorities to engage in the required relationships even when some individual members do not want them to. If cooperation between authorities would better enable subjects of both authorities to conform to the reasons that apply to them, then they should cooperate even if some of their individual subjects believe otherwise.[60] The presence of authority enables subjects to achieve things that they could not (or would not) on their own, and authority can also concretize members' moral duties. In theories of independent authority, this broadly perfectionist account would be subject to the well-known criticisms from liberal theory. Yet when we conceive of authority as relative, arising out of the interaction of subjects with non-subjects and the overlapping subjection of peoples to different authorities, then putting the onus upon authorities to help secure compliance with reason is not primarily about paternalist or perfectionist direction of subjects, rather it is about: (i) enabling

---

[59] Although it is possible to conceive of peoples whose social organization does not involve political or legal authority of some form, it would be a stretch to see such groups (probably small-scale associations or kinship groups in which there are forms of private authority) as the kinds of groups who claim and may be entitled to self-determination. Thus, the peoples who claim or have interactive self-determination will normally have authorities that actually conduct the inter-peoples' interactions and manage their relationships.

[60] There is a practical constraint upon the practice of relative authority in circumstances where members of overlapping or interacting communities refuse to cooperate despite the requirements of reason. If it were so far out of alignment that it led to resistance and the breakdown of authority itself, then authority would cease to exist in circumstances where members of overlapping or interacting communities refuse to cooperate despite the requirements of reason.

subjects of these multiple authorities to avoid practical conflicts and to trust that they can follow 'their' authority and plan around its directives (without worrying that this will run them afoul of other authorities); and (ii) protecting the legitimate relationships that exist between shared subjects or interactive non-subjects and their respective authorities.

4. The Crown and Māori as Relative Authorities

The relative authority approach is particularly useful in the New Zealand case, where any of the standard arguments for or against indigenous self-determination run up against the facts of deep interaction, territorial integration, and entwined relationships. It enables an analysis of those relationships to be presented as an evaluation of the legitimacy of the parties, not just as evidence of good or bad faith, health, or pathologies in the relationships themselves.[61] It is also more useful than multiculturalist arguments, which offer powerful justifications for protection of immigrant cultures in pluralist societies, but are less convincing when addressing the relationships between multiple cultures which each see themselves as 'at home' in a single state.[62] Indeed, the Treaty of Waitangi itself can be seen as an expression and commitment to relative authority; it is a confirmation of the entanglement of the legitimacy of Crown and Māori authorities, but it does not indicate how they can each realize their authority.

The key outstanding questions are: what does right reason (including reasons for action and reasons for decision) require of all New Zealanders in their relationships with each other; and how can the relevant interacting or overlapping authorities help serve conformity to those requirements? There will no doubt be disagreement about what right reason requires, so any required processes of engagement must also incorporate concern for disagreement and respect for contending reasonable views.[63] To break it down further, this requires asking: how do requirements of right reason apply to actual social and political circumstances in which there is reasonable disagreement about

---

[61] Compare Palmer, *The Treaty of Waitangi in New Zealand's Law and Constitution*, 298–312, setting the objective not as legitimacy per se, but 'healthy relationships' between the Crown and Māori.

[62] See, eg Raz, 'Multiculturalism', 196–197: 'multiculturalism warns us against the dangers of each one of us understanding the universal in terms of him- or her- self, a danger which is particularly great when the other is an alien in our country, when we are at home, and he is not'.

[63] To clarify, I accept here that there is value pluralism between the different communities, and that the communities themselves are not monolithic. Within and among Māori communities there is as much disagreement and political difference as there is in and among the wider population of New Zealanders.

their content? In short, what does 'political morality' require of Crown and Māori authorities?

a. Justified relationships and specific problems

This can be tested first in relation to specific concrete questions on which authorities can help their subjects better conform to the reasons that apply to them. There are many examples where the state's construction of a public good, such as a road or a prison, or extraction of a public resource, such as minerals, has been contrary to Māori law in the areas where the construction or extraction takes place. Many of these clashes have come before the courts or the Waitangi Tribunal, while others have featured in political negotiations between parties in Parliament, or between the Crown and the tribes directly affected. Some have been the subject of all of these procedures.[64] When these clashes arise, applying the relative authority test makes it possible to work out what is required, or, in other words, what is a justified relationship between the Crown and Māori authorities. Under the relative authority test there are three requirements:

(i) The relationship between the authorities must improve or at least not diminish the prospects of conformity to reason for Māori and other New Zealanders, recognizing that these reasons might be different and/or that the same reasons might apply differently to members of these communities.

(ii) The relationship must be consistent with the values protected by the procedures conferring standing upon each authority—ie the autonomy and respect for disagreement that is protected by representative democracy, and the autonomy and the values of tikanga Māori that are protected by relationships of rangatiratanga.

(iii) There must be no overriding undefeated reasons against having that relationship. The most likely candidate would be reasons of necessity which, for instance, would override having a dialogical cooperative relationship if there was an overriding need for an immediate decision.

To put these into a concrete scenario, imagine an example of resource extraction, in which the applicable substantive reasons include the value of the resource to the general public, and the value of the resource to a particular Māori tribe. These values can be commensurable in terms of the economic wealth that the resources instantiate, but they can be incommensurable when

---

[64] For an example of a dispute of this type which tracked through these different dispute resolution procedures, see Nicole Roughan, 'The Association of State and Indigenous Law: A Case Study in "Legal Association" ' (2009) 59 *University of Toronto Law Journal* 135, 147–152.

they also involve cultural practices and beliefs about the special role or inherent value of land and resources.

Assume first that the economic reasons are equally weighted on both sides, and that there are valid cultural reasons on both sides that are incommensurable. In that case, the most justified relationship will be a relationship of cooperation in which authorities participate together to decide how the different incommensurable reasons can be best accommodated or compromised. Reason does not dictate an outcome, but the relative authority condition makes it clear that the state cannot justifiably ignore Māori authorities, or exclude them by force, and vice versa, because to do so would undermine the shared/overlapping subjects' conformity to reason and the standing which each individual or community has conferred upon its representatives.

There are a number of different methods such cooperation might take. Examples from practice include co-management agreements, (often between local governments and local hapu/iwi, but also larger-scale arrangements between the Crown and one or more hapu/iwi).[65] These arrangements are imperfect and always evolving, but it is significant that there are now a number of different models upon which direct Crown–Māori cooperation can be negotiated. Other examples have been developed in non-environmental policy settings, notably in education, justice, and health, and there are guidelines for Ministries and other Crown entities about best practice for entering into formal cooperative arrangements with Māori authorities.[66]

A recent case of this sort presents a powerful illustration of relative authority.[67] In 2013, the Supreme Court heard a dispute over the Crown's plans to sell a minority shareholding in a state-owned hydro-energy company, whose water use permits allow use of water resources that are the subject of ongoing claims to the Waitangi Tribunal. Both the relevant Māori authorities and the Waitangi Tribunal itself, however, were concerned that

---

[65] See, eg the arrangements negotiated by the Crown with Waikato-Tainui iwi for co-management of the Waikato River and resources. The procedures established under the Deed of Settlement with Waikato-Tainui include: a single co-governance entity with five members each appointed by the Crown and iwi (including other iwi—Te Arawa, Maniapoto, and Tuwharetoa—who are members of the Waikato River Authority and with whom the Crown has negotiated separate settlements), with responsibility for achieving restoration of the Waikato River; and joint management agreements and requirements for iwi participation in specified planning decisions related to the river. The arrangements are given effect in the Waikato-Tainui Raupatu Claims (Waikato River) Settlement Act 2010.

[66] See Palmer, *The Treaty of Waitangi in New Zealand's Law and Constitution*, 143–144 and 223–225. At 223 Palmer calls the Cabinet-approved set of guidelines 'a fascinating mixture of facilitating well-intentioned relationship-building, realistic appreciation about the difficulty of doing this and the importance of mitigating legal risk in doing it'.

[67] *New Zealand Māori Council v Attorney-General* [2013] NZSC 6 (hereafter '*Asset Sales*').

the company's partial sale would 'materially impair' the Crown's ability to meet its statutory obligations to act consistently with the principles of the Treaty of Waitangi.[68] Under New Zealand law, particular Māori authorities can have rights (including forms of ownership rights) in the riverbeds and adjoining lands, and have spiritual and environmental interests, but not full ownership rights, in the waters themselves. This much was all accepted by the Crown, just as the Māori authorities accepted that modern practicalities and cultural preferences support the use of water as an energy resource. That is, there were cultural and economic reasons in each direction.

The example will need to be evaluated in full elsewhere, but several elements are striking. First is the apparently reasonable nature of the concessions made by both sides, which may indeed reflect recognition of their relative authority and an attempt to realize their legitimacy through appropriate relationships. The Māori Council accepted that the modern need to use water resources for energy generation created a limit upon what claimants could reasonably be expected to receive by way of Treaty settlements relating to those water resources, while the Crown indicated that there may be proprietary interests in the water itself, and was open to considering proprietary interests short of full ownership. As the court summarized, the Crown is 'prepared to encourage and facilitate joint ventures in the generation of electricity using waters in which Maori are interested in the future. It is also prepared to negotiate co-governance and co-management arrangements under which Maori have a substantial say in the control of particular rivers through Treaty settlements'.[69]

Second, there is a key element of relative authority recognized within the Supreme Court's ruling itself. In a unanimous decision, the court held that the proposed sale of shares was reviewable for its compliance with the principles of the Treaty, but that the sale would not make a 'material difference' to the outcome of ongoing Treaty claims challenging Crown action or rights to the relevant water resources.[70] The court accepted the Crown's undertakings 'that it will not rely on the privatization of the generating companies so as to diminish any claimed rights'.[71] It then found that, given the availability of a range of co-management and other cooperative arrangements which could preserve a degree of Māori authority, and the willingness of the Crown to undertake such arrangements: 'in the current legal and social environment,

---

[68] Interim Waitangi Tribunal Report Released on the National Freshwater and Geothermal Resources Claim, 24 August 2012.
[69] Interim Waitangi Tribunal Report Released on the National Freshwater and Geothermal Resources Claim, para 103.
[70] *Asset Sales*, para 64.   [71] *Asset Sales*, paras 104, 105.

Maori can be confident that their claims will be addressed' notwithstanding the partial share sale.[72]

The correctness or otherwise of the decision itself is not the point here; rather, the example illustrates the kinds of ways in which a balance of reasons can be weighed up so as to require a relationship of negotiated cooperation on the part of the interacting relative authorities.

Stepping back into the hypothetical case, the example can then be changed so that there is no special cultural reason on the side of the wider political community, but there is for the relevant Māori communities, and furthermore there are alternative sites that could be used to extract the resources. In those circumstances the justified relationship will be one of coordination in which the Crown defers to the Māori authorities regarding the resources or site of significance, and if those authorities so decide, uses an alternative site for their extraction plans. Such deference is justified because it enhances or at least avoids diminishing the prospects of conformity to reason for the shared or interactive subjects. The Crown should, at the least, tolerate Māori control of this matter in order to better enable Māori subjects of those authorities to conform to the cultural reasons that apply to them, and to respect the authority they have conferred upon their leaders. Yet that deference is still consistent with the standing that has been conferred upon the state because it can go ahead with its plans, just in a different place. It is, effectively, a no-loss situation.

Things get more difficult if the example is changed again, so that this time there is no alternative site or resource available, yet circumstances still necessitate that the project go ahead. That structure will likely apply only in extreme fact situations —for instance, a drought causing crop and livestock failure so that all nationwide fish stocks (including those under tribal control) need to be tapped in order to feed the population.[73] A valid argument of necessity would rule out any relationship that would prevent the necessary action. By definition, necessity trumps self-determination just as it trumps other valuable practices, if there is no way of performing the necessary act consistently with them. The tricky part is working out when claims of necessity are valid. Legal doctrine, political theory, and philosophical argument give some guidance, but must be tempered by remembering that necessity only trumps self-determination and other values if it is inconsistent with them.

---

[72] *Asset Sales*, paras 115, 147–148.

[73] Like all arguments of necessity, there will almost always be counter-arguments that the action is not actually necessary (ie here, the alternative action could include resort to importing large quantities of vegetable proteins). It is therefore useful to adopt the legal conception of reasonable necessity, which requires the absence of options that are reasonably available.

It is possible that many problems of necessity can be addressed cooperatively rather than exclusively, thus preserving the legitimacy of each authority by promoting conformity to reason for all the subjects (by doing the act that is necessary) while preserving the procedural justifications that each authority carries. For instance, faced with a crisis of food security, it is hard to imagine any tribal authority refusing to participate in a cooperative co-management scheme that made the necessary resources available, and, indeed, if it did refuse, it would cease to have legitimate authority for its citizens, who have reason to help both themselves and their co-subjects who are in need.

The final variation arises when the balance of commensurable reasons favours going ahead with the project, and there are no incommensurable reasons that have been left outside that equation. For instance, if there is no specific cultural reason for action on either side, or one single cultural reason that is shared between the cultures, there remains just a question of economic value. In that case, the substantive requirements for legitimate authority are clear, but the procedural element of the relativity condition remains active, so that while the project should go ahead, it must involve all the relevant authorities. This could be through cooperation, making the project a joint project and sharing its resulting value, or through a coordination system to resolve any disagreements. The choice of method must then be informed by the wider relationship and its context.

b. Constitutional issues

All of these actual and hypothetical examples take place in the context of wider and continuing relationships, in which there are lasting and more fundamental constitutional questions at stake. The requirements of relative authority therefore need to be applied not only to dealing with specific problems, but also to the question of how the overall relationship between Crown and Māori authorities should be conducted. This focuses attention upon all the reasons relevant to constitutional questions about the status of iwi/hapū authority, the extent of self-determination, the role of the Treaty of Waitangi, the character and structure of representation and participation, the processes of administering and controlling the power of the state, and the pathways for constitutional reform. In New Zealand, none of these constitutional elements is enshrined or entrenched; they are all subject to the incremental and dialogical methods of development and reform, which characterize New Zealand's customary constitution.[74]

---

[74] Matthew SR Palmer, 'What Is New Zealand's Constitution and Who Interprets It? Constitutional Realism and the Importance of Public Office-Holders' (2006) 17 *Public Law Review* (Aust) (2006).

An illustration can be found in the example of Tuhoe, a central North Island tribe which has one of the most persuasive claims to extensive self-determination, because Tuhoe were not given the opportunity to sign the Treaty of Waitangi in 1840 and, they argue, have never consented to the Crown's authority or engaged in relationships that would legitimize that authority. To the contrary, Tuhoe has suffered a history of injustices perpetuated by the Crown, which, according to the relative authority account, would preclude the Crown's legitimate authority over tribe members for much of the history of interaction.[75] Tuhoe's claim is to an autonomous political relationship with the Crown—they are not seeking to isolate themselves or deprive their members of contact with the rest of New Zealand and New Zealanders, which is important to the economic well-being and civil freedoms of tribe members.[76]

The relative authority approach affirms that however geographically and culturally isolated Tuhoe is, it is not isolated enough to stop its members being overlapping or at least interactive subjects of the Crown. This does not depend upon pragmatics or upon the defences of liberal democratic values—rather, the interaction or overlap of subjects is established by looking at the reasons that apply to them. In the case of Tuhoe, members of the tribe share reasons to commit to joint projects with the wider community (and indeed other tribes) whenever the tribal authorities could not fulfil those projects alone. These are the reasons applying to co-subjects of a political community or the separate subjects of interacting communities. For instance, and without attempting to provide a definitive or exhaustive list, the balance of reasons likely supports having the following:

- Common systems of private law and criminal justice. These are necessary to provide for dispute-resolution and protect social interaction beyond the tribal membership, but they do not preclude the operation of parallel tribal justice mechanisms and do not mean that the common justice system should consist only of state-made law. To the contrary, where rules of Māori law would produce results that are more in accordance with the reasons that apply to all parties, then those rules should be applied.[77]

---

[75] These matters are currently the subject of a claim before the Waitangi Tribunal. The first part of the tribunal's report is a damning account of the Crown's actions towards Tuhoe, which include land confiscations, scorched earth tactics, and physical brutality. See Waitangi Tribunal, Wai 894: *Te Urewera Pre-Publication* (2009).

[76] Any attempt to restrict that interaction or deprive new generations of those opportunities would not only be impractical or even impossible, but it would have to involve unreasonable and unjustified restrictions on the lives of tribe members. Along with most other self-determination claimants, Tuhoe are not seeking to build their own illiberal communities.

[77] Much has been written about the justifications for, content of, and effectiveness of tribal justice systems and procedures. See, eg Juan Tauri, 'Explaining Recent Innovations in New Zealand's Criminal

- A common taxation and welfare system which spreads the benefits and burdens of distributive justice amongst the wider population. Again, this does not preclude internal and specific tribal redistribution processes.
- Access to a common public health system, which also centralizes the costs of providing this public good without precluding alternative health systems that can be established internally to the tribe.
- Access to common education services which, although not necessarily requiring a common curriculum, must prepare children adequately to participate fully in the lives of all the communities of which they are members.[78]

The relationship between the Crown and Tuhoe must be consistent with helping subjects conform to these reasons.

The relative authority condition also requires that relationships between the authorities be consistent with upholding the values supported by reasons for decision. These include but are not limited to the following:

- The 'standing' principle: authority is conferred by communities upon their representatives/leaders through justified procedures which give effect to values of autonomy and self-determination.
- The self-determination principle: self-determination acts as a qualification on the Crown's standing because the authority conferred upon the Crown by subjects it shares with another authority is relative authority, not exclusive authority. Relative authority requires either procedures to manage the interaction of separate domains, or cooperation and coordination over the co-design/management/delivery of law and policy.
- The dialogue principle: action over matters of common concern between relative authorities should normally be made through cooperative or dialogically coordinative processes rather than hierarchical relationships.[79] This requires participation in common institutions and mutual responsiveness to each others' separate institutions.

These procedural and substantive reasons can then be applied to examine the existing constitutional and political relationship between the Crown and Māori authorities—either Tuhoe specifically or in general. This is not the

---

Justice System: Empowering Maori or Biculturalising the State?' (1999) 32 *Australian and New Zealand Journal of Criminology* 153; Valmaine Toki, 'Will Therapeutic Jurisprudence Provide a Path Forward for Maori?' (2005) 13 *Waikato Law Review: Taumauri* 169.

[78] This principle is fundamental to the recent revival of Māori education services and providers, from early childhood programmes through to university education, which are provided in the Māori language, and where the curriculum includes an emphasis upon matauranga Māori (knowledge) without being isolated to those forms of knowledge and knowing.

[79] The exception is when there is an overriding reason (of necessity) which requires hierarchical arrangements.

place to work out a full evaluation of the constitutional relationship, but as a preliminary assessment, it seems the existing arrangements are not sufficient to uphold the legitimacy of the relative authorities.

The Māori seats in Parliament, which are often upheld as the key procedure for protecting the special constitutional status of Māori, are an important attempt at realizing the dialogue principle in which relative authorities participate in common institutions, but they are insufficient because they make the interaction of authorities into a numbers game, and they do not require or generate the mutual responsiveness that is necessary for legitimate relative authority. In the past, Members of Parliament holding those seats have often been required to compromise what is best for their constituencies in the process of building numbers to support nationwide policies. This is not a criticism of those compromises, which are an inevitable part of the tension involved in representative democracies, but it reveals that Parliament is not, in that sense, a common institution; it is an institution of the state in which Māori are guaranteed seats but not necessarily voice. Furthermore, Māori representatives in Parliament are not the only Māori authorities who need to be engaged, nor do the Māori seats give effect to those values by which Māori confer authority on their leaders who have nothing to do with Parliament.

Specific arrangements that have been negotiated between tribal authorities and the Crown to share control or management of particular resources are more successful on this front. They have the advantage of being sensitive to the differences between Māori authorities, which cannot be dealt with as a single or homogenous set, and requiring mutual responsiveness and recognition of each others' standing. The results tend to give some effect to self-determination while maintaining mechanisms to deal with any failures of cooperation or coordination. The Supreme Court's decision in the *Asset Sales* case,[80] and the positions and concessions adopted by both parties in that litigation, are reflective of the extent to which current arrangements seek to achieve legitimate relative authority.

Yet the success of specific arrangements and the reasonableness of arguments and outcomes in specific legal challenges do not address the wider constitutional picture of mutually dependent legitimacy.[81] They are limited to specific fields of policy and, thus far, are mostly practised within the environmental

---

[80] *New Zealand Māori Council v Attorney-General* [2013] NZSC 6.
[81] In the 'Asset Sales' case, notably, the Supreme Court identifies the fundamental character of the dispute but expressly cautions against drawing any broader implications out of its decision because it was taken under some urgency and without the benefit of a decision from the court immediately below: see *New Zealand Māori Council v Attorney-General* [2013] NZSC 6, para 5. This seems an unfortunate but understandably pragmatic dodging of a potentially rich consideration of relative authority in the wider constitutional relationship.

management sphere. Negotiations also depend upon the willingness of all parties to engage in them, and to do so in good faith. Recent trends for relatively productive agreements cannot be relied upon to continue, just as any recent trends for law-making and judicial decisions sensitive to relative authority cannot be relied upon. As Palmer notes, 'surprises' in the Crown–Māori relationship can occur without warning, causing harmful and unjustified reactions.[82]

The contingency of political and legal sensitivity to the requirements of relative authority suggests that other mechanisms and approaches are necessary to ensure that the conditions of relative authority are met. Various suggestions have been put forward, including an upper chamber of Parliament to deal with inter-cultural constitutional matters, or a council made up of Māori and non-Māori representatives to hear constitutional questions arising from the Treaty relationship; and/or a 'Treaty of Waitangi court' that would interpret and apply the Treaty of Waitangi as a legal instrument. Many suggestions emphasize processes that require the communities to justify and explain themselves to one another and, if need be, come to terms where there are differences.[83] Sometimes suggestions are made in conjunction with arguments for a new republican form of government, in a grand constitutional reform that would repatriate the Head of State and open the way for some sort of Presidential (or co-Presidential) structure. The precise character and extent of such constitutional changes is beyond the scope of this study; but the implication of relative authority is that some combination of procedural and substantive relationship-management mechanisms would be needed in order to produce legitimate relative authority. A joint representative institution would likely be necessary in order to satisfy the procedural requirements for legitimate relative authority, so that one authority could not speak for or exclude the other, and a special (perhaps legislative, perhaps judicial) institution would

---

[82] A recent example involves legislation passed by the former New Zealand centre-left government, which removed the right of iwi and hapū to access the courts to hear claims of customary title to the foreshore and seabed. The legislation was passed in response to public concern after an appellate court decision which held that at least some of these claims had not been extinguished: *Attorney-General v Ngati Apa* [2003] 3 NZLR 643. After a series of negotiations and consultations with Māori political representatives and some of the tribes concerned, and hearing expert recommendations and public submissions which criticized the Act as unjustifiably discriminatory, the current (centre-right) New Zealand government repealed the legislation and restored rights to seek customary interests in the courts, but through legislation that is almost as substantively and procedurally problematic as that which it has replaced.

[83] The expatriate historian, JGA Pocock, has described this process as one of 'recounting histories in one another's hearing' and reconstituting the policy as a marae (a meeting ground) 'where challenge is constantly being turned into greeting and strangers into guests and fellow counselors': see JGA Pocock, 'The Treaty between Histories', in Andrew Sharp and Paul McHugh (eds), *Histories, Power and Loss: Uses of the Past—a New Zealand Commentary* (Bridget Williams Books, 2001), 94.

be necessary in order to review and resolve differences over common concerns in order to best pursue substantive legitimacy.

All of this speculation reveals that seeing the Crown and Māori as relative authorities does not determine exactly how they are going to secure a legitimate relationship, but it establishes that the relationship is not only about best practices, healthy partnerships, fiduciary principles, or even Treaty obligations; it is about the very existence of authority in circumstances of plurality, and the conditions of its legitimacy.

Bibliography

Ahdieh, Robert, 'From Federalism to Intersystemic Governance: The Changing Nature of Modern Jurisdiction' (2007) 57 *Emory Law Journal* 1

Alexy, Robert, 'The Dual Nature of Law' (2010) 23 *Ratio Juris* 167

Alford, RP, '*Roper v. Simmons* and Our Constitution in International Equipoise' (2005) 53 *UCLA Law Review* 53

Allan, TRS, *Law, Liberty, and Justice: The Legal Foundations of British Constitutionalism* (Clarendon Press, 1993)

Allan, TRS, 'Constitutional Dialogue and the Justification of Judicial Review' (2003) 23 *OJLS* 563

Anscombe, GEM, 'On the Source of the Authority of the State' (1978) 20 *Ratio* 1

Avbelj, Matej and Komárek, Jan, 'Four Visions of Constitutional Pluralism' (2008) 4 *European Constitutional Law Review* 524

Avbelj, Matej and Komárek, Jan, 'Four Visions of Constitutional Pluralism—Symposium Transcript' (2008) 2 *European Journal of Legal Studies* 325

Avbelj, M and Komárek, J, *Constitutional Pluralism in the European Union and Beyond* (2012)

Baquero Cruz, J, 'Legal Pluralism and Institutional Disobedience', in M Avbelj and J Komárek (eds), *Constitutional Pluralism in the European Union and Beyond* (Hart Publishing, 2012)

Barber, NW, 'Legal Pluralism and the European Union' (2006) 12 *European Law Journal* 306

Barcham, Manuhuia, *(De)Constructing the Politics of Indigeneity* (Duncan Ivison *et al.* eds, Cambridge University Press, 2000)

Bartelson, Jens, 'The Concept of Sovereignty Revisited' (2006) 17 *European Journal of International Law* 463

Bellamy, Richard, 'Sovereignty, Post-Sovereignty and Pre-Sovereignty: Three Models of the State, Democracy and Rights within the EU', in Neil Walker (ed), *Sovereignty in Transition* (Hart Publishing, 2003)

Benhabib, Seyla, *Democracy and Difference: Contesting the Boundaries of the Political* (Princeton University Press, 1996)

Benhabib, Seyla, *The Rights of Others: Aliens, Residents, and Citizens* (Cambridge University Press, 2004)

Benvenisti, Eyal, *Margin of Appreciation, Consensus, and Universal Standards* (1998–1999) 31 *New York University Journal of International Law and Politics* 843

Benvenisti Eyal and Downs, George, 'National Courts, Domestic Democracy and the Evolution of International Law' (2009) 20 *European Journal of International Law* 59

Berman, Paul Schiff, 'Global Legal Pluralism' (2007) 80 *Southern California Law Review* 1155

Berman, Paul Schiff, 'Federalism and International Law through the Lens of Legal Pluralism' (2008) 73 *Missouri Law Review* 1151

Berman, Paul Schiff, 'The New Legal Pluralism' (2009) 5 *Annual Review of Law and Social Science* 225

Berman, Paul Schiff, 'Towards a Jurisprudence of Hybridity' (2010) *Utah Law Review* 11

Berman, Paul Schiff, *Global Legal Pluralism: A Jurisprudence of Law Beyond Borders* (Cambridge University Press, 2012)

Bermann, GA et al., *Transatlantic Regulatory Cooperation: Legal Problems and Political Prospects* (Oxford University Press, 2000)

Besson, Samantha, 'Sovereignty in Conflict' (2004) 8(15) *European Integration Online Papers*

Besson, Samantha, *The Morality of Conflict: Reasonable Disagreement and the Law* (Hart Publishing, 2005)

Besson, Samantha, 'Review Article: Democracy, Law and Authority' (2005) 2 *Journal of Moral Philosophy* 89

Besson, Samantha, 'The Authority of International Law—Lifting the State Veil' (2009) 31 *Sydney Law Review* 343

Besson, Samantha, 'European Legal Pluralism after Kadi' (2009) 5 *European Constitutional Law Review* 237

Besson, Samantha, 'Institutionalizing Global Demoi-Cracy', in Lukas H Meyer (ed), *Justice, Legitimacy and Public International Law* (Cambridge University Press, 2009)

Besson, Samantha, 'Whose Constitution(S)? International Law, Constitutionalism and Democracy', in Jeffrey L Dunoff and Joel P Trachtman (eds), *Ruling the World?: Constitutionalism, International Law, and Global Governance* (Cambridge University Press, 2009)

Bickel, Alexander M, *The Least Dangerous Branch: The Supreme Court at the Bar of Politics* (2nd edn, Yale University Press, 1986)

Blake, Michael, 'Distributive Justice, State Coercion, and Autonomy' (2001) 30 *Philosophy and Public Affairs* 257

Boast, Richard and Erueti, Andrew, *Māori Land Law* (2nd edn, LexisNexis, 2004)

Bodin, Jean, *Six Books of the Commonwealth* (MJ Tooley trans, B Blackwell, 1955)

Bogdandy, Armin, *The Exercise of Public Authority by International Institutions* (Cambridge University Press, 2010)

Bogdandy, Armin and Dann, Philipp, 'International Composite Administration' (2008) 9 *German Law Journal* 2013

Bratman, Michael E, 'Shared Cooperative Activity' (1992) 101 *The Philosophical Review* 327

Brookfield, FM, *Waitangi and Indigenous Rights: Revolution, Law, and Legitimation* (Auckland University Press, 1999)

Broude, Tomer and Shany, Yuval, *The Shifting Allocation of Authority in International Law* (Hart Publishing, 2008)

Buchanan, Allen, *Secession: The Morality of Political Divorce from Fort Sumter to Lithuania and Quebec* (Westview Press, 1991)

Buchanan, Allen, *Justice, Legitimacy, and Self-Determination: Moral Foundations for International Law* (Oxford University Press, 2007)

Buchanan, Allen, 'The Legitimacy of International Law', in Samantha Besson and John Tasioulas (eds), *The Philosophy of International Law* (Oxford University Press 2010)

Buchanan, Ruth, 'Reconceptualizing Law and Politics in the Transnational: Constitutional and Legal Pluralist Approaches' (2009) 3 *Socio-Legal Review* 1; available at <http://www1.nls.ac.in/ojs-2.2.3/index.php/slr/article/view/72>

Calliess, Peter and Zumbansen, Peer, *Rough Consensus and Running Code: A theory of Transnational Private Law* (Hart Publishing, 2010)

Celano, Bruno, 'Are Reasons for Action Beliefs?', in Lukas H Meyer *et al.* (eds), *Rights, Culture and the Law: Themes from the Legal and Political Philosophy of Joseph Raz* (Oxford University Press, 2003)

Charters, Claire, 'A Self-Determination Approach to Justifying Indigenous Peoples' Participation in International Law and Policy Making' (2010) 17 *International Journal on Minority and Group Rights* 215

Charters, Claire and Stavenhagen, Rodolfo, *Making the Declaration Work: The United Nations Declaration on the Rights of Indigenous Peoples* (Transaction Publishers, 2009)

Christiano, Tom, 'Authority', in Edward N Zalta (ed), *Stanford Encyclopedia of Philosophy*, (Spring 2013 edition) available at <http://plato.stanford.edu/archives/spr2013/entries/authority/>

Christiano, Tom, 'The Authority of Democracy' (2004) 12 *Journal of Political Philosophy* 266

Claes, M and de Witte, B, 'Report on the Netherlands', in A Sweet, A-M Slaughter and J Weiler (eds), *The European Court and National Courts* (Hart Publishing, 1998)

Cleveland, Sarah, 'Our International Constitution' (2006) 31 *Yale Journal of International Law* 1

Coleman, Jules L, *The Practice of Principle: In Defence of a Pragmatist Approach to Legal Theory* (Oxford University Press, 2001)

Coleman, Jules L, 'The Architecture of Jurisprudence' (2011) 121 *Yale Law Journal* 1

Connolly, William E, *Identity/Difference: Democratic Negotiations of Political Paradox* (University Of Minnesota Press, 2002)

Cotterrell, Roger, 'Transnational Communities and the Concept of Law' (2008) 21 *Ratio Juris* 1

Cover, Robert M, Nomos and Narrative (1983) 97 *Harvard Law Review* 4

Craig, Paul, 'Proportionality, Deference, Wednesbury: Taking up Michael Taggart's Challenge: Proportionality, Rationality and Review II' (2010) *New Zealand Law Review* 265

Craig, Paul P and De Búrca, Grainne, *EU Law: Text, Cases, and Materials* (Oxford University Press, 2008)

Culver, Keith Charles and Giudice, Michael, *Legality's Borders: An Essay in General Jurisprudence* (Oxford University Press, 2010)

Cutler, A Claire, *Private Power and Global Authority* (Cambridge University Press, 2003)

Darwall, Stephen, *The Second-Person Standpoint: Morality, Respect, and Accountability* (Harvard University Press, 2006)

Darwall, Stephen, 'The Value of Autonomy and Autonomy of the Will' (2006) 116 *Ethics* 263

Darwall, Stephen, 'Authority and Second-Personal Reasons for Acting', in David Wall and Steven Sobel (eds), *Reasons for Action* (Cambridge University Press, 2009)

Darwall, Stephen, 'Authority and Reasons: Exclusionary and Second-Personal' (2010) 120 *Ethics* 257

D'Aspremont, Jean, 'The Foundations of the International Legal Order' (2007) 18 *Finnish Yearbook of International Law* 219

Davies, Margaret, 'Pluralism and Legal Philosophy' (2006) 57 *Northern Ireland Legal Quarterly* 577

De Búrca, Grainne, 'The EU, the European Court of Justice and the International Legal Order after *Kadi*' (2009) 51 *Harvard International Law Journal* 1

De Jouvenel, Bertrand, *Sovereignty: An Inquiry into the Political Good* (Cambridge University Press, 1957)

De Sousa Santos, Boaventura, 'Law: A Map of Misreading Toward a Postmodern Conception of Law' (1987) 14 *Journal of Law and Society* 279

Delmas-Marty, Mireille, *Ordering Pluralism: A Conceptual Framework for Understanding the Transnational Legal World* (Hart Publishing, 2009)

Dickson, Julie, 'How Many Legal Systems? Some Puzzles Regarding the Identity, Conditions of, and Relations between, Legal Systems in the European Union' (2008) 2 *Problema* 9

Dunoff, Jeffrey L, 'A New Approach to Regime Interaction', in Margaret A Young (ed), *Regime Interaction in International Law: Facing Fragmentation* (Cambridge University Press, 2012)

Dunoff, Jeffrey L and Trachtman, Joel P, *Ruling the World?: Constitutionalism, International Law, and Global Governance* (Cambridge University Press, 2009)

Durie, Mason, *Te Mana, Te K Wanatanga: The Politics of Self Determination* (Oxford University Press, 1998)

Dworkin, Ronald, *Law's Empire* (Belknap Press, 1986)

Dworkin, Ronald, 'Thirty Years On' (2002) 115 *Harvard Law Review* 1655

Dworkin, Ronald, *Justice in Robes* (Belknap Press, 2006)

Edmundson, William A, 'Political Authority, Moral Powers and the Intrinsic Value of Obedience' (2010) 30 *OJLS* 179

Eleftheriadis, Pavlos, 'Pluralism and Integrity' (2010) 23 *Ratio Juris* 365

Elliott, Mark, 'The Human Rights Act 1998 and the Standard of Substantive Review' (2001) *The Cambridge Law Journal* 301

Endicott, Timothy A, 'The Logic of Freedom and Power', in S Besson and J Tasioulas (eds), *The Philosophy of International Law* (Oxford University Press, 2010)

Estlund, David M, *Democratic Authority: A Philosophical Framework* (Princeton University Press, 2008)

Esty, DC, 'Bridging the Trade-Environment Divide' (2001) 15 *The Journal of Economic Perspectives* 113

Fallon, Richard H, 'The Core of an Uneasy Case for Judicial Review' (2008) 121 *Harvard Law Review* 1693

Finnis, John, *Natural Law and Natural Rights* (Clarendon Press, 1980)
Fischer-Lescano, A and Teubner, G, 'Regime-Collisions: The Vain Search for Legal Unity in the Fragmentation of Global Law' (2003) 25 *Michigan Journal of International Law* 999
Flathman, Richard E, *The Practice of Political Authority* (University of Chicago Press, 1980)
Friedman, Richard B, 'On the Concept of Authority in Political Philosophy', in Richard E Flathman (ed), *Concepts in Social and Political Philosophy* (Macmillan, 1973)
Fuller, Lon L, *The Morality of Law* (Yale University Press, 1964)
Fuller, Lon L, 'Human Interaction and the Law' (1969) 14 *American Journal of Jurisprudence* 1
Gaillard, Emmanuel, *Legal Theory of International Arbitration* (Martinus Nijhoff Publishers, 2010)
Galanter, Marc, 'Justice in Many Rooms: Courts, Private Ordering, and Indigenous Law' (1981) 19 *Journal of Legal Pluralism* 1
Galligan, DJ, *Law in Modern Society* (Oxford University Press, 2007)
Gardner, John, 'How Law Claims, What Law Claims', in Matthias Klatt (ed), *Institutional Reason: The Jurisprudence of Robert Alexy* (Oxford University Press, 2010)
Garlicki, Lech, 'Cooperation of Courts: The Role of Supranational Jurisdictions in Europe' (2008) 6 *International Journal of Constitutional Law* 509
Gauthier, David P, *Morals by Agreement* (Clarendon Press, 1986)
Geddis, Andrew, 'A Dual Track Democracy? The Symbolic Role of the Maori Seats in New Zealand's Electoral System' (2006) 5 *Election Law Journal* 347
Goodin, Robert E, 'What Is So Special About Our Fellow Countrymen?' (1988) 98 *Ethics* 663
Gover, Kirsty and Baird, Natalie, 'Identifying the Māori Treaty Partner' (2002) 52 *University of Toronto Law Journal* 39
Green, Leslie, *The Authority of the State* (Clarendon Press, 1988)
Green, Leslie, 'The Duty to Govern' (2007) 13 *Legal Theory* 165
Green, Leslie, 'Positivism and the Inseparability of Law and Morals' (2008) 83 *NYU Law Review* 1035
Greve, Michael S, 'Against Cooperative Federalism' (2000) 70 *Mississippi Law Journal* 557
Griffiths, John, 'What Is Legal Pluralism' (1986) 24 *Journal of Legal Pluralism and Unofficial Law* 1
Habermas, Jurgen, *Between Facts and Norms: Contributions to a Discourse Theory of Law and Democracy* (MIT Press, 1996)
Hall, Rodney Bruce and Biersteker, Thomas J, 'Theorizing Private Authority: The Emergence of Private Authority in the International System', in *The Emergence of Private Authority in Global Governance* (Cambridge University Press, 2002)
Halpin, Andrew, 'Conceptual Collisions' (2001) 2 *Jurisprudence* 507
Hampton, Jean, *Hobbes and the Social Contract Tradition* (Cambridge University Press, 1988)
Hampton, Jean, *Political Philosophy* (Westview Press, 1997)

Handl, Günther and Zekoll, Joachim, *Beyond Territoriality: Transnational Legal Authority in an Age of Globalization* (Martinus Nijhoff Publishers, 2012)

Hart, HLA, 'Commands and Authoritative Legal Reasons', in Joseph Raz (ed), *Authority* (New York University Press, 1990)

Hart, HLA, *The Concept of Law* (2nd edn, Clarendon Press, 1994)

Hayward, J, 'Local Government and Maori: Talking Treaty?' (1999) 50 *Political Science* 182

Hershovitz, Scott, 'Legitimacy, Democracy, and Razian Authority' (2003) 9 *Legal Theory* 201

Hershovitz, Scott, 'Accountability and Political Authority' (2006) *Minn Law Review* 1012

Hershovitz, Scott, 'The Role of Authority' (2011) 7 *Philosophers' Imprint*; available at <http://quod.lib.umich.edu/p/phimp>

Higgins, Rosalyn, 'A Babel of Judicial Voices? Ruminations from the Bench' (2006) 55 *International and Comparative Law Quarterly* 791

Himma, Kenneth Einar, 'Law's Claim of Legitimate Authority', in Jules L Coleman (ed), *Hart's Postscript: Essays on the Postscript to the Concept of Law* (Oxford University Press, 2001)

Hobbes, T, *Leviathan* (JCA Gaskin ed, Oxford University Press, 1998)

Hogg, Peter W and Bushell, Allison A, 'The Charter Dialogue between Courts and Legislatures' (1997) 35 *Osgoode Hall Law Journal* 75

Hogg, Peter W et al., 'Charter Dialogue Revisited—or "Much Ado About Metaphors"' (2007) 45 *Osgoode Hall Law Journal* 1

Hohfeld, Wesley Newcomb, *Fundamental Legal Conceptions* (Yale University Press, 1964)

Hope, Simon, 'The Roots and Reach of Rangatiratanga' (2004) 56 *Political Science* 23

International Law Commission, *Conclusions of the Work of the Study Group on the Fragmentation of International Law: Difficulties Arising from the Diversification and Expansion of International Law* (United Nations, 2006)

Ivison, Duncan, et al., *Political Theory and the Rights of Indigenous Peoples* (Cambridge University Press, 2000)

Jackson, Moana, *The Māori and the Criminal Justice System/He Whaaipanga Hou* (New Zealand Department of Justice, 1987–1988) (in two parts)

Jacobsen, T, et al., *Re-Envisioning Sovereignty: The End of Westphalia?* (Ashgate Publishing Co, 2008)

Jessup, Philip C, *Transnational Law* (Yale University Press, 1956)

Joseph, Philip A, 'The Maori Seats in Parliament', New Zealand Business Roundtable (2008)

Kawharu, Merata, 'Local Maori Development and Government Policies' (2001) *Social Policy Journal of New Zealand* 1

Keating, Michael, *Plurinational Democracy: Stateless Nations in a Post-Sovereignty Era* (Oxford University Press, 2004)

Kelsen, Hans, *General Theory of Law and State* (Harvard University Press, 1945)

Kingsbury, Benedict, 'Reconciling Five Competing Conceptual Structures of Indigenous Peoples' Claims in International and Comparative Law' (2001) 34 *New York University Journal of International Law and Policy* 189

Kingsbury, Benedict *et al.*, 'The Emergence of Global Administrative Law' (2005) 68 *Law of Contemporary Problems* 15

Kirby, Michael, 'Transnational Judicial Dialogue, Internationalisation of Law and Australian Judges' (2008) 9 *Melbourne Journal of International Law* 171

Knop, Karen, 'Here and There: International Law in Domestic Courts' (1999) 32 *NYU Journal of International Law and Policy* 501

Knowles, Dudley, 'The Domain of Authority' (2007) 82 *Philosophy* 23

Koh, Harold Hongju, 'Transnational Legal Process' (1996) *Neb Law Review* 75

Koh, Harold Hongju, 'Why Do Nations Obey International Law?' (1997) 106 *Yale Law Journal* 2599

Koh, Harold Hongju, 'Why Transnational Law Matters' (2005) 24 *Penn St International Law Review* 745

Kokott, Juliane and Sobotta, Christoph, 'Constitutional Core Values and International Law' (2012) 23 *European Journal of International Law* 1015

Koskenniemi, Marti, 'The Fate of Public International Law: Between Technique and Politics' (2007) 70 *MLR* 1

Kramer, Matthew H, *In Defense of Legal Positivism: Law without Trimmings* (Oxford University Press, 1999)

Krasner, Stephen D, *Sovereignty: Organized Hypocrisy* (Princeton University Press, 1999)

Krasner, Stephen D, 'The Hole in the Whole: Sovereignty, Shared Sovereignty, and International Law' (2003) 25 *Michigan Journal of International Law* 1075

Krehoff, Bernd, 'Legitimate Political Authority and Sovereignty: Why States Cannot Be the Whole Story' (2008) 14 *Res Publica* 283

Krisch, Nico, 'The Case for Pluralism in Postnational Law' in De Búrca and Weiler (eds) *The Worlds of European Constitutionalism* (Cambridge University Press, 2012)

Krisch, Nico, *Beyond Constitutionalism: The Pluralist Structure of Postnational Law* (1st edn, Oxford University Press, 2010)

Krisch, Nico and Kingsbury, Benedict, 'Introduction: Global Governance and Global Administrative Law in the International Legal Order' (2006) 17 *European Journal of International Law* 1

Kumm, Mattias, 'Who Is the Final Arbiter of Constitutionality in Europe?: Three Conceptions of the Relationship between the German Federal Constitutional Court and the European Court of Justice' (1999) 36 *Common Market Law Review* 351

Kumm, Mattias, 'The Legitimacy of International Law: A Constitutionalist Framework of Analysis' (2004) 15 *European Journal of International Law* 907

Kumm, Mattias, 'Democratic Constitutionalism', in Sujit Choudhry (ed), *The Migration of Constitutional Ideas* (Cambridge University Press, 2005)

Kumm, Mattias, 'The Jurisprudence of Constitutional Conflict: Constitutional Supremacy in Europe before and after the Constitutional Treaty' (2005) 11 *European Law Journal* 262

Kumm, Mattias, 'The Cosmopolitan Turn', in Joel P Trachtman and Jeffrey Dunoff (eds), *Ruling the World* (Cambridge University Press, 2009)

Kumm, Mattias, 'Conflicts of Authority' (unpublished 2012)

Kumm, Mattias and Komárek, Jan, 'Rethinking Constitutional Authority', in Matej Avbelj and Jan Komárek (eds), *Constitutional Pluralism in the European Union and Beyond* (Hart Publishing, 2012)

Kuo, MS, 'Between Fragmentation and Unity: The Uneasy Relationship between Global Administrative Law and Global Constitutionalism' (2008) 10 *San Diego International Law Journal* 439

Kymlicka, Will, *Multicultural Citizenship: A Liberal Theory of Minority Rights* (Clarendon Press, 1996)

Kymlicka, Will, 'Liberal Theories of Multiculturalism', in Lukas H Meyer *et al.* (eds), *Rights, Culture, and the Law: Themes from the Legal and Political Philosophy of Joseph Raz* (Oxford University Press, 2003)

Laclau, Ernesto and Mouffe, Chantal, *Hegemony and Socialist Strategy: Towards a Radical Democratic Politics* (2nd edn, Verso, 2001)

Ladenson, Robert, 'In Defense of a Hobbesian Conception of Law' (1980) 9 *Philosophy and Public Affairs* 134

Lake, David A, 'Delegating Divisible Sovereignty: Sweeping a Conceptual Minefield (2007) 2 *The Review of International Organizations* 219

Lake, David A, 'Escape from the State of Nature: Authority and Hierarchy in World Politics' (2007) 32 *International Security* 47

Lister, Matthew, 'The Legitimating Role of Consent in International Law' (2100) 11 *Chicago Journal of International Law* 663

Lorenzetti, Ricardo, *Global Governance: Dialogue between Courts* (Eui edn, European University Institute, 2010)

Lowenfeld, Andreas F, 'Forum Shopping, Antisuit Injunctions, Negative Declarations, and Related Tools of International Litigation' (1997) *American Journal of International Law* 314

MacCormick, Neil, 'Beyond the Sovereign State' (1993) 56 *MLR* 1

MacCormick, Neil, 'The Maastricht-Urteil: Sovereignty Now' (1995) 1 *European Law Journal* 259

MacCormick, Neil, 'Liberalism, Nationalism and the Post-Sovereign State' (1996) 44 *Political Studies* 553

MacCormick, Neil, *Questioning Sovereignty: Law, State, and Nation in the European Commonwealth* (Oxford University Press, 1999)

MacCormick, Neil, *Institutions of Law* (Oxford University Press, 2007)

Maduro, Miguel, 'Contrapunctual Law: Europe's Constitutional Pluralism in Action', in Neil Walker (ed), *Sovereignty in Transition* (2003)

Maduro, Miguel, 'The Importance of Being Called a Constitution: Constitutional Authority and the Authority of Constitutionalism' (2005) 3 *International Journal of Constitutional Law* 332

Maduro, Miguel, 'Three Claims of Constitutional Pluralism', in M Avbelj and J Komárek (eds), *Constitutional Pluralism in the European Union and Beyond* (2012)

Margalit, Avishai and Raz, Joseph, 'National Self-Determination' (1990) 87 *The Journal of Philosophy* 439

Marmor, Andrei, *Positive Law and Objective Values* (Oxford University Press, 2001)

Marmor, Andrei, *Law in the Age of Pluralism* (Oxford University Press, 2007)
Marmor, Andrei, 'An Institutional Conception of Authority' (2011) 39 *Philosophy and Public Affairs* 238
Marmor, Andrei, *Philosophy of Law* (Princeton University Press, 2011)
Marmor, Andrei, 'Farewell to Conceptual Analysis Jurisprudence', in Wil Waluchow and Sciaraffa Stefan (eds), *Philosophical Foundations of the Nature of Law* (2013)
Martin, Margaret, 'Raz's the Morality of Freedom: Two Models of Authority' (2010) *Jurisprudence* 63
McBride, Mark, 'Darwall Versus Raz on Practical Authority' (2011) 3 *Public Reason* 73
McHugh, PG, '"Treaty Principles": Constitutional Relations Inside a Conservative Jurisprudence' (2008) 39 *Victoria University Wellington Law Review* 39
McLachlan, Campbell, *Lis Pendens in International Litigation* (Hague Academy of International Law (ed), Martinus Nijhoff, 2009)
McLean, Janet, '"Crown Him with Many Crowns": The Crown and the Treaty of Waitangi' (2008) 6 *New Zealand Journal of Public and International Law* 35
McVeigh, Shaun and Dorsett, Shaunnagh, 'Questions of Jurisdiction', in *Jurisprudence of Jurisdiction* (Shaun McVeigh (ed), 2006)
McWhinney, Edward, 'Self-Determination of Peoples and Plural-Ethnic States' (2002) 294 *Recueil des Cours—Academie de Droit International* 167
Merry, Sally Engle, 'Legal Pluralism' (1988) 22 *Law and Society Review* 869
Michaels, Ralf, 'Global Legal Pluralism' (2009) 5 *Annual Review of Law and Social Science* 243
Miller, David, *On Nationality* (Clarendon Press, 1995)
Moore, Michael S, 'Authority, Law and Razian Reasons' (1988) 62 *California Law Review* 827
Moore, Michael S, *Educating Oneself in Public: Critical Essays in Jurisprudence* (Oxford University Press, 2000)
Mouffe, Chantal, *On the Political* (Routledge, 2005)
New Zealand Law Commission, *Māori Custom and Values in New Zealand Law* (Study Paper 9, Wellington, 2001)
Nussbaum, MC, 'Non-Relative Virtues: An Aristotelian Approach', in Martha C Nussbaum and Amartya Sen (eds), *The Quality of Life* (Oxford University Press, 1993)
Oberthür, Sebastian and Schram Stokke, Olav (eds), *Managing Institutional Complexity: Regime Interplay and Global Environmental Change* (MIT Press, 2011)
Orange, Claudia, *The Treaty of Waitangi* (2nd edn, Bridget Williams Books, 2011)
Orebech, Peter, 'EU Competency Confusion: Limits, Extension Mechanisms, Split Power, Subsidiarity, and Institutional Clashes' (2003) 13 *Journal of Transnational Law and Policy* 99
Oxford English Dictionary, 'Relative, N, Adj, and Adv' (Oxford University Press, 3rd edition, 2009)
Palmer, Geoffrey WR and Palmer, Matthew, *Bridled Power: New Zealand Government under M.M.P.* (3rd edn, Oxford University Press, 1997)

Palmer, Matthew SR, 'What Is New Zealand's Constitution and Who Interprets It? Constitutional Realism and the Importance of Public Office-Holders' (2006) 17 *Public Law Review* 133

Palmer, Matthew SR, *The Treaty of Waitangi in New Zealand's Law and Constitution* (Victoria University Press, 2008)

Perry, Stephen R, 'The Works of Joseph Raz: Second-Order Reasons, Uncertainty and Legal Theory' (1989) 62 *Southern California Law Review* 913

Peters, Anne, 'Dual Democracy', in Jan Klabbers *et al.* (eds), *The Constitutionalization of International Law* (2009)

Petersen, Hanne, *Legal Polycentricity Consequences of Pluralism in Law* (Ashgate, 1995)

Pocock, JGA, 'The Treaty between Histories', in Andrew Sharp and Paul McHugh (eds), *Histories, Power and Loss: Uses of the Past—a New Zealand Commentary* (Bridget Williams Books, 2001)

Pogge, Thomas W, 'Cosmopolitanism and Sovereignty' (1992) 103 *Ethics* 48

Posner, Elliot, 'Making Rules for Global Finance: Transatlantic Regulatory Cooperation at the Turn of the Millennium' (2009) 63 *International Organization* 665

Postema, GJ, 'Custom in International Law: A Normative Practice Account', in A Perreau-Saussine, and J B Murphy (eds), *The Nature of Customary Law* (Cambridge University Press, 2007)

Postema, GJ, 'Custom, Practice, and the Law' (forthcoming, *Duke Law Review*, 2012)

Prantl, Jochen, 'Informal Groups of States and the UN Security Council' (2005) 59 *International Organization* 559

Rawls, John, *Political Liberalism* (Columbia University Press, 1993)

Rawls, John, *The Law of Peoples: With 'the Idea of Public Reason Revisited'* (Harvard University Press, 2001)

Raz, Joseph, 'Authority, Law and Morality' (1985) 68 *The Monist* 295

Raz, Joseph, *The Morality of Freedom* (Clarendon Press, 1986)

Raz, Joseph, 'Government by Consent', in J Rowland Pennock and John W Chapman (eds), *Authority Revisited* (New York University Press, 1987)

Raz, Joseph, *Authority* (New York University Press, 1990)

Raz, Joseph, *Ethics in the Public Domain* (Oxford University Press, 1994)

Raz, Joseph, 'Multiculturalism' (1998) 11 *Ratio Juris* 193

Raz, Joseph, *Practical Reason and Norms* (2nd edn, Oxford University Press, 1999)

Raz, Joseph, 'On the Authority and Interpretation of Constitutions', in Larry Alexander (ed), *Constitutionalism: Philosophical Foundations* (Cambridge University Press, 2001)

Raz, Joseph, 'Reasoning with Rules' (2001) 54 *Current Legal Problems* 1

Raz, Joseph, 'Comments and Responses', in Lukas H Meyer (ed), *Rights, Culture and the Law: Themes from the Legal and Political Philosophy of Joseph Raz* (Oxford University Press, 2003)

Raz, Joseph, 'Personal Practical Conflicts', in Peter Baumann and Monika Betzler (eds), *Practical Conflicts: New Philosophical Essays* (Cambridge University Press, 2004)

Raz, Joseph, 'The Problem of Authority: Revisiting the Service Conception' (2006) 90 *Minn Law Review* 1003

Raz, Joseph, *The Authority of Law* (2nd edn, Oxford University Press, 2009)
Raz, Joseph, *Between Authority and Interpretation: On the Theory of Law and Practical Reason* (Oxford University Press, 2009)
Raz, Joseph, 'On Respect, Authority, and Neutrality: A Response' (2010) 120 *Ethics* 279
Resnik, Judith, 'Afterword: Federalism's Options', Symposium Issue (1996) *Yale Law and Policy Review/Yale Journal on Regulation* 465
Resnik, Judith, 'Foreign as Domestic Affairs: Rethinking Horizontal Federalism and Foreign Affairs Preemption in Light of Translocal Internationalism' (2007) 57 *Emory Law Journal* 31
Resnik, Judith, 'Law as Affiliation: "Foreign" Law, Democratic Federalism, and the Sovereigntism of the Nation-State (2008) 6 *International Journal of Constitutional Law* 33
Ripstein, Arthur, 'Authority and Coercion' (2004) 32 *Philosophy and Public Affairs* 2
Roach, K, 'A Dialogue About Principle and a Principled Dialogue: Justice Iacobucci's Substantive Approach to Dialogue' (2007) 57 *University of Toronto Law Journal* 449
Rosen, Arie, 'The Normative Fallacy Regarding Law's Authority', in Wil Waluchow and Stefan Sciaraffa (eds), *Philosophical Foundations of the Nature of Law* (Oxford University Press, 2013)
Rosenfeld, Michael, 'Rethinking Constitutional Ordering in an Era of Legal and Ideological Pluralism' (2008) 6 *International Journal of Constitutional Law* 415
Roughan, Nicole, 'Te Tiriti and the Constitution: Rethinking Citizenship, Justice, Equality and Democracy' (2005) 3 *New Zealand Journal of Public and International Law* 285
Roughan, Nicole, 'The Association of State and Indigenous Law: A Case Study in "Legal Association"' (2009) 59 *University of Toronto Law Journal* 135
Roughan, Nicole, 'The Relative Authority of Law: A Contribution to "Pluralist Jurisprudence"', in M Del Mar (ed), *New Waves in Philosophy of Law* (Palgrave Macmillan, 2011)
Sassen, Saskia, *Losing Control?: Sovereignty in an Age of Globalization* (Columbia University Press, 1996)
Scanlon, Thomas, *What We Owe to Each Other* (Belknap Press of Harvard University Press, 1998)
Schapiro, Robert A, 'Federalism as Intersystemic Governance: Legitimacy in a Post-Westphalian World' (2007) 57 *Emory Law Journal* 115
Scheffler, Samuel, 'Conceptions of Cosmopolitanism' (1999) 11 *Utilitas* 255
Schultz, Thomas, 'Some Critical Comments on the Juridicity of the *Lex Mercatoria*' (2008) 10 *Yearbook of Private International Law* 667
Seuffert, Nan, 'Jurisdiction and Nation-Building: Tall Tales in Nineteenth-Century Aotearoa/New Zealand', in Shaun McVeigh (ed), *Jurisprudence of Jurisdiction* (Routledge, 2007)
Shany, Yuval, *The Competing Jurisdictions of International Courts and Tribunals* (Oxford University Press, 2004)

Shapiro, Scott J, 'Authority', in Scott J Shapiro and Jules L Coleman (eds), *Oxford Handbook of Jurisprudence and Philosophy of Law* (Oxford University Press, 2002)
Shapiro, Scott J, 'Law, Plans, and Practical Reason' (2002) 8 *Legal Theory* 387
Shapiro, Scott J, *Legality* (Harvard University Press, 2010)
Sharp, Andrew, 'Blood, Custom, and Consent: Three Kinds of Māori Groups and the Challenges They Present to Governments' (2002) 52 *University of Toronto Law Journal* 9
Sharp, Andrew, 'Traditional Authority and the Legitimation Crisis of Urban Tribes: The Waipareira Case' (2003) 6 *Ethnologies Comparee;* available at <http://recherche.univ-montp3.fr/cerce/r6/a.s.htm>
Shelton, Dinah, 'Normative Hierarchy in International Law' (2006) 100 *The American Journal of International Law* 291
Simmons, A John, *Moral Principles and Political Obligations* (Princeton University Press, 1979)
Simmons, A John, 'Associative Political Obligations' (1996) 106 *Ethics* 247
Simmons, A John, *Justification and Legitimacy: Essays on Rights and Obligations* (Cambridge University Press, 2001)
Slaughter, Anne-Marie, *A New World Order* (Princeton University Press, 2004)
Stone Sweet, Alec, 'Constitutionalism, Legal Pluralism, and International Regimes' (2009) 16 *Indiana Journal of Global Legal Studies* 621
Stone Sweet, Alec, 'A Cosmopolitan Legal Order: Constitutional Pluralism and Rights Adjudication in Europe' (2012) 1 *Journal of Global Constitutionalism* 53
Taggart, Michael, 'Proportionality, Deference, *Wednesbury*' (2008) III *New Zealand Law Review* 423
Tamanaha, Brian Z, *A General Jurisprudence of Law and Society* (Oxford University Press, 2001)
Tamanaha, Brian Z, 'Understanding Legal Pluralism: Past to Present, Local to Global' (2008) 30 *Sydney Law Review* 375
Tamir, Yael, *Liberal Nationalism* (Princeton University Press, 1995)
Tasioulas, John, 'The Legitimacy of International Law', in Samantha Besson and John Tasioulas (eds), *The Philosophy of International Law* (Oxford University Press, 2010)
Tauri, Juan, 'Explaining Recent Innovations in New Zealand's Criminal Justice System: Empowering Maori or Biculturalising the State?' (1999) 32 *Australian and New Zealand Journal of Criminology* 153
Taylor, Charles and Gutmann, Amy, *Multiculturalism: Examining the Politics of Recognition* (Princeton University Press, 1994)
Teubner, Gunther, 'Global Bukowina: Legal Pluralism in the World-Society', in Gunther Teubner (ed), *Global Law without a State* (Dartmouth Publishing Company, 1997)
Toki, Valmaine, 'Will Therapeutic Jurisprudence Provide a Path Forward for Maori?' (2005) 13 *Waikato Law Review: Taumauri* 169
Tremblay, Luc B, 'The Legitimacy of Judicial Review: The Limits of Dialogue between Courts and Legislatures' (2005) 3 *International Journal of Constitutional Law* 617

Tully, James, *Strange Multiplicity: Constitutionalism in an Age of Diversity* (Cambridge University Press, 1995)
Twining, WL, *General Jurisprudence* (Cambridge University Press, 2009)
Twining, WL, 'Institutions of Law from a Global Perspective', in Maksymilian Del Mar and Zenon Bankowski (eds), *Law as Institutional Normative Order* (Ashgate Publishing Co, 2009)
Vermeule, Adrian, 'Judicial Review and Institutional Choice' (2001) 43 *William & Mary Law Review* 1557
Vermeule, Adrian, 'Second Opinions and Institutional Design' (2011) 97 *Virginia Law Review* 1435
von Benda-Beckmann, Franz, 'Who's Afraid of Legal Pluralism (2002) 47 *Journal of Legal Pluralism and Unofficial Law* 37
von Bogdandy, Armin, 'General Principles of International Public Authority: Sketching a Research Field', in Armin von Bogdandy (ed) *et al.*, *The Exercise of Public Authority by International Institutions: Advancing International Institutional Law* (Springer, 2010)
von Bogdandy, Armin *et al.*, *The Exercise of Public Authority by International Institutions: Advancing International Institutional Law* (Springer, 2009)
von Daniels, D, *The Concept of Law from a Transnational Perspective* (Ashgate Publishing Co, 2010)
Waitangi Tribunal, *Wai 414: Te Whanau O Waipareira Report* (1998)
Waldron, Jeremy, 'Special Ties and Natural Duties' (1993) 22 *Philosophy and Public Affairs* 3
Waldron, Jeremy, *Law and Disagreement* (Clarendon Press, 1998)
Waldron, Jeremy, *The Dignity of Legislation* (Cambridge University Press, 1999)
Waldron, Jeremy, 'Authority for Officials', in Lukas H Meyer *et al.* (eds), *Rights, Culture and the Law: Themes from the Legal and Political Philosophy of Joseph Raz* (Oxford University Press, 2003)
Waldron, Jeremy, 'Some Models of Dialogue between Judges and Legislators', in Grant Huscroft and Ian Brodie (eds), *Constitutionalism in the Charter Era* (LexisNexis, 2004)
Waldron, Jeremy, 'Foreign Law and the Modern Ius Gentium' (2005) 119 *Harvard Law Review* 129
Waldron, Jeremy, 'The Core of the Case against Judicial Review' (2006) 115 *Yale Law Journal* 1346
Waldron, Jeremy, 'Legal Pluralism and the Contrast between Hart's Jurisprudence and Fuller's', in Peter Cane (ed), *The Hart–Fuller Debate in the 21st Century* (Hart Publishing, 2010)
Waldron, Jeremy, *Separation of Powers or Division of Power?* (New York University School of Law, Public Law Research Paper No 12–20, 2012)
Walker, Neil, 'Flexibility within a Metaconstitutional Frame: Reflections on the Future of Legal Authority in Europe', in Grainne De Búrca and Joanne Scott (eds), *Constitutional Change in the EU: From Uniformity to Flexibility?* (Hart Publishing, 2000)
Walker, Neil, 'The Idea of Constitutional Pluralism' (2002) 65 *MLR* 317

Walker, Neil, 'Late Sovereignty in the EU', in Neil Walker (ed), *Sovereignty in Transition* (Hart Publishing, 2003)

Walker, Neil, *Sovereignty in Transition* (Hart Publishing, 2003)

Walker, Neil, 'Beyond Boundary Disputes and Basic Grids: Mapping the Global Disorder of Normative Orders' (2008) 6 *International Journal of Constitutional Law* 373

Waluchow, WJ, 'Authority and the Practical Difference Thesis' (2000) 6 *Legal Theory* 45

Weil, Prosper, 'Towards Relative Normativity in International Law?' (1983) 77 *The American Journal of International Law* 413

Weiler, Joseph HH, 'The Transformation of Europe' (1991) 100 *Yale Law Journal* 2403

Weiler, Joseph HH, 'Does Europe Need a Constitution? Demos, Telos and the German Maastricht Decision' (1995) 1 *European Law Journal* 219

Weiler, Joseph HH, *The Constitution of Europe: 'Do the New Clothes Have an Emperor?' And Other Essays on European Integration* (Cambridge University Press, 1999)

Weiler, Joseph HH, 'Prologue: Global and Pluralist Constitutionalism—Some Doubts', in G De Búrca and J Weiler (eds), *The Worlds of European Constitutionalism* (Cambridge University Press, 2012)

Weiler, Joseph HH and Marlene Wind, *European Constitutionalism Beyond the State* (Cambridge University Press, 2003)

Weithman, PJ, 'Contractualist Liberalism and Deliberative Democracy' (1995) 24 *Philosophy and Public Affairs* 314

Willem van Rossem, Jan, 'Interaction between EU Law and International Law in the Light of *Intertanko* and *Kadi*' (2009) 40 *Netherlands Yearbook of International Law* 183

Williams, David V, 'Wi Parata Is Dead, Long Live Wi Parata', in Andrew Erueti and Claire Charters (eds), *Maori Property Rights and the Foreshore and Seabed: The Latest Frontier* (Victoria University Press, 2007)

Wolff, Robert Paul, 'The Conflict between Authority and Autonomy', in Joseph Raz (ed), *Authority* (New York University Press, 1990)

Young, Iris Marion, 'Polity and Group Difference: A Critique of the Ideal of Universal Citizenship' (1989) 99 *Ethics* 250

Young, Iris Marion, *Justice and the Politics of Difference* (Princeton University Press, 1990)

Young, Iris Marion, *Inclusion and Democracy* (Oxford University Press, 2002)

Young, Iris Marion, 'Two Concepts of Self-Determination', in Stephen May *et al.* (eds), *Ethnicity, Nationalism, and Minority Rights* (Cambridge University Press 2004)

Young, Margaret A, *Regime Interaction in International Law: Facing Fragmentation* (Cambridge University Press, 2012)

Zumbansen, Peer, 'Transnational Law', in JM Smits (ed), *Elgar Encyclopedia of Comparative Law* (Edward Elgar Publishing, 2006)

Zumbansen, Peer, 'Transnational Legal Pluralism' (2010) 1 *Transnational Legal Theory* 141

Zumbansen, Peer, 'Defining the Space of Transnational Law: Legal Theory, Global Governance and Legal Pluralism' (2011) 15 *Law of Contemporary Problems* 5

Index

autonomy 22, 30–3, 38, 41, 63, 79–80, 112, 118–19, 127–31, 140–1, 176, 225, 237, 243

Berman, Paul Schiff 7, 69, 76, 173
Besson, Samantha 32, 40–2, 54, 62, 66–7, 79–80, 117, 176–8, 181–2, 203–4
Buchanan, Allen 80–1, 186

claim/claiming 56–7, 82, 142, 151–5, 158, 160
coercion 24–6, 157
conflicts of authority 8–10, 56–9, 75–6, 78, 89, 102, 105–15, 120–2, 130–2, 142–5, 195, 197, 201, 204–5, 234–6
consent 21, 31–5, 77, 80, 88–9, 120–2, 180–6
constitutional pluralism 8, 61–5, 69–70, 77–8, 146, 193–207
constitution
  de facto 47, 89, 93, 95–100
contractualism 34–5
cooperative authorities 8–10, 48, 51–3, 67, 86, 103, 122, 139–41, 158–62
Culver, Keith 70–1, 168

Daniels, Detlef von 71–2, 168
Darwall, Stephen 21–2, 36–7, 40, 127–8
de facto authority 9, 15, 29–30, 37, 107–8
de facto constitution *see* constitution, de facto
deference 48–9, 88–94, 98–9, 102–3, 121–2, 167, 208, 210, 240
democracy 31–2, 35, 40, 119
dialogue 55–6, 162, 167, 211–2, 214
disjunctive v integrated authorities 47–9, 50, 52, 65, 87, 93, 95–6, 100–2
Dworkin, Ronald 169, 25, 198

European courts 57, 60–2, 167, 201–4

federalism 45–7, 54, 57, 68, 213–15
Finnis, John 36–8, 40–1

Giudice, Michael 70–1, 155
governance reasons *see* reasons, governance
graduated authority 77–8, 81, 199–200

Herhovitz, Scott 21–2, 36–7, 40–1, 116, 120–1, 127
Hobbes, Thomas 21–2, 32

identification problem 8, 114–122, 126, 135–6, 144, 159, 166, 200
incommensurability *see* reasons, incommensurable
indigenous authority 159, 161, 215–9, 230–1, 233, 236–7
institutional settlement, principle of 89–92, 101–4
international law
  and domestic law 189–90, 203–4
  authority of 174–8, 180–8
  courts and tribunals 54, 62, 175, 182
  legal status of 156, 174–5
  private 50–1
  public 50, 54, 61–3, 66–7, 69, 79–80, 155–6
  subjects of 175–8

judicial review 142, 202–4, 210–12
jurisdiction 5, 12, 28, 46, 68, 121, 151–2, 159

Koskenniemi, Marti 62–3
Krisch, Nico 64–5, 78–9, 146–7, 196
Kumm, Mattias 69–70, 77–8, 81, 184–5, 189–90, 196–200, 207

legality 2–3, 67–72, 149–50, 168–9, 214

MacCormick, Neil 64–5, 70–1
Maduro, Miguel 63, 193–5, 197, 201–7

pluralist jurisprudence 1–2, 10, 69–74, 149–50, 167–70
plurality
  contra pluralism 2–3, 44–5
  types of 44–7, 64–5
  value of 145–8, 163–6
private v public authority 28–9, 73–4, 191–2

rankings problem 105, 114–5, 122, 125, 135, 144, 200

Raz, Joseph
  dependence thesis 38, 72, 95, 112, 116
  normal justification thesis (NJT) 27, 36–41, 79–80, 89–92, 94–7, 100, 116, 122, 127
  on authority of law 152–7, 159–60
  on de facto conditions for authority 37, 107–8
  on multiculturalism 227–30
  on the independence condition 39–40, 109, 110–12
  preemption thesis 22–3, 115–17
reasons
  exclusionary 23–4, 38
  for action 23, 38, 112, 133
  for decision 111–16, 126–7, 130–4, 140–2
  governance 130–1, 134–9, 141–5, 234–5
  incommensurability of 109–15, 133, 135–6, 176, 237–8
  procedural 112–4, 130–2, 139, 142, 234
  side-effects 112–4, 116, 130–2, 140–1, 234–5
relativity condition 6, 10, 136–43, 158, 167, 198–9, 207, 241

self-determination 131, 146–8, 163–5, 216–7, 225–36
  Māori 240–4

separation of powers 209–10
Shapiro, Scott 41, 97, 151–2
Side-effects *see* reasons, side-effects
sociology of law 42, 45, 67–8, 73, 75, 169
sovereignty 12–14, 65–8, 77, 155, 178, 215–7, 224–6
subsidiarity principle 66–7, 77, 92, 176, 181, 185
standards 126, 128–9, 135
standing 21–2, 126–30, 138–41, 234–5, 237–8, 240, 243–4
subsidiarity 66–7, 77, 92, 176, 181, 185

Tamanaha, Brian Z 67–8, 175
transnational law 76, 190–2
Treaty of Waitangi 217–21
Twining, William 67–8, 72

Waldron, Jeremy 87, 89–95, 97–8, 99, 101–3
Walker, Neil 43–4, 65, 76–7, 146–8, 100, 196

Young, Iris Marion 228, 233–6

Zumbansen, Peer 3, 73–4